Thinking Sociologically

THINKING
SOCIOLOGICALLY

ZYGMUNT BAUMAN

Basil Blackwell

Copyright © Zygmunt Bauman 1990

First published 1990

Basil Blackwell Ltd
108 Cowley Road, Oxford, OX4 1JF, UK

Basil Blackwell, Inc.
3 Cambridge Center
Cambridge, Massachusetts 02142, USA

British Library Cataloguing in Publication Data
A CIP catalogue record for this book is available from the British Library.

Library of Congress Cataloging in Publication Data
Bauman, Zygmunt.
    Thinking sociologically / Zygmunt Bauman.
        p. cm.
    Includes bibliographical references + index.
    ISBN 0−631−16361−1 — ISBN 0−631−16362−X (pbk.)
    1. Sociology.   I. Title.
  HM51.B364   1990
  301−dc20   90−160
                                                    CIP

Typeset in 11 on 13 pt Ehrhardt
by Setrite Typesetters Limited
Printed in Great Britain by Billing & Sons Ltd., Worcester.

Contents

Acknowledgements

Tim Goodfellow, Simon Prosser, Tracy Traynor, Kate Chapman and Helen Jeffrey all contributed, each in her or his own way (through exciting ideas, gentle prodding, competent guidance, thorough editing and sheer dedication to the project) to the creation of this book. The authorship of the book would not be properly ascertained without their names being mentioned.

There were countless people whose names it is impossible to list without whom this book would never have been conceived, written and produced. Colleagues and students above all: this book has been born of talking and listening to them. Thinking and writing, however private, is a social affair.

Introduction:

Sociology — What For?

One can conceive of sociology in a number of ways. The simplest way is to think of a long line of library shelves, tightly packed with books. All books have the word 'sociology' in their titles, or in subtitles, or in their list of contents (this is why the librarian put them on these shelves in the first place). The books carry the names of their authors, who describe themselves as sociologists (that is, are classified as sociologists in their official titles of teachers or researchers). Thinking of these books and their authors, one thinks of a body of knowledge accumulated over the long years during which sociology has been practised and taught. And so one thinks of sociology as a sort of binding tradition — a certain volume of information all newcomers to the field, whether they want to become practising sociologists or merely to avail themselves of whatever sociology may offer, must first consume, digest, appropriate. Or, better still, one thinks of sociology in a way that includes the constant influx of newcomers (new books are always being added to the shelves, after all): one thinks of it as of a continuing activity — a going concern, a constant testing of the received lore of wisdom against new experience, a constant adding to the accumulated knowledge and changing of it in the process.

This way of thinking about sociology seems natural and obvious. This is, after all, how we tend to respond to any question of the type 'What is an X?' If, for instance, asked, 'What is a lion?', we point our finger towards a particular animal in a zoo cage, or to a picture in a book. Asked by a non-English speaker, 'What is a pencil?', we pick a particular object from our pockets and show it. In both cases we seek and point out a link between a certain word and a certain object. We treat words as *referring* to objects, standing for objects; each word sends us to a specific object, be it an animal or a writing tool. Finding such an object to which the word in question refers (that is, finding the word's *referent*) is a correct and useful answer to the original question. Once I have obtained such an answer, I know how to use a heretofore unfamiliar word: in reference to what, in what connection, under what conditions. The kind of answer we are talking about teaches me precisely this: how to use a given word.

What the answer does not give me is knowledge about the object itself, the one that has been pointed out to me as the referent of the word I asked about. I know only what the object looks like, so that in future I'll be able to recognize it as one that the word stands for. Thus there are limits — and pretty narrow ones — to what the finger-pointing method may teach me. Having found out what object the word refers to, I'd probably right away be prompted to ask the next questions: 'In what way is this object peculiar? In what way does it differ from other objects, so that referring to it by a separate name is justified?' This is a lion. But this is not a tiger. This is a pencil. But this is not a pen. If calling this animal a lion is correct, but calling it a tiger is not, there must be something that lions have that tigers do not (this something makes the lions be what the tigers are not). There must be some *difference* that sets the lions apart from the tigers. Only by discovering this difference can we know what the lions truly are — as distinct from knowing what the object the word 'lion' stands for.

And so we cannot be fully satisfied with our preliminary answer to the question about sociology. We need to think further. Having satisfied ourselves that the word 'sociology' stands for a certain body of knowledge, and for certain practices which use this knowledge while simultaneously adding to it, we must now ask further questions about that knowledge and those practices. What is there about them that makes them distinctly 'sociological'? What makes them different from other bodies of knowledge and other knowledge-using/producing practices?

Indeed, the first thing we find out when looking at the library shelves filled with sociology books is that they are surrounded by other shelves, all bearing names different from that of 'sociology'. In most university of college libraries one would probably discover that the closest neighbours are the shelves carrying the labels 'history', 'political science', 'law', 'social policy', 'economics'. The librarians who arranged such shelves close to each other probably had the readers' comfort and convenience in mind. They assumed (or so we may guess) that the readers browsing through sociology shelves would occasionally reach for a book placed on, say, history or political science shelves; and that this may happen more often than searching the contents of, say, physics or mechanical engineering shelves. In other words, the librarians assumed that the subject-matter of sociology is somewhat nearer to that of the bodies of knowledge for which names like 'political science' or 'economics' stand; perhaps also that the difference between sociology books and the books placed in their immediate vicinity is somehow less pronounced, clear-cut and uncontentious than the differences between sociology and, say, chemistry or medicine.

Whether these thoughts crossed their minds or not, the librarians did the right thing. The bodies of knowledge they made into neighbours have got much in common. They are all concerned with the *human-made* world: with the part of the world, or the aspect of the world, that bears an imprint of human activity, which would not exist at all but for the actions of human beings. History, law, economics, political science, sociology all discuss human actions and their consequences. This much they share, and for this reason they truly belong together. If, however, all these bodies of knowledge explore the same territory, what, if anything, sets them apart? What is 'that difference which makes the difference' — the one that justifies the division and separate names? On what basis do we insist that, all the similarities and sharing of grounds and interests notwithstanding, history is not sociology, and neither is political science?

Off-hand, we are all prompted to give a simple answer to those questions: divisions between bodies of knowledge must reflect the divisions in the world they investigate. It is the human actions, or the aspects of the human actions, which differ from each other, and the divisions between bodies of knowledge merely take cognizance of this fact. Thus, we will be tempted to say, history is about the actions which took place in the past and are no more, while sociology concentrates on the current ones, or on such general qualities of actions as do not change with time; anthropology tells us of human actions in societies spatially remote and different from our own, while sociology focuses its attention on actions that take place in our society (whatever that may mean), or such aspects of action which do not vary from one society to another. In the case of some other close relatives of sociology, the 'obvious' answer will be somewhat less obvious — but one can still try: and so political science mostly discusses such actions as pertain to power and the government; economics deals with the actions related to the use of resources as well as production and distribution of goods; law is interested in the norms that regulate human behaviour and in the way such norms are articulated, made obligatory and enforced ... We can see by now that were we to continue in a similar way, we would be bound to conclude that sociology is a sort of residual discipline, feeding on what other disciplines left unattended. The more the other disciplines took under their own microscopes, the less remained for sociologists to talk about; as if 'out there', in the human world, there was a limited number of facts waiting to be split, and picked up, depending on their intrinsic character, by specialistic branches of investigation.

The trouble with such an 'obvious' answer to our question is that, like most other beliefs which appear to us self-evident and obviously true, it remains obvious only as long as we refrain from looking closely at all the assumptions one must tacitly make to accept it. So let us try to trace back the stages by which we came to see our answer obvious.

Where did we get the idea that human actions divide into a certain number of distinct types in the first place? From the fact that they have been classified in such a way and that each file in this classification has been given a separate name (so that we know when to speak of politics, when of economics, and when of legal matters — and what to find where); and from the fact that there are groups of credible experts, knowledgeable and trustworthy people, who claim exclusive rights to study, to give an informed opinion, to guide or advise some types of actions rather than others. But let us pursue our inquiry one step further: how do we know at all what the human world is 'by itself', that is, before it has been split into economics, politics or social policy, and independently of such a split? Most certainly, we have not learned it from our own life experience. One does not live now in politics, then in economics; one does not move from sociology to anthropology when travelling from England to South America, or from history to sociology when one grows a year older. If we can separate such domains in our experience, if we can tell that this action here and now belongs to politics while another has an economic character, it is only because we have been taught to make such distinctions beforehand. What we really know, therefore, is not the world itself, but what we are doing with the world; we are putting in practice, so to speak, our *image* of the world, a model put neatly together from the building blocks we got from the language and our training.

And so we may say that it is not the natural division of the human world that is reflected in the differences between scholarly disciplines. It is, on the contrary, the division of labour between scholars who deal with human actions (a division backed and reinforced by the mutual separation of respective experts, and the exclusive rights each group enjoys to decide what does and what does not belong to the area they command) that is projected onto the mental map of the human world that we carry in our minds and then deploy in our deeds. It is that division of labour that gives structure to the world we live in. If we want, therefore, to crack our mystery and find the secret location of 'that difference which makes the difference', it would be better to look at the practices of the self-same disciplines which seemed to us in the beginning modestly to reflect the natural structure of the world. We may now guess that it is these very practices which differ between themselves in the first place; that if there is a reflection, it goes in the direction exactly opposite to the one we supposed.

How do the practices of various branches of study differ from each other? To start with, there is little difference — or no difference — between their attitudes towards whatever they selected as their objects of study. They all claim obedience to the same rules of conduct when dealing with their respective objects. They all try hard to collect all relevant *facts*; they all try to make sure that they get their facts right, that the facts have been checked and rechecked and so the information about them is reliable; they all try to put the propositions they make about the facts in a form in which they can be clearly, unambiguously understood and tested against evidence from which they claim to derive and also against any evidence that may become available in the future; they all try to pre-empt or eliminate contradictions between the propositions they make or uphold, so that no two propositions are made that cannot be true at the same time. In short, they all try to live up to their promises; to obtain and present their findings in a *responsible* way (that is, the way believed to lead to the *truth*). And they are prepared to be criticized — and retract their assertions — if they do not. So there is no difference in how the task of the experts and their trade mark — the scholarly responsibility — are understood and practised. We would probably fail to find a difference in most other aspects of scholarly practices too. All people claiming to be and confirmed as scholarly experts seem to deploy similar strategies to collect and to process their facts: they observe things they study either in their natural habitat (for instance, human beings in their 'normal' daily life at home, on public occasions, at their place of work or entertainment) or under specially designed and tightly controlled experimental conditions (when, for instance, human reactions are watched in purposely designed settings, or people are prompted to respond to questions designed to eliminate unwelcome interference); alternatively, they use as their facts the recorded evidence of similar observations made in the past (for example, parish records, census data, police archives). And all scholars share the same general rules of logic to draw and validate (or invalidate) the conclusions from the facts they amassed and verified.

It seems, therefore, that our last hope of finding the sought-after 'difference which makes the difference' is in the kind of questions typical for each branch of inquiry — questions that determine the points of view (*cognitive perspectives*) from which human actions are looked at, explored and described by scholars belonging to different disciplines — and in the *principles* used to order the information such questioning has generated and to assemble that information into a model of a given section or aspect of human life.

At a very rough approximation, economics, for example, would look primarily at the relationship between the costs and effects of human action. It would probably look at human action from the point of view of the management of scarce resources that the actors want access to and to use to their best advantage. So it would see the relationships between actors as aspects of the creation and exchange of goods and services, regulated by offer and demand. It would, eventually, arrange its findings into a model of the process through which resources are created, obtained and allocated among various demands. Political science, on the other hand, would be interested more often than not in that aspect of human action that changes, or is changed by, the actual or anticipated conduct of other actors (an impact usually discussed under the name of power or influence). It would consider human actions from the point of view of the asymmetry of such power and influence: some actors emerge from interaction with their behaviour changed more profoundly than that of their partners. It would probably organize its findings around concepts like power, domination, authority, etc. — all referring to the differentiation of the chances of obtaining what the sides in the relationship are striving for.

Such concerns of economics and political science (much as the interests pursued by the rest of the human sciences) are by no means alien to sociology. You will find this out the moment you look into any list of recommended reading for sociology students: it will most certainly contain quite a few works written by scholars who call themselves, and are classified as, historians, political scientists, anthropologists. And yet sociology, like other branches of social study, has its own cognitive perspective, its own set of questions for interrogating human actions, as well as its own set of principles of interpretation.

As a first and tentative summation, we may say that what sets sociology apart and gives it its distinctive character is the habit of viewing human actions as *elements of wider figurations*: that is, of a non-random assembly of actors locked together in a web of *mutual dependency* (dependency being a state in which the probability that the action will be undertaken and the chance of its success change in relation to what other actors are, or do, or may do). Sociologists would ask what consequences this being locked together would have for the possible and the actual behaviour of human actors. Such interests shape the object of sociological inquiry: figurations, webs of mutual dependence, reciprocal conditioning of action and expansion or confinement of actors' freedom are the most prominent preoccupations of sociology. Single actors, like you and me, come into the view of sociological study in their capacity as units, members or partners in a network of interdependence. The central question of sociology, one could say, is: in what sense does it matter that in whatever they do or may do people are dependent on other people; in what sense does it matter that they live always (and cannot but live) in the company of, in communication with, in an exchange with, in competition with, in cooperation with other human beings? It is this kind of question (and not a separate collection of people or events selected for the purpose of study, nor some set of human actions neglected by other lines of investigation) that constitutes the particular area of sociological discussion and defines sociology as a relatively autonomous branch of human and social sciences. Sociology, we may conclude, is first and foremost a *way of thinking* about the human world; in principle one can also think about the same world in different ways.

Among these other ways from which the sociological way of thinking is set apart, a special place is occupied by so-called **common sense**. Perhaps more than other branches of scholarship, sociology finds its relation with common sense (that rich yet disorganized, non-systematic, often inarticulate and ineffable knowledge we use to conduct our daily business of life) fraught with problems decisive for its standing and practice.

Indeed, few sciences are concerned with spelling out their relationship to common sense; most do not even notice that common sense exists, let alone that it presents a problem. Most sciences settle for defining themselves in terms of boundaries that separate them from or bridges that connect them with other sciences — respectable, systematic lines of inquiry like themselves. They do not feel they share enough ground with common sense to bother with drawing boundaries or building bridges. Their indifference is, one must admit, well justified. Common sense has next to nothing to say of the matters of which physics, or chemistry, or astronomy, or geology speak (and whatever it has to say on such matters comes courtesy of those sciences themselves, in so far as they manage to make their recondite findings graspable and intelligible for lay people). The subjects dealt with by physics or astronomy hardly ever appear within the sight of ordinary men and women: inside, so to speak, yours and my daily experience. And so we, the non-experts, the ordinary people, cannot form opinions about such matters unless aided — indeed, instructed — by the scientists. The objects explored by sciences like the ones we have mentioned appear only under very special circumstances, to which lay people have no access: on the screen of a multi-million-dollar accelerator, in the lens of a gigantic telescope, at the bottom of a thousand-feet deep shaft. Only the scientists can see them and experiment with them; these objects and events are a monopolistic possession of the given branch of science (or even of its selected practitioners), a property not shared with anybody who is not a member of the profession. Being the sole owners of the experience which provides the raw material for their study, the scientists are in full control over the way the material is processed, analysed, interpreted. Products of such processing would have to withstand the critical scrutiny of other scientists — but their scrutiny only. They will not have to compete with public opinion, common sense or any other form in which non-specialist views may appear, for the simple reason that there is no public opinion and no commonsensical point of view in the matters they study and pronounce upon.

With sociology it is quite different. In sociological study there are no equivalents of giant accelerators or radiotelescopes. All experience which provides raw material for sociological findings — the stuff of which sociological knowledge is made — is the experience of ordinary people in ordinary, daily life; an experience accessible in principle, though not always in practice, to everybody; and experience that, before it came under the magnifying glass of a sociologist, had already been lived by someone else — a non-sociologist, a person not trained in the use of sociological language and seeing things from a sociological point of view. All of us live in the company of other people, after all, and interact with each other. All of us have learned only too well that what we get depends on what other people do. All of us have gone more than once through the agonizing experience of a communication breakdown with friends and strangers. Anything sociology talks about was already there in our lives. And it must have been, otherwise we should be unable to conduct our business of life. To live in the company of other people, we need a lot of knowledge; and common sense is the name of that knowledge.

Deeply immersed in our daily routines, though, we hardly ever pause to think about the meaning of what we have gone through; even less often have we the opportunity to compare our private experience with the fate of others, to see the *social* in the *individual*, the *general* in the *particular*; this is precisely what sociologists can do for us. We would expect them to show us how our individual *biographies* intertwine with the *history* we share with fellow human beings. And yet whether or not the sociologists get that far, they have no other point to start from than the daily experience of life they share with you and me — from that raw knowledge that saturates the daily life of each one of us. For this reason alone the sociologists, however hard they might have tried to follow the example of the physicists and the biologists and stand aside from the object of their study (that is, look at your and my life experience as an object 'out there', as a detached and impartial observer would do), cannot break off completely from their insider's knowledge of the experience they try to comprehend. However hard they might try, sociologists are bound to remain on both sides of the experience they strive to interpret, inside and outside at the same time. (Note how often the sociologists use the personal pronoun 'we' when they report their findings and formulate their general propositions. That 'we' stands for an 'object' that includes those who study and those whom they study. Can you imagine a physicist using 'we' of themselves and the molecules? Or astronomers using 'we' to generalize about themselves and the stars?)

There is more still to the special relationship between sociology and common sense. The phenomena observed and theorized upon by modern physicists or astronomers come in an innocent and pristine form, unprocessed, free from labels, ready-made definitions and prior interpretations (that is, except such interpretations as had been given them in advance by the physicists who set the experiments that made them appear). They wait for the physicist or the astronomer to name them, to set them among other phenomena and combine them into an orderly whole: in short, to give them *meaning*. But there are few, if any, sociological equivalents of such clean and unused phenomena which have never been given meaning before. Those human actions and interactions that sociologists explore had all been given names and theorized about, in however diffuse, poorly articulated form, by the actors themselves. Before sociologists started looking at them, they were objects of commonsensical knowledge. Families, organizations, kinship networks, neighbourhoods, cities and villages, nations and churches and any other groupings held together by regular human interaction have already been given meaning and significance by the actors, so that the actors consciously address them in their actions as bearers of such meanings. Lay actors and professional sociologists would have to use the same names, the same language when speaking of them. Each term sociologists may use will already have been heavily burdened with meanings it was given by the commonsensical knowledge of 'ordinary' people like you and me.

For the reason explained above, sociology is much too intimately related to common sense to afford that lofty equanimity with which sciences like chemistry or geology can treat it. You and I are allowed to speak of human interdependence and human interaction, and to speak with authority. Don't we all practise them and experience? Sociological discourse is wide open: no standing invitation to everybody to join, but no clearly marked borders or effective border guards either. With poorly defined borders whose security is not guaranteed in advance (unlike sciences that explore objects inaccessible to lay experience), the sovereignty of sociology over social knowledge, its right to make authoritative pronouncements on the subject, may always be contested. This is why drawing a boundary between sociological knowledge proper and the common sense that is always full of sociological ideas is such an important matter for the identity of sociology as a cohesive body of knowledge; and why sociologists pay this matter more attention than other scientists.

We can think of at least four quite seminal differences between the ways in which sociology and common sense — your and my 'raw' knowledge of the business of life — treat the topic they share: human experience.

To start with, sociology (unlike common sense) makes an effort to subordinate itself to the rigorous rules of **responsible speech**, which is assumed to be an attribute of science (as distinct from other, reputedly more relaxed and less vigilantly self-controlled, forms of knowledge). This means that the sociologists are expected to take great care to distinguish — in a fashion clear and visible to anybody — between the statements corroborated by available evidence and such propositions as can only claim the status of a provisional, untested guess. Sociologists would refrain from misrepresenting ideas that are grounded solely in their beliefs (even the most ardent and emotionally intense beliefs) as tested findings carrying the widely respected authority of science. The rules of responsible speech demand that one's 'workshop' — the whole procedure that has led to the final conclusions and is claimed to guarantee their credibility — be wide open to an unlimited public scrutiny; a standing invitation ought to be extended to everyone to reproduce the test and, be this the case, prove the findings wrong. Responsible speech must also relate to other statements made on its topic; it cannot simply dismiss or pass by in silence other views that have been voiced, however sharply they are opposed to it and hence inconvenient. It is hoped that once the rules of responsible speech are honestly and meticulously observed, the trustworthiness, reliability and eventually also the practical usefulness of the ensuing propositions will be greatly enhanced, even if not fully guaranteed. Our shared faith in the credibility of beliefs countersigned by science is to a great extent grounded in the hope that the scientists will indeed follow the rules of responsible speech, and that the scientific profession as a whole will see to it that every single member of the profession does so on every occasion. As to the scientists themselves, they point to the virtues of responsible speech as an argument in favour of the superiority of the knowledge they offer.

The second difference is related to the **size of the field** from which the material for judgement is drawn. For most of us, as non-professionals, such a field is confined to our own life-world: things we do, people we meet, purposes we set for our own pursuits and guess other people set for theirs. Rarely, if at all, do we make an effort to lift ourselves above the level of our daily concerns to broaden the horizon of experience, as this would require time and resources most of us can ill afford or do not feel like spending on such effort. And yet, given the tremendous variety of life conditions, each experience based solely on an individual life-world is necessarily partial and most likely one-sided. Such shortcomings can be rectified only if one brings together and sets against each other experiences drawn from a multitude of life-worlds. Only then will the incompleteness of individual experience be revealed, as will be the complex network of dependencies and interconnections in which it is entangled — a network which reaches far beyond the realm which could be scanned from the vantage point of a singular biography. The overall result of such a broadening of horizons will be the discovery of the intimate link between individual biography and wide social processes the individual may be unaware of and surely unable to control. It is for this reason that the sociologists' pursuit of a perspective wider than the one offered by an individual life-world makes a great difference — not just a quantitative difference (more data, more facts, statistics instead of single cases), but a difference in the quality and the uses of knowledge. For people like you or me, who pursue our respective aims in life and struggle for more control over our plight, sociological knowledge has something to offer that common sense cannot.

The third difference between sociology and common sense pertains to the way in which each one goes about **making sense** of human reality; how each one goes about explaining to its own satisfaction why this rather than that happened or is the case. I imagine that you (much as myself) know from your own experience that you are 'the author' of your actions; you know that what you do (though not necessarily the results of your actions) is an effect of your intention, hope or purpose. You normally do as you do in order to achieve a state of affairs you desire, whether you wish to possess an object, to receive an accolade from your teachers, or to put an end to your friends' teasing. Quite naturally, the way you think of your action serves you as a model for making sense of all other actions. You explain such actions to yourself by imputing to others intentions you know from your own experience. This is, to be sure, the only way we can make sense of the human world around us as long as we draw our tools of explanation solely from within our respective life-worlds. We tend to perceive everything that happens in the world at large as an outcome of somebody's intentional action. We look for the persons responsible for what has happened and, once we have found them, we believe our inquiry has been completed. We assume somebody's goodwill lies behind every event we like and somebody's ill intentions behind every event we dislike. We would find it difficult to accept that a situation was not an effect of intentional action of an identifiable 'somebody'; and we would not lightly give up our conviction that any unwelcome condition could be remedied if only someone, somewhere, wished to take the right action. Those who more than anyone else interpret the world for us — politicians, journalists, commercial advertisers — tune in to this tendency of ours and speak of the 'needs of the state' or 'demands of the economy', as if the state or the economy were made to the measure of individual persons like ourselves and could have needs or make demands. On the other hand, they portray the complex problems of nations, states and economic systems (deeply seated in the very structures of such figurations) as the effects of the thoughts and deeds of a few individuals one can name, put in front of a camera and interview. Sociology stands in opposition to such a personalized world-view. As it starts its survey from *figurations* (networks of dependencies) rather than from individual actors or single actions, it demonstrates that the common metaphor of the motivated individual as the key to the understanding of the human world — including our own, thoroughly personal and private, thoughts and deeds — is inappropriate. When thinking sociologically, one attempts to make sense of the human condition through analysing the manifold webs of human interdependency — that toughest of realities which explains both our motives and the effects of their activation.

Finally, let us recall that the power of common sense over the way we understand the world and ourselves (the immunity of common sense to questioning, its capacity for self-confirmation) depends on the apparently self-evident character of its precepts. This is turn rests on the routine, monotonous nature of daily life, which informs our common sense while being simultaneously informed by it. As long as we go through the routine and habitualized motions which fill most of our daily business, we do not need much self-scrutiny and self-analysis. When repeated often enough, things tend to become familiar, and familiar things are self-explanatory; they present no problems and arouse no curiosity. In a way, they remain invisible. Questions are not asked, as people are satisfied that 'things are as they are', 'people are as they are', and there is precious little one can do about it. Familiarity is the staunchest enemy of inquisitiveness and criticism — and thus also of innovation and the courage to change. In an encounter with that familiar world ruled by habits and reciprocally reasserting beliefs, sociology acts as a meddlesome and often irritating stranger. It disturbs the comfortingly quiet way of life by asking questions no one among the 'locals' remembers being asked, let alone answered. Such questions make evident things into puzzles: they **defamiliarize** the familiar. Suddenly, the daily way of life must come under scrutiny. It now appears to be just one of the possible ways, not the one and only, not the 'natural', way of life.

Questioning and disrupting the routine may not be to everybody's liking; many would resent the challenge of defamiliarization as it calls for rational analysis of things which thus far just 'went on their way'. (One may recall Kipling's centipede who walked effortlessly on all her hundred legs until a sycophantic courtier began to praise her exquisite memory, which allowed her never to put down the thirty-seventh leg before the eighty-fifth, or the fifty-second before the nineteenth ... Brutally made self-conscious, the hapless centipede was unable to walk any more ...) Some may feel humiliated: what they have known and were proud of has now been devalued, perhaps even shown worthless and ridiculed, giving a shock of the kind no one enjoys. And yet however understandable the resentment, defamiliarization also has benefits to offer. Most importantly, it may open up new and previously unsuspected possibilities of living one's life with more self-awareness, more comprehension — perhaps also with more freedom and control.

To everyone who thinks that living life in a conscious way is worth the effort, sociology would be a welcome help. While remaining in a constant and intimate conversation with common sense, sociology aims at overcoming its limitation; it strives to open up the possibilities that common sense naturally tends to close down. When addressing and challenging our shared commonsensical knowledge, sociology may prompt and encourage us to re-assess our experience, to discover many more of its possible interpretations, and to become in the end somewhat more critical, less reconciled to things as they are at present or as we believe them to be (or, rather, never consider them not to be).

One could say that the main service the art of thinking sociologically may render to each and every one of us is to make us more *sensitive*; it may sharpen up our senses, open our eyes wider so that we can explore human conditions which thus far had remained all but invisible. Once we understand better how the apparently natural, inevitable, immutable, eternal aspects of our lives have been brought into being through the exercise of human power and human resources, we will find it hard to accept once more that they are immune and impenetrable to human action — our own action included. Sociological thinking is, one may say, a power in its own right, an *antifixating* power. It renders flexible again the world hitherto oppressive in its apparent fixity; it shows it as a world which could be different from what it is now. It can be argued that the art of sociological thinking tends to widen the scope, the daring and the practical effectiveness of your and my *freedom*. Once the art has been learned and mastered, the individual may well become just a bit less manipulable, more resilient to oppression and regulation from outside, more likely to resist being fixed by forces that claim to be irresistible.

To think sociologically means to understand a little more fully the people around us, their cravings and dreams, their worries and their misery. We may then better appreciate the human individuals in them and perhaps even have more respect for their rights to do what we ourselves are doing and to cherish doing it: their rights to choose and practise the way of life they prefer, to select their life-projects, to define themselves, and — last but not least — vehemently defend their dignity. We may realize that in doing all those things other people come across the same kind of obstacles as we do and know the bitterness of frustration as well as we do. Eventually, sociological thinking may well promote solidarity between us, a solidarity grounded in mutual understanding and respect, solidarity in our joint resistance to suffering and shared condemnation of the cruelty that causes it. If this effect is achieved, the cause of freedom will be strengthened by being elevated to the rank of a *common* cause.

Thinking sociologically may also help us to understand other forms of life, inaccessible to our direct experience and all too often entering the commonsensical knowledge only as stereotypes — one-sided, tendentious caricatures of the way people different from ourselves (distant people, or people kept at a distance by our distaste or suspicion) live. An insight into the inner logic and meaning of the forms of life other than our own may well prompt us to think again about the alleged toughness of the boundary that has been drawn between ourselves and others, between 'us' and 'them'. Above all, it may prompt us to doubt that boundary's natural, preordained character. This new understanding may well make our communication with the 'other' easier than before, and more likely to lead to mutual agreement. It may replace fear and antagonism with tolerance. This would also contribute to our freedom, as there are no guarantees of my freedom stronger than the freedom of all, and that means also of such people as may have chosen to use their freedom to embark on a life different from my own. Only under such conditions may our own freedom to choose be exercised.

For the reasons just spelled out, the strengthening of individual freedom through grounding it in the solid foundation of collective freedom may be seen as having a **destabilizing** effect on the existing power relations (which are normally represented by their guardians as *the* social order). This is why charges of 'political disloyalty' are all too often made against sociology by governments and other power-holders in control of the social order (particularly by the governments bent on confining the freedom of their subjects and undermining their resistance to such rulings as — for them to be obeyed — must be presented to the public as 'necessary', 'inevitable', or 'the only reasonable ones'). When witnessing a renewed campaign against the 'subversive impact' of sociology, one can safely assume that another assault on the subjects' capacity to resist coercive regulation of their lives is under preparation. Such campaigns more often than not coincide with tough measures aimed at the extant forms of self-management and self-defence of collective rights — at, in other words, the collective foundations of individual freedom.

It has been said that sociology is the power of the powerless. This is not always the case, though. There is no guarantee that having acquired sociological understanding one can dissolve and disempower the resistance put up by the 'tough realities' of life; the power of understanding is no match for the pressures of coercion allied with resigned and submissive common sense. And yet were it not for that understanding, the chance of successful management of one's life and the collective management of shared life conditions would be slimmer still.

This book has been written with one aim in mind: to help an ordinary person like you and me to see through our experience, and to show how the apparently familiar aspects of life can be interpreted in a novel way and seen in a different light. Each chapter is addressed to an aspect of daily life, to dilemmas and choices we confront routinely while having little time or opportunity to think about them in depth. Each chapter is meant to prompt such thinking; not to 'correct' your knowledge, but to expand it; not to replace an error with unquestionable truth, but to encourage critical scrutiny of beliefs hitherto uncritically held; to promote a habit of self-analysis and of questioning the views that pretend to be certainties.

This book is therefore intended for personal use — as a help in understanding the problems that arise in our daily lives as human beings. It differs in this respect from many other books about sociology: it is organized according to the logic of daily life, rather than according to the logic of the scholarly discipline that studies it. Quite a few topics that occupy professional sociologists because of the problems they confront in their own 'form of life' (that is, the life of professional sociologists) are mentioned only briefly or omitted entirely. On the other hand, things often at the edge of the main body of sociological wisdom have been given prominence in proportion to their centrality in lay life. Thus no comprehensive picture of sociology as it is practised and taught in academic institutions will emerge. To gain such a comprehensive picture, the reader will need to reach for other texts; some advice to this effect is given at the end of this book.

The book meant to comment on our daily experience cannot be more systematic than the experience itself. Hence the narrative goes in circles rather than developing in a straight line. Some topics return later, to be looked upon once again in the light of what we have discussed in the meantime. This is how all effort of understanding works. Each step in understanding makes a return to previous stages necessary. What we thought we understood in full reveals new question marks we previously failed to notice. The process may never end; but much may be gained in its course.

Chapter One

Freedom and Dependence

Being free and unfree at the same time is perhaps the most common of our experiences. It is also, arguably, the most confusing. No doubt it is one of the most profound puzzles of the human condition which sociology attempts to unravel. Indeed, much in the history of sociology may be explained as an on-going effort to solve this puzzle.

I am free: I can choose and I do make my own choices. I can go on reading this book or I can stop reading it and make myself a cup of coffee. Or forget it all and go for a walk. More than that; I can abandon the whole project of studying sociology and obtaining a college degree, and start looking for a job instead. Because I can do all those things, going on reading this book and sticking to my original intention to study sociology and to graduate are surely the results of my choices; they are courses of action I have selected from among available alternatives. Making decisions testifies to my freedom. Indeed, **freedom** means the ability to decide and choose.

Even if I do not spend much time thinking about my choices and take my decisions without properly surveying alternative courses of action, now and again I am reminded of my freedom by others. I am told, 'This has been your decision, no one but you is responsible for the consequences', or, 'No one forced you to do so, you have only yourself to blame!' If I do something which other people do not allow or normally abstain from doing (if, so to speak, I break a rule), I may be punished. The punishment will confirm that I am *responsible* for what I have done; it will confirm that I could, if I wanted to, refrain from breaking the rule. I could, for example, arrive promptly at the tutorial instead of making myself absent without good reason. Sometimes I am told of my freedom (and hence of my responsibility) in a form which I may find more difficult to accept than in previous examples. I may be told, for instance, that remaining unemployed is entirely my own fault and that I could make a living if only I tried hard enough. Or that I could have become an altogether different person if only I had stretched myself more and applied myself more earnestly to my task.

If these last examples were not enough to make me pause and wonder whether I am indeed free and in control of my life (I might have looked for a job in earnest but not have been able to find one as there was none on offer; or I might have tried hard to enter a different carrer, yet been barred entry to where I wished to go), I have surely experienced many other situations which showed me in no unclear way that my freedom is, in fact, limited. Such situations taught me that to decide on my own what goal to pursue, and to have an intention to pursue it with all my heart, is one thing; it is an entirely different thing, however, to be able to act on my words and reach the purpose I sought.

First of all, I learn that other people may strive for the same goals as I do, but not all can reach them, since the amount of available prizes is limited, that is, smaller than the number of people pursuing them. If this is the case, I will find myself engaged in a competition, the outcome of which will not wholly depend on my efforts alone. I may, for example, compete for a college place, only to find out that there are twenty candidates for every place available, and that most of them have all the qualifications required and use their freedom sensibly — do precisely the things which prospective students are prompted and expected to do. In addition, I will find that the results of my actions and theirs depend on someone else — on people who decide how many places are available and judge the skills and the efforts of the applicants. Such people set the rules of the game; they are, at the same time, the referees: they have the last say in the selection of the winner. They possess the right of discretion — their own freedom to choose and to decide, this time about my own and my competitors' fate. Their freedom seems to draw the boundaries of mine. I depend on the way they decide their own actions — because their freedom to choose introduces an element of uncertainty in my own situation. It is a factor over which I have no control and which nevertheless heavily influences the outcome of my efforts. I am dependent on them because they are in control of this uncertainty. At the end of the day, it is they who pronounce the verdict as to whether my efforts have been good enough and justify my admission.

Secondly, I learn that my determination and goodwill are just not enough if I lack the means to act upon my decision and see it through. I may, for example, 'follow the jobs' and decide to move to the South of the country where jobs are abundant, but then find that house prices and rents in the South are exorbitant and much beyond my means. Or I may wish to escape the squalor of inner-city dwellings and move to a healthier, greener area of the suburbs, yet again find out than I cannot afford the move because houses in better and more-coveted locations cost more than I can afford. Again, I may be dissatisfied with the kind of education my children are offered in their school and wish them to be better taught than they are. Yet there are no other schools available in the area where I live and I am told that if I wish to secure a better education for my children I ought to send them to a richer, better-equipped private school and pay the fees, often higher than my total income. What all such examples (as well as many others you can easily supply yourself) demonstrate is that freedom of choice does not by itself guarantee freedom to act effectively on one's choice; still less does it secure freedom to attain the intended results. To be able to act freely, I need resources in addition to free will.

Most commonly, such resources are money. But they are not the only resources on which freedom of action depends. I may find out that freedom to act on my wishes depends not on what I *do*, or not even on what I *have*, but on what I *am*. For example, I may be refused entry to a certain club, or employment in a certain office, because of my qualities — like race, or sex, or age, or ethnicity, or nationality. None of these attributes depends on my will or action, and no amount of freedom will enable me to change them. Alternatively, my access to the club, or the employment, or the school may depend on my past achievements (or lack of them) — acquired skills, or a diploma, or the length of previous service, or the nature of my accumulated experience, or the local dialect I learned in my childhood and never bothered to refine. In such cases, I may conclude that the requirements do not coincide with the principle of my free will and responsibility for my actions, as the absence of skill or a distinguished service record are the lasting consequences of my past choices. And yet there is nothing I can do now to change it. My freedom today is limited by my freedom of yesterday; I am '**determined**' — constrained in my present freedom — by my past actions.

Thirdly, I may find out (as I surely will, sooner or later) that as I was, say, born British and as English is my mother tongue, I feel most comfortable, most at home in Britain and among English-speaking people. Elsewhere, I am not sure what the effects of my action would be, I am uncertain what to do and thus feel unfree. I cannot communicate easily, I do not understand the meaning of things other people do, and I am not sure what I should do myself to express my own intentions and achieve the results I am after. I experience a similarly upsetting feeling in many other situations — not just when visiting another country. Coming from a working-class family, I may feel ill at ease among rich, middle-class neighbors. Or being a Catholic, I may find that I cannot live according to more libertarian, relaxed habits which accept divorces and abortions as ordinary facts of life. Had I time to think about experiences of this kind, I would probably come to the conclusion that the group in which I feel most at home also sets limits to my freedom — makes me dependent on it for my freedom. It is inside this group that I am capable of exercising my freedom most fully (that means that only inside this group can I assess the situation correctly and select the course of action that the others approve of and that fits the situation well). The very fact that I am adjusted so well to the conditions of action inside the group to which I belong, however, constrains my freedom of action in the vast and poorly charted, often off-putting and frightening space beyond the confines of that group. Having trained me in its ways and means, my group enables me to practise my freedom. Yet by the same token it limits this practice to its own territory.

As far as my freedom goes, therefore, the group of which I am a member plays an ambivalent role. On one hand it *enables* me to be free; on the other it *constrains* me by drawing the borders of my freedom. In enables me to be free as it imparts the sort of desires which are both acceptable and 'realistic' inside my group, teaches me to select the ways of acting which are appropriate to the pursuit of such desires, and gives me the ability to read the situation properly and hence to orient myself correctly to the actions and intentions of others who infuence the outcome of my efforts. At the same time it fixes the territory within which my freedom may be properly exercised, as all the many assets I owe to it, all the invaluable skills I acquired from my group turn from advantages into liabilities the moment I venture beyond the boundary of my own group and find myself in an environment where different desires are promoted, different tactics are deemed appropriate, and the connections between other people's conduct and their intentions are not like those I have come to expect.

This is not, however, the only conclusion I would have drawn, had I been able and willing to think through my experience. I would discover something more bewildering still: that usually the very group which plays such an ambivalent and yet crucial role in my freedom is not one which I have myself freely chosen. I am a member of such group because I was born into it. The territory of my freedom itself is not a matter of free choice. The group which made me a free person and which continues to guard the realm of my freedom took command over my life (my desires, my purposes, the actions I would take and the actions I would refrain from, etc.) uninvited. Becoming a member of that group was not an act of my freedom. On the contrary, it was a manifestation of my **dependence**. I never decided to be French, or to be black, or to be middle-class. I may accept my fate with equanimity or resignation; or I may make it into destiny: relish it, enthusiastically embrace it, and decide to make the best of it — advertising my Frenchness, feeling proud of the beauty of being black, or living my life carefully and prudently as a decent middle-class person is expected to. If I want, however, to change what the group made me and to become someone else, I will have to exert myself to the utmost. The change would require much more effort, self-sacrifice, determination and endurance than are normally needed for living placidly and obediently in conformity with the upbringing offered by the group into which one was born. I will find then that my own group is the most awesome adversary I must conquer to win my fight. The contrast between the ease of swimming with the stream and the difficulty of changing sides is the secret of that hold which my natural group has over me; it is the secret of my dependence on my group.

If I look closely and try to write down an inventory of all those things I owe to the group to which I — for better or worse — belong, I'll end up with quite a long list. For the sake of brevity I may divide all the items on the list into four broad categories. First, the distinction I make between the **ends** worth pursuing and those that are not worth my trouble. If I happened to be born into a middle-class family, the chances are that gaining a higher education would seem to me an indispensable condition of a proper, successful, satisfying life — yet if chance made me a working-class child, the odds are that I would agree to leave school early, aiming at a job which does not necessarily call for a lengthy study, but which would allow me to 'enjoy life' right away, and later perhaps to support my family. And so I take from my group the purpose to which I should apply my capacity for 'free choice'. Second, the **means** I use in pursuing whatever end my group has taught me to pursue. These means are also supplied by the group, and once supplied they form my 'private capital', which I can use in my efforts: the speech and the 'body language' with which I communicate my intentions to others, the intensity with which I apply myself to some ends as distinct from others, and — in general — the forms of conduct considered appropriate to the task in hand. Third, the criteria of **relevance**, the art of distinguishing between things or people relevant and irrelevant to the project I set out to complete. My group guides me to set apart my allies from my enemies or rivals as well as from those who are neither, and whom I may therefore leave out of the account, disregard and treat with disdain. Last but not least, my 'map of the world' — things charted on my map as against such things as may be visible on other people's maps but on my map are represented only by blank spaces. Among other roles such a map plays in my life, it selects the set of conceivable life itineraries — the set of realistic **life-projects** — suitable for 'people like me'. All in all, I owe to my group quite a lot; all that enormous knowledge which helps me through the day and without which I would be totally unable to conduct my daily business.

In most cases, as a matter of fact, I am not aware that I possess all that knowledge. If asked, for example, what the code is through which I communicate with other people and decipher the meaning of their actions towards me, I would, in all probability, be taken aback; I probably would not quite understand what I had been asked to do, and when I did comprehend the question, I would not be able to explain that code (much as I am incapable of explaining the simplest rules of grammar, while using the language they guide competently, fluently and with little difficulty). All the same, the knowledge required to fight my way through daily tasks and challenges is somewhere within me. I somehow have it at my disposal, if not in the form of *rules* I can recite, then as a set of practical *skills* I use effortlessly day by day throughout my life.

It is thanks to such knowledge that I feel secure and need not look far for the right thing to do. If I am in command of all that knowledge without in fact being aware of it, it is because I acquired most of its basic precepts in my early childhood, time of which one does not remember much. And so I can say little, if anything, about the way I acquired that knowledge, dipping into my own experience or personal recollections. It is precisely thanks to this forgetting of my origins that my knowledge is so well settled, that it has such a powerful grip over me, that I take it for granted as the 'natural' thing and seldom feel like questioning it. To find out how the knowledge of everyday life is in fact produced and then 'handed in' by the group, I need to consult results of research conducted by professional psychologists and sociologists. When I consult them, I find the results are often disturbing. What seemed to be obvious, evident, and natural is now revealed as a collection of beliefs which have no more than the authority of one group among many to stand on.

Perhaps no one has contributed more to our understanding of this **internalization** of group standards than the American social psychologist **George Herbert Mead**. To describe the process of acquisition of the essential skills of social life the concepts he coined are mainly used. Most famous among these are the concepts of **I** and **Me**, which refer to the duality of the self, to its split into two: an external part (more exactly, a part that is seen by the person as coming from outside, from the society which surrounds it, in the form of demands to be met and patterns to be followed), the 'Me' of the self, and another part, the 'I', which is the self's inner core, from where those external, social demands and expectations are scrutinized, assessed, taken stock of and ultimately spelled out. The role played by the group in shaping the self is accomplished through the 'Me' part. Children learn that they are looked upon, evaluated, chastised, prompted to behave in a particular way, pushed into line if they depart from the required way. This experience sediments in the child's growing self as an image of the *expectations* the others have of him or her. They — the others — obviously have a way of distinguishing between a proper and an improper conduct. They approve of the proper behaviour and punish the wrong one as a *deviation* from the norm. Memories of rewarded and penalized actions blend gradually into the unconscious understanding of the *rule* — of what is and what is not expected — into the 'Me', which is nothing other than the self's image of the others' image of itself. Moreover, the 'others' are not just any others who happen to be around. From the multitude of people with whom the child comes into contact, some are picked up by the self as *significant others* — those whose evaluations and responses count more than anybody else's, being more persistently or more poignantly felt, and hence more effective.

From what has been said so far a wrong conclusion may be drawn, that the development of the self through learning and training is a passive process; that it is the others and only they who do the job, that the child is filled with instructions and — with the help of stick or carrot — cajoled, pressed and drilled into following them obediently. The truth of the matter is, however, different. The self develops in an interaction between the child and its environment. Activity and initiative mark both sides of the interaction. It could hardly be otherwise. One of the first discoveries every child must make is that the 'others' differ among themselves. They rarely see eye to eye, they give commands which clash with each other and cannot be obeyed at the same time. In many cases, satisfying one command cannot but mean defying another. One of the first skills the child must learn is to discriminate and select, which cannot be acquired unless supported by the ability to resist and withstand pressure, take a stand, act against at least some of the external forces. In other words, the child learns to *choose* and to take *responsibility* for his or her own action. The 'I' part of the self represents precisely these abilities. Because of the contradictory and inconsistent content of the 'Me' (contradictory signals about the expectations of various significant others), the 'I' must stand aside, at a distance, look at the external pressures internalized in the 'Me' as if from outside; scan them, classify and evaluate. In the end, it is the 'I' which makes the choice and thus becomes the true, rightful 'author' of the ensuing action. The stronger the 'I', the more *autonomous* becomes the *personality* of the child. The strength of the 'I' expresses itself in the persons's ability and readiness to put the social pressures internalized in the 'Me' to the test, check their true power and their limits, challenge them — and bear the consequences.

A crucial task in the separation of the 'I' from the 'Me' (that is, in the emergent ability of the self to visualize, scrutinize and monitor the demands of the significant others) is performed by the child's activity of *role playing*. By playfully assuming the roles of the others, for instance the father or mother, and experimenting with their behaviour (including their conduct towards the child itself), the child learns the art of looking at action as at an *assumed* role, something one can do or not do; action means doing what the situation requires, and it may change with the situation. This somebody, who acts, is not truly me — not the 'I'. As children grow and their knowledge of various roles accumulates, they may engage in *games*, which, unlike the playing, include the element of cooperation and coordination with other role players. Here the child experiments with the art most central to a truly autonomous self: that of selecting the appropriate course of action in response to the action of others and to lure or force the others to act as one would wish them to. Through play and games, the child simultaneously acquires habits and skills instilled by the social world outside, and the ability to act in that world as a free — an autonomous and responsible — person. In the course of this acquisition, a child develops the peculiar ambiguous attitude which we all know well; *having* a self (looking at one's own behaviour as if from outside, praising it or disapproving of it, attempting to control and, if necessary, correct it), and *being* a self (asking myself, 'what am I really like?' and 'Who am I?', occasionally rebelling against a model other people try to impose upon my life, and striving instead to achieve what I think of as 'the authentic life', life conforming to my true identity). I experience the contradiction between freedom and dependence as an inner conflict between what I wish to do and what I feel obliged to do because of what the significant others have made, or intend to make, of me.

The significant others do not mould the child's self out of nothing; rather, they impress their image on the 'natural' (pre-social or, more precisely, pre-educational) predispositions of the child. Though such natural predispositions − *instincts* or *drives* − play on the whole a lesser role in human life than in the life of the other animals, they are still present in the biological endowment of each newly born human being. What instincts there are, is a moot question. The scholars differ in their opinions, and their views range from an attempt to explain most of the ostensibly socially induced conduct by biological determinants, to the belief in the almost unlimited potential of the social processing of human behaviour. Still, most scholars would support the claim of a society to its right to set and enforce standards of acceptable behaviour, as well as the argument which backs up this claim: that socially administered training is indispensable because the natural predispositions of men make cohabitation either impossible or unacceptably coarse and dangerous. Most scholars agree that the pressure of some natural drives is particularly powerful and hence must be dealt with, one way or the other, by any human group. *Sexual* and *aggresive* drives are most often named as those which groups may omit to control only at their peril. Scholars point out that were such drives given a free rein, they would result in conflicts of an intensity no group could bear and render social life all but impossible.

All surviving groups must have developed, so we are told, effective ways of taming, bridling, suppressing or otherwise controlling manifestations of such drives. **Sigmund Freud**, the founder of **psychoanalysis**, suggested that the whole process of self-development and the social organization of human groups may be interpreted in the light of the need, and the practical effort required, to control the expression of socially dangerous drives, particularly the sexual and the aggressive instincts. Freud suggested that the instincts are never annihilated; they cannot be destroyed, they can only be 'repressed', driven into the **subconscious**. What keeps them in that limbo is the **superego**, the internalized knowledge of demands and pressures exerted by the group. The superego has been metaphorically described by Freud as a 'garrison left in a conquered city' by the victorious army of society, in order to keep the suppressed instincts — the subconscious — in permanent obedience. The **ego** itself is hence permanently suspended between two powers: the instincts which have been driven into the subconscious yet remain potent and rebellious, and the superego (akin to Mead's 'Me'), which presses the ego (akin to Mead's 'I') to keep the drives subconscious and prevent their escape from confinement. **Norbert Elias**, the German-British sociologist who followed up Freud's hypotheses with comprehensive historical research, has suggested that the experience of the self we all have arises precisely from such double pressure to which we are all exposed. Our previously mentioned ambiguous attitude towards our respective selves is the result of the ambivalent position in which the two pressures, acting in opposite directions, cast us. Living in a group, *I* have to control *myself*. The self is something to be controlled, and I am the one to control it . . .

That all societies control the natural predispositions of their members and strain to contain the range of permissible interactions is beyond question. What is less certain is whether only the morbid, anti-social aspects of the natural endowment are suppressed in the process (though this is exactly what the powers speaking in the name of society aver). As far as we know, there is no conclusive evidence that human beings are naturally aggressive and therefore must be bridled and tamed. What tends to be interpreted as the outburst of natural aggression is more often than not an outcome of callousness or hatred — both attitudes traceable to their social rather than genetic origin. In other words, while it is true that groups train and control the conduct of their members, it does not necessarily follow that they make such conduct more humane and moral. It only means that, as a result of this drilling and surveillance and correcting, the conduct better conforms to the patterns recognized as proper for a given kind of social group and enforced by it.

The processes of the 'I' and 'Me' formation, of the suppression of instincts and the production of the superego, are often given the name of **socialization**. I have been socialized (that is, transformed into a being capable of living in society) inasmuch as I have been made, through internalizing social pressures, fit to live and act in a group; inasmuch as I have acquired the skills to behave in the way society allows, and thus to be 'free', to bear the responsibility for my action. Those significant others who played such an important role in the acquisition of these skills may therefore be seen as the socializing agents. But who are they? We have seen that the force which truly operates in the development of the self is the child's *image* of the intentions and expectations other people have, not necessarily the intentions and expectations they themselves entertain; and that the child itself performs the selection of significant others from among the many persons who appear within its vision. True, the child's freedom to select is not complete; some 'others' may force their way into the child's world more effectively than other 'others', and interfere with the selection. And yet while growing in a world populated by groups acting at cross purposes and pursuing different modes of life, the child can hardly avoid choosing; if the demands of others are contradictory and cannot be met at the same time, some of them must be paid more attention than others and so assigned more significance.

The need to assign significance (relevance) *differentially* is not confined to the plight of the child. You and I experience this need virtually daily. Day by day I must select between the demands of family, friends or bosses, each wishing me to do something at the same time. I have to risk the displeasure of some friends whom I cherish and respect in order to placate some others whom I like equally strongly. Whenever I express political views, I can be pretty sure that some people I know and care about would not like them and would bear a grudge against me for expressing them. There is little I can do to ward off such unpleasant consequences of my choices. Assigning relevance means, unavoidably, assigning irrelevance; selecting some people as significant means, inescapably, proclaiming someone else insignificant, or at least less significant. This very often means risking someone's resentment. The risk grows with the degree to which the environment in which I live is **heterogeneous** — conflict-ridden, split into groups of diverging ideals and modes of life.

Making a selection of significant others in such an environment means choosing one group among many as my **reference group**; a group against which I measure my own behaviour, which I accept as the standard for my whole life or a particular aspect of life. From what I know of the reference group of my choice, I will evaluate my behaviour and draw conclusions about its worthiness, its quality. I will derive from that knowledge the comforting feeling that what I am doing is right, or the unpleasant awareness that my action should have been different from what it was. I will try to follow the example of the reference group in the way I speak, in the words I use, in the way I dress. I will try to learn from that group whether and in what circumstances to be bold or irreverent, and when to go along obediently with the shared standards. From the image I hold of my reference group I will draw advice concerning the things which are worth my attention and such as are beneath me. All this I will do as if I sought the approval of my reference group; as if I wished to obtain its acceptance of me as its member, as 'one of them', its satisfaction with my style of life; as if I were trying to avoid the harsh measures the reference group may apply to bring me into line or retaliate for my rule-breaking.

And yet it is by and large *my* selection and analyses, conclusions and actions which make the reference group such a potent agent in shaping my conduct. Often the groups themselves are blissfully unaware of my attention, of my efforts to imitate what I think is their mode of life and apply what I think is their standards. Some of the groups, to be sure, may be justly called **normative reference groups** — as they do indeed, at least on occasion, set the norms for my conduct, watch what I do and thus are in a position to 'normatively influence' my actions by rewarding or punishing them, confirming or correcting. Particularly prominent among such groups are the family, friends in whose company I spend a large part of my time, my teachers, my superiors in the place of my work, my neighbors whom I cannot avoid meeting frequently and from whom I cannot easily hide. Being in a position to respond to my action does not make them, however, automatically my reference groups. They become such only when selected by me — when I respond to their attention with assigning them significance, when I care for their wardenship. I may still disregard their pressure (even if at my own peril) and choose to follow the standards they condemn. I may, for instance, deliberately defy my neighbours' ideas about the proper design of front gardens, or about the kind of people one should receive at home and the time of the day they should be received. I may also challenge my friends' dislike of overdoing the study and their preference for taking it easy as far as one's duties are concerned. I may 'play it cool' when deep involvement and passion are called for by the group. In order to exercise their normative influence, even the normative reference groups therefore need my consent to treat them as my reference groups and, for one reason or another, to refrain from resisting their pressure, to conform to their demands.

My decision to be bound is all the more in evidence in the case of **comparative reference groups** — groups of which I am not a member, as I remain, so to speak, beyond their reach. I see the comparative groups without being seen by them. Assigning relevance is in this case one-sided: I consider their actions and standards significant, while they hardly pay any attention to my existence. Because of the distance between us, they are often physically incapable of invigilating and evaluating my actions; for that reason they cannot punish me for my deviation, but neither can they reward me for my conformity. Since, thanks to the mass media and television in particular, all of us are more and more exposed to the flood of information about the diverse ways of life, everything points to the increasing role of comparative reference groups in shaping contemporary selves. The mass media transmit information about reigning fashions and latest styles with enormous speed, and reach the most distant corners of the world. By the same token, they also stamp authority on the patterns they make visually accessible: surely modes of life that deserve to be shown on such media and to be watched by millions of people around the world are worth consideration and, if possible, imitation . . . .

I believe our discussion so far has conveyed the right impression that the process of socialization is not confined to the childhood experience. In fact, it never ends; it goes on throughout one's life, always bringing freedom and dependence into a complex interaction with each other. Sociologists sometimes speak of the **secondary socialization**, to distinguish the continuous transformation of the self which takes place in later life from the internalization of elementary social skills in childhood. They focus attention on situations in which the insufficiency or inadequacy of the former − the **primary** − socialization happens to be dramatically exposed and sharply brought into relief: when, for instance, a person emigrates to a distant country with strange customs and unfamiliar language, and so must not only acquire new skills, but unlearn the old ones which have now turned into a handicap; or when a person brought up in remote countryside migrates to a large city and feels lost and helpless among the dense traffic, rushing crowds and the indifference of passers-by and neighbours. It has been suggested that radical changes of this kind are likely to cause acute anxiety and, indeed, high incidence of nervous breakdowns and even mental ailments. It has also been pointed out that a situation of secondary socialization with equally dramatic consequences may be brought about by the change in external social conditions, rather than mobility of the individual. Sudden economic depression, the onset of mass unemployment, outbreak of war, destruction of life savings by rampant inflation, loss of security through withdrawal of the right to a benefit or on the contrary a rapid rise in prosperity and opportunities for improvement, opening up new, unthought-of possibilities − all provide examples of such cases. They all 'invalidate' the achievements of preceding socialization and require a radical restructuring of one's behaviour, which in its turn calls for new skills and new knowledge.

Examples of both kinds help us to visualize the problems brought about by secondary socialization, as they present them in their sharpest and most acute form. Yet in a less spectacular mode each of us confronts the secondary socialization problems virtually daily; most certainly we experience them whenever we change a school, go to university or leave it, take up a new job, change from being a single to a married person, acquire a house of our own, move house, become parents, turn into old-age pensioners, and so on. It is perhaps better to think of socialization as a continuing process, rather than to split it into two separate stages. The dialectics of freedom and dependence starts at birth and ends only with death.

The balance between the two partners in this continuous dialectical relationship shifts, however. In early childhood there is little, if any, freedom to choose the group one is dependent on. One is born into a particular family, locality, neighbourhood, class or country. One is assumed, without being asked, to be a member of a particular nation or one of the two socially accepted sexes. With age (that means with a growing collection of skills and resources of action) the choice widens; some dependencies may be challenged and rejected, others sought and assumed voluntarily. And yet freedom is never complete. Remember that all of us tend to become determined by our own past actions; because of them, we find ourselves at every moment in a position in which some choices, however attractive, are unattainable, while the costs of change are exorbitant and off-putting. There is too much to be 'de-learned' too many habits to be forgotten. The skills and resources which could be acquired only at an earlier stage were neglected at that time, and now it is too late to make up for the lost opportunity. By and large, we find the feasibility and the likelihood of a 'new break' increasingly remote beyond a certain age.

Neither is the balance the same for all human beings. Remember the role which the available resources play in making choice a viable, realistic proposition. Remember too the role of the 'horizons' set by the original social location for later life-projects and such ends as one may find attractive enough to pursue. It is enough to consider the role of these two factors, to understand that while all people are free and cannot but be free (that is, they are bound to take responsibility for whatever they do), some are more free than others: their horizons (range of choice) are wider, and once they have made up their minds as to the kind of life-project they wish to pursue, they have most of the resources (money, connections, education, refined speech habits, etc.) such a project requires; they are freer than others to desire, to act upon their wishes, and to achieve the results they want.

We can say that the ratio between freedom and dependence is an indicator of the relative position a person, or a whole category of persons, occupies in society. What we call privilege appears, under closer scrutiny, a higher degree of freedom and a lesser degree of dependence. The obverse is true for those who bear the name of disprivileged.

Chapter Two

Us and Them

Adam Smith, an acute observer of the paradoxes of social life, commented once that 'in civilized society [a person] stands of all times in need of the cooperation and assistance of great multitudes, while his whole life is scarce sufficient to gain the friendship of a few friends'.

Think of all those unknown and uncountable multitudes whose actions are indispensable to make your life liveable (those whose labour was used to bring your daily measure of cornflakes on to your plate; those who keep watch on the state of the motorway surface so you can develop the 70 mph speed without fearing gaping holes round the corner; those who, by obeying the rules of joint living, make it possible for you to walk the streets without fear of assault, or breathe the air without being afraid of poisoning by toxic fumes). Think of all those huge multitudes who, equally unknown to you, nevertheless put constraints upon your freedom to select the life of your liking (those who wish to possess the same commodity you are after and hence allow the merchandising companies to keep the price high; those who find robots more profitable than living employees and hence trim your chances of finding a job which suits you; those who — preoccupied as they are with their own ends — bring about that foul air, noise, clogged roads, smelly water you can do little to escape). Compare the sheer size of such multitudes with a list of people you have met, whom you can recognize by face, whose names you can remember. No doubt you will find out that among all those people who influence your life, the people you know or know of constitute a very small section of those whom you have never met and heard of. How small that section is, you will never know . . .

As I think of them, members of the human race (past, present or future) appear to me in different capacities. Some I meet quite often and hence seem to know intimately; I believe I know what I may and what I may not expect of them, how to make sure that I get from them what I expect and desire, how to make sure that they react to my actions the way I would like them to. With such people I *interact*; we *communicate* — we talk to each other, share our knowledge, and debate things of common interest with a hope of reaching agreement. Some others I meet only on occasion; our meetings take place on the whole in special circumstances, when either myself or the other person wishes to obtain or exchange particular, quite specific services (I seldom meet my teacher other than during lectures or tutorials; I meet a certain shop assistant only when I buy my groceries; I see my dentist, luckily, very seldom — when my teeth need repair). My relations with such people may be called functional. In my life, these people perform a **function**; our interaction is reduced to certain aspects of my own (and, I presume, also of their) interests and activities. In most cases, I am not interested in such aspects of the other person as do not bear on the function I expect that person to perform. And so I do not inquire about the family life of the shop assistant, about the hobbies of the dentist, about the artistic taste of my teacher of political science. I expect a similar consideration from them in exchange. I would treat their inquiries as an unwarranted intrusion into what, in relation to them, I see as my *privacy*. Should such an intrusion occur, I would resist it — as a case of abusing or breaching the unwritten terms of reference of our relationship, which is, after all, no more than an *exchange* of a particular service. Finally, others still I meet hardly at all. I know of them; I know they exist, but as they do not seem directly relevant to my daily business, I do not seriously consider the possibility of communicating with them directly. In fact, I seldom devote them more than a fleeting thought.

Alfred Schutz, a German-American sociologist who founded the so-called phenomenological school in sociology, suggested that from any individual point of view all other members of the human race may be plotted along an imaginary line, a continuum measured by **social distance**, which grows as social intercourse shrinks in its

volume and intensity. Taking myself (the ego) as the starting point
of such a line, I may say that those plotted nearest to me are my
consociates; people with whom I truly enter direct, face-to-face relations. My consociates occupy only a small stretch of a larger sector
populated by my *contemporaries* — people who live at the same time
as I do and with whom I can, at least potentially, establish such face-
to-face relations. My practical experience of such contemporaries is
varied, of course. It ranges all the way from a personalized knowledge
to a knowledge limited to my ability to assign people to *types* — as no
more than specimens of a category (old people, blacks, Jews, South
Americans, the rich, football hooligans, soldiers, bureaucrats and the
like). The more distant from myself is the given point on the
continuum, the more generalized, typified is my awareness of the
people who occupy it, as well as my reaction to them: my mental
attitude towards them if we do not meet, or my practical conduct if
we do. In addition to my contemporaries, however, there are (at
least within my mental map of the human race) my *predecessors* and
my *successors*. They differ from my contemporaries in that my communication with them is incomplete, one-sided, and is bound to
remain such — for the time being, or perhaps for ever. The predecessors may pass messages to me (we tend to call such messages
tradition, preserved by *historical memory*), but I cannot answer them
back. With the successors, it is the other way around; I, together
with my contemporaries, leave messages for them, contained as it
were in what we conjointly or individually build or write — yet I do
not expect them to answer me back. Note that none of the listed
categories is fixed once and for all. They have 'porous' boundaries;
individual people may and do change their location, moving from
one category to another, travelling towards my end of the continuum
or away from it, shifting from the contemporaries to the predecessors
or from the successors to the contemporaries.

The two types of proximity — mental and physical — do not
necessarily overlap. In densely populated areas, like urban centres,
we remain at any moment physically close to a great number of
people with whom we feel little spiritual link; as we will find out in
chapter 3, in the congested space of the city physical proximity goes
hand in hand with spiritual remoteness (indeed, living in a city calls

for a complex art of 'neutralizing' the impact of physical nearness, lest it should embroil us in a mental overload and impose moral obligations too voluminous for us to carry; all city dwellers learn and practise this art). Mental or moral proximity consists of our capacity (and willingness) to experience **fellow-feeling**: to perceive other persons as subjects like us, with their own objectives and the right to pursue them, with emotions similar to ours and similar ability to feel pleasure and suffer pain. Fellow-feeling normally includes *empathy*: the ability, and willingness, to put oneself in the other person's position, to see things through someone else's eyes. It also entails the capacity for *commiseration* — for enjoying other person's joys and being sad because of the other person's sorrows. This kind of fellow-feeling is the surest sign (in fact, the very meaning) of mental and moral proximity. It fades and peters out as the distance grows.

Among all the distinctions and divisions which enable me to visualize the 'breaks in continuity', to perceive divisions where a smooth continuum would otherwise be, to divide people into categories calling for different attitudes and different behaviour, one division stands out and has more impact on my relations with others than all the rest of the divisions I carry in my head and embody in my conduct. This is the distinction between 'us' and 'them'. 'We' and 'they' do not stand just for two separate groups of people, but for the distinction between two totally different attitudes — between emotional attachment and antipathy, trust and suspicion, security and fear, cooperativeness and pugnacity. 'We' stands for the group to which I belong. What happens inside this group, I understand well — and since I understand, I know how to go on, I feel secure and at home. The group is, so to speak, my natural habitat, the place where I like to be and to which I return with a feeling of relief. 'They', on the contrary, stands for a group to which I either cannot or do not wish to belong. My vision of what is going on in that group is thereby vague and fragmentary, I poorly comprehend its conduct, and hence what that group is doing is to me by and large unpredictable and by the same token frightening. I am inclined to suspect that 'they' repay my reservations and anxiety in the same currency, reciprocate my suspicions and resent me as much as I disapprove of them. I expect them therefore to act against my interests, to seek to do me harm and bring me misfortune, to rejoice in my misery.

The distinction between 'us' and 'them' is sometimes presented in sociology as one between **in-group** and **out-group**. This pair of opposite attitudes is inseparable; there can be no 'in-group' feeling without an 'out-group' sentiment, and vice versa. The two members of the conceptual-behavioural opposition complement and condition each other; they acquire all their meaning from that opposition. 'Them' are not 'us', and 'us' are not 'them'; 'we' and 'they' can be understood only together, in their mutual conflict. I see my in-group as 'us' only because I think of some other group as 'them'. The two opposite groups sediment, as it were, in my map of the world on the two poles of an antagonistic relationship, and it is this *antagonism* which makes the two groups 'real' to me and makes credible that inner unity and coherence I imagine they possess.

The opposition is, first and foremost, a tool which I employ to draw the chart of my world (my principle of classification, the frame assigning to others their places in my map of the divided universe). I use it to differentiate between my own and the neighbouring school; or between 'my' and the competing football side, complete with its troublesome fans; or between the well-off and hence presumably decent taxpayers like me and the 'spongers' who wish to live at other people's expense; or between my peace-loving friends who wish nothing but to enjoy themselves, and the police, determined to make it impossible; or between us, law-abiding, respectable citizens, and the 'rabble' who defy all rules and dislike all order; or between us, reliable, hard-working adults and the wild, idle adolescents; or between us, young people who want to find our room in the world and make it a better place to live in, and the old who stick to their outdated and obsolete ways; or between my benevolent and well-wishing nation and its aggressive, evil and scheming neighbours.

We and they, in-group and out-group, derive in each case our respective characteristics, as well as our distinctive emotional colouring, from our mutual antagonism. One can say that this antagonism defines both sides of the opposition. One can also say that each side derives its identity from the very fact that we see it as being engaged in antagonism with its opposite. From these observations, we can draw a truly amazing conclusion: an out-group is precisely that imaginary opposition to itself which the in-group needs for its self-identity, for its cohesiveness, for its inner solidarity and emotional security. The readiness to cooperate within the confines of the in-group needs, as it were, a prop in the form of a refusal to cooperate with an adversary. One can even say that the actual presence of a group which truly behaves like one would expect an out-group to behave is neither here nor there; were there no such group, it would have been invented – for the sake of the coherence and integration of the group which must postulate an enemy to draw and to guard its own boundaries and to secure loyalty and cooperation within. It is as if I needed the fear of a wilderness in order to feel securely at home somewhere. There must be an 'out' for the 'in' to be truly appreciated.

It is the **family** (not necessarily the one we know from our own, not always happy, experience, but one like we imagine 'an ideal family' to be, or want such a family to be, or dream it to be) which serves most often as a model for that mutual sympathy and assistance which we tend to ascribe to, or demand from, or hope to obtain from, an in-group. The ideals which colour attitudes towards most in-groups are those of solidarity, mutual confidence and 'common bind' (that is, having an obligation to help, even at one's own expense, whenever the other side needs assistance, and acting on it). This is how one would expect the members of an ideal family to behave towards each other. Ideal relations of parents towards their children supply a pattern for love and care, for using one's superior strength or power only in the interest of the weaker side of the relationship. Ideal relations between husband and wife provide an example of complementarity; only together, through offering each other the services at which he or she is best, may they attain the purpose they both value and seek. Ideal relations between siblings offer a prototype of selfless cooperation, of joining forces in a common cause, of a solidary behaviour of the type 'one for all, all for one'. You have probably noticed time and again that people who wish to evoke mutual loyalty in their audience are fond of using the metaphor of brotherhood or sisterhood and address their listeners as 'brothers' or 'sisters'. Feelings of national solidarity and the readiness to sacrifice oneself for the nation are prompted by references to the native country as 'our mother' or 'the fatherland'.

Mutual help, protection and friendship are therefore the imaginary rules of the in-group life. When we think of the others whom we count among the 'we-group', we hope that were there a disagreement among them, they would behave as if a solution useful to them all, and universal consent to it, were in principle both desirable and attainable. We hope that they would set about negotiating the solution in a friendly mood, peacefully, mindful of the commonality of their interests. Falling out with each other would be seen, contrariwise, as a temporary mishap, which could be averted if only all sides 'saw all the facts of the matter' and were allowed to express their true feelings instead of permitting themselves to be misled by assorted trouble-makers (most probably agents of 'the other side', the 'infiltrators' who only pretend to belong to 'us'). All this makes us perceive of relationships of the in-group type as emotionally warm, suffused with mutual sympathy and thus inspiring in everyone the loyalty and determination needed for the solidary defence of the group against all and sundry.

It goes without saying that we would not take lightly any adverse opinions about those with whom we identify as with co-members of our we-group. If we hear such opinions, we will probably do our best to refute them and defend the good name of the 'unjustly accused'. Were we confronted with proof that people belonging to the in-group have behaved in a less than impeccable fashion, we would try hard to explain the facts away, or to dismiss them as malicious gossip, evidence of ill will or an invention of hostile propaganda. The opposite, of course, applies to all such accusations we may charge against 'them'. Such charges, for a change, are true. They must be true. They had better be true . . .

What all this amounts to is the feeling which *precedes* all reflection and argument: the feeling of a community, or an in-group, which is a pleasant place to be, which is truly one's home, and whose boundaries ought to be defended at any price, just as one's home tends to be. Here, inside, things may sometimes be difficult, but one can always find a solution in the end. People may seem harsh and selfish, but one can count on their help in case of need. Above all, one can understand them and be certain of being understood by them. Mistaken reading of their behaviour is unlikely. All in all, one enjoys the comforting feeling of security; if there is a danger, it will surely be spotted in time and then 'we' will join forces to fight it.

This is what we feel — even if we do not say it in so many words or even if we have never spelled it out for ourselves — whenever we speak of 'us'. We *feel* it, and it is this feeling which counts and not what all these people whom we include in the 'we' really do. Of their practices we sometimes know little, particularly if the spiritual closeness is not matched by physical proximity, by frequent encounters, by constant intercourse, by **face-to-face** contact.

Although our images of all in-groups, large and small, share certain crucial features, the groups to which we apply such images differ sharply in themselves. Some in-groups are small in size; so small, in fact, that all persons included may closely observe each other through most of the day, in most of their activities, while their interactions are frequent and intense. These are face-to-face groups. The family (particularly a family living under one roof) offers the most obvious, indeed primary, example. But one can also think of a close group of dedicated friends, spending as much time as they can afford in each other's presence and constantly longing for each other's company. Though the composition of the family is only partly of our own choice, while we may choose, change or abandon a group of friends according to our will, both groups, thanks to their manageable size, are as intimate as only face-to-face contact allows. In such groups, we may effectively test our expectations and ideal images against what the others really do and how they do it. We may even try to bring the behaviour of our companions closer to the ideal if we find that their actual conduct is not quite up to the standard we expect. We can rebuke and punish them for what we do not like, and praise and reward them for what we do. In such cases, our ideal image acquires tangible, 'material' power. Through our corrective actions, it exerts constant pressure on what all the members of the we-group do. In the end, it may even keep reality in line with the norms we approve of, make it as we have imagined it and wished it to be. This is not the case, however, if the in-group is so large and scattered that one meets but few of its assumed members face-to-face.

Class, gender and nation are typical examples of this second category of in-group. Though we often imagine them as if they were much like the small, intimate groups we know, only on a bigger scale, 'writ large', they partake of none of the small-group intimacy; their unity is carried mostly in the heads of those who think of them as 'us'. They are fully and truly *imaginary communities* (or, rather, they are imaginary *as* communities; the traits they have in common do not by themselves guarantee that the solidary action and mutual understanding which we rightly and credibly associate with genuine we-groups will indeed take place). In fact, collections of people of the same occupational standing and income, of the same sex, of the same language and customs, may be and most often are torn apart by deep conflicts of interests, split into warring factions, divided by beliefs and objectives which cannot be easily reconciled. All such cracks in their unity are but thinly painted over by the 'we' image. If I use 'us' to talk about a particular class, gender or nation, I give priority to what unites us (or what I believe and would wish to unite us) over what divides us. It is as if I were appealing to other members of an imaginary community (like many a nationalist leader does in his patriotic pep-talk): forget the differences, stop quarrelling, remember we have a lot in common, and what we have in common is much more important than anything which divides us, so let us close our ranks and join the common cause.

Lacking the cement of face-to-face contact, classes, genders and nations do not become in-groups by themselves. They must be *made* so, and often despite powerful forces that tear them apart. The image of a class, of a gender, of a nation as a community, as a unified, concerted and harmonious body of like-minded people who feel similar, must be imposed on the reality with which it jars. The imposition demands that contrary evidence is suppressed or dismissed as false or irrelevant. It also demands unmitigated, relentless preaching of unity. To be effective, it needs a permanent, disciplined and resourceful body of activists, a sort of professional spokespersons for the community, whose practices give flesh to the imaginary unity of interests and beliefs. This body (for instance, a political party, a trade union, a feminist association, a national liberation committee, governments of national states) formulates what it means to belong to the community. It makes a case for unity, pointing out the real or imaginary traits in which all members allegedly share (common historical tradition, or common oppression, or common language and customs) as sufficient grounds for cooperation. If it can afford it, it also deploys its resources to promote conformity with the model it preaches, and to punish or ostracize dissidents and deviants. In short, it is the action of such bodies which *precedes* the formation of large-scale in-groups. And so the idea of class struggle and the militants who promote it precedes that solidarity of class action which stems from viewing class as an in-group. Similarly, nationalism (the idea that loyalty to the nation takes priority over all other loyalties) precedes the emergence of unified national units.

However formidable the bodies which promote the idea of community, and however hard they work, their hold on reality remains inevitably fragile and vulnerable. Because it lacks the substance of a dense network of face-to-face intercourse, the unity of a large-scale community must be upheld by constant appeals to beliefs and emotions. Hence the tremendous importance of drawing and maintaining a boundary. No effort to induce loyalty in a large-scale in-group stands a chance of success if the building of solidarity with the proposed in-group is not associated with preaching and practising hostility to an out-group. The call to close the ranks is always a call to close ranks against an enemy.

The image of the enemy is painted in colours as lurid and frightening as the colours of one's own group are soothing and pleasurable. The enemies are a cunning and scheming lot. They are implacably hostile even if they mask as friendly neighbours, or are prevented from putting their deeds where their hearts are. Were they allowed to have it their way, they would have invade, conquer, enslave, exploit: openly, if they are strong enough, or surreptitiously, if forced to hide their true intentions. One has to remain therefore forever vigilant – to keep the powder dry, as they used to say, to arm oneself and to modernize one's weapons, to be strong so that the enemy notices and admits its weakness and gives up its ill intentions.

Enmity, suspicion and aggressiveness against the out-group (generally represented as a necessary response to the other side's hostility and ill will) result in and are in turn enhanced by **prejudice**. Prejudice means a flat refusal to admit any virtues the enemies may possess, coupled with an inclination to magnify their real and imaginary vices. All the actions of the declared enemies are interpreted in such a way as to blacken their image further, and iniquitous motives are read into them, as if according to the principle 'Whatever you do or say will be taken down and used as evidence against you'. Prejudice prevents one from accepting the possibility that the intentions of the out-group may be honest, or that the enemies may mean what they say and their offer of peace may be sincere and devoid of ulterior motives. In the fight against the 'evil empire' every move of the enemy, however ostensibly peaceful or downright innocuous, is put under a magnifying glass in order to detect its wicked purpose.

Prejudice also manifests itself in double moral standards. What the members of the in-group deserve as of right will be an act of grace and benevolence if done for the people of the out-group; conversely, what in the case of in-group members is commended as an act of praiseworthy selflessness is played down and dismissed as a matter of 'ordinary human decency' if committed by an out-group member. Most importantly, one's own atrocity against out-group members does not seem to clash with moral conscience, while severe condemnation is demanded in cases where much milder acts have been perpetrated by the enemy. Prejudice prompts people to approve of such means used in the promotion of their own cause as they would never agree to accept as justified by the out-group's purposes. Identical actions are called by different names, alternatively loaded with praise and condemnation, depending on which side has undertaken them. Think of such pairs of concepts as freedom fighters and terrorists, protesters and trouble-makers, revolution and riots. These and similar subterfuges allow us to insist — stubbornly, repeatedly and with a clear conscience — that justice is fairly and squarely on the in-group's side.

Inclination to prejudice is not uniformly distributed. It has been observed time and again that some people are particularly prone to perceive the world in terms of sharp, irreconcilable oppositions, and to resent passionately anyone who is or seems to be different from themselves. Such a disposition manifests itself in *racist* attitudes and actions — or, more generally, in *xenophobia*, the hatred of everything 'foreign'. People who entertain high levels of prejudice are normally also stringently and compulsively on the side of uniformity. They are ill prepared to endure any deviation from strict rules of conduct and hence favour a strong power capable of keeping people in line. People characterized by this set of attitudes are said to possess an *authoritarian personality*. Why some people have such a personality, while others can live happily surrounded by a wide variety of styles of life and remain tolerant to even formidable differences, has not been convincingly explained. It may well be that what we describe as an expression of an authoritarian personality is just the outcome of a social situation in which its alleged holders have been cast. Better understood, on the other hand, are such variations in the range and intensity of prejudice as are related to the context in which the affected persons live and act.

Thus the disposition to 'buy' the idea of sharp boundaries between in-group and out-group and jealousy guard the integrity of the first against the threat ostensibly carried by the second seems to be closely related to the feeling of *insecurity*, generated by a drastic change in the habitual and familiar life conditions. Such a change naturally makes life more difficult. As the situation becomes more uncertain and less predictable, it tends to be experienced as dangerous and thus frightening. What people have learned as the efficient and effective way to go about their business of life suddenly becomes less reliable; people feel that they have lost control of the situation, which they previously believed they could handle. The change is therefore resented. The need to defend 'the old ways' (that is, the *familiar* and comfortable ways) is strongly felt, and the resulting aggression is directed against newcomers: those who were not present when the old ways were still securely entrenched but are around now, when the old ways have come under attack or are fast losing their usefulness. The newcomers, in addition, are different anyway; they have their own style of life and so are a tangible embodiment of change. It seems easy to put two and two together; the newcomers are to blame for the change itself, for the fading of old security, the devaluation of old habits, the uncertainty of the present situation and the disasters the future may bring.

Norbert Elias presented a comprehensive analysis of his prejudice-generating situation in his theory of the **established** and the **outsiders**. An influx of outsiders always presents a challenge to the way of life of the established population, however tiny the objective difference between the newcomers and the old inhabitants. Tension arising out of the necessity to make room for the newcomers, and from the outsiders' need to find room for themselves, prompts each side to exaggerate the differences. Often minute traits, which under different circumstances could have passed unnoticed, are now dwelled upon and represented as obstacles to cohabitation. They become an object of abomination and are used as proof that strict separation is unavoidable, and mixing unthinkable. Anxiety and hostile feelings reach boiling-point on both sides, yet the established have, on the whole, better resources to act upon their prejudices. They can also invoke the rights they have acquired to the place by the sheer length of habitation ('this is the land of our forefathers'): outsiders are not just alien and different, they are also 'invaders', intruders, with no entitlement to be there.

The complex relationship between the established and the outsiders goes a long way towards explaining a large variety of the conflicts between in-group and out-group and, more generally still, the cases of widespread and intense prejudice. The birth of modern antisemitism in the nineteenth-century Europe and its wide reception can be understood as the result of a coincidence between the high speed of change in a rapidly industrializing society and the emancipation of the Jews, who emerged from the ghettos or separate Jewish quarters and closed communities to mix with the Gentile population of the cities and enter 'ordinary' occupations. The masses of craftsmen and shopkeepers who were about to lose their habitual existence because of the competition of factories and merchandising companies eagerly accepted the arrival of the strangers previously unseen in their streets as a cogent explanation of the earth-shattering calamity. Similarly, the loss of traditional grounds of security that followed the gradual falling apart of the empire, the destruction of the familiar urban landscape in the course of urban redevelopment in post-war Britain, and the later disappearance of industry to which the skills and life-expectations of many people were geared, generated widespread anxiety which has been subsequently focused on the newcomers from the West Indies or Pakistan; hence the surge of antagonism towards the harbingers of the earthquake — sometimes expressed in an overtly racist form, sometimes deceivingly masked as resistance to 'alien culture' (think of the protest against halal meat 'on humanitarian grounds', or against integrated education in the schools under the pretext that chapatti are served instead of traditional pancakes). To take one more example: for several decades in the second half of the nineteenth century, anxiety and frustration of skilled workers, faced with the threat to the security of their jobs presented by the rapid mechanization of factories and the consequent 'de-skilling' of working operations, was turned against the influx of workers who called themselves 'general', but were immediately dubbed 'unskilled' by the established trade unions. The unskilled were barred entry to trade unions and refused trade-union protection until such time as they finally succeeded in winning trade-union rights against the resistance of the skilled.

Similar processes may be observed in our own times whenever there is change and the opportunities to continue in the old ways are rapidly shrinking. We read of the vehement resistance of one or another unionized group of workers to sharing jobs with members of another union; disputes about demarcation of job entitlements have been arguably the most frequent causes of recent strikes. Perhaps the most spectacular case of the established inclination to construe the newcomers as dangerous outsiders is the notorious male resistance to women's claims of equal rights in employment and in competition for positions of social influence. The entry of women into once secure male preserves puts in question heretofore unchallenged rules, and with that introduces a strongly resented element of unsettling confusion into a previously unambiguous setting. The feminist demand for equal rights evinces feelings of danger, which trigger off angry responses and aggressive postures.

The bitterness of the established — outsiders antagonism, as well as the gravity of its likely consequences, are further exacerbated by the fact that the pugnacity of the established elicits a symmetrical response from the group cast in the position of the outsiders — which, if anything, detracts from the probability of an armistice. An

American anthropologist **Gregory Bateson** suggested the name of **schismogenesis** for the chain of actions and reactions which follows: hostile attitudes, so to speak, supply their own proof through evoking hostile behaviour. As each action calls for a still stronger reaction, both sides willy-nilly drift towards a deep and lasting schism. Whatever control or influence either side might initially have had over mutual relations is now lost. 'The logic of the situation' takes over.

Bateson distinguished between two types of schismogenesis. In the case of **symmetrical schismogenesis**, each side reacts to the signs of strength of the adversary. Whenever the adversary shows power and determination, a still stronger manifestation of power and resolve is sought. What both sides fear most of all is to be seen as weak or hesitating. Think of the slogans 'deterrence must be credible', or 'the aggressor must be shown that aggression does not pay'; some strategists have even suggested that the launching mechanism of nuclear missiles ought to be automatic, to convince the enemy that no last-moment pangs of conscience would stop a nuclear retaliation in case of a hostile action. Symmetrical schismogenesis breeds self-assertiveness on both sides of the conflict and virtually destroys the possibility of rational argument and agreement. Think of the self-exacerbating antagonism between partners in marriage; as each side wishes to have its way rather than compromise, and as each side assumes that only a demonstration of a stronger will and of resolve not to show weakness may achieve this purpose, original petty differences of opinion swell into a chasm so deep that neither side is able to bridge it. Neither side remembers now the original reason for conflict; both sides, instead, are incensed by the bitterness of their present fight. The mutual recriminations and manifestations of superiority slip beyond control and the marriage ends up in divorce: the further chain of interaction is broken.

Complementary schismogenesis develops from exactly opposite assumptions, yet it leads to identical results: namely, to the breakdown of the relationship. The schismogenetic sequence of actions is complementary when one side strengthens its resolve at the sign of weakness on the other side, while the other side weakens its resistance when confronted with manifestations of growing strength on the opposite side. Typically, this is the tendency of any interaction between a domineering and a submissive partner. Self-assurance and self-confidence of one partner feed on symptoms of timidity and submissiveness of the other. In turn, the latter's meekness grows together with the self-assertiveness and arrogance of the first. Cases of complementary schismogenesis are as varied in their content as they are numerous. On one extreme, one can think of a gang terrorizing an entire neighbourhood into unconditional submission and then − convinced of its own omnipotence by complete absence of resistance − raising its demands beyond the capacity of its victims to pay. This will either drive the victims to desperation and ignite their rebellion, or prompt them to move out of the territory blackmailed by the gang. On the other extreme, one can think of the patron− client relationship. The dominant majority (national, racial, cultural, religious) may accept the presence of a minority on condition that the latter studiously demonstrates its acceptance of the dominant values and eagerness to live by the dominant rules. The minority would be keen to please and thereby to curry the rulers' favour − only to discover that the volume of concessions the dominant group demands tends to grow with that group's confidence that its rules and values have been surrendered to and are unlikely to be contested. The minority learns as well that as a means of earning acceptance as an equal partner, the strategy of effacing one's own distinctiveness is counterproductive. The minority will be driven either to escape into its own ghetto, or to change its strategy to one modelled on symmetrical schismogenesis. Whatever the choice, the breakdown of the relationship will be the likely outcome.

Fortunately − so Bateson reminds us − there is also a third type of framework in which interaction may take place: that of **reciprocity**. Reciprocity combines, in a sense, features of the two previously discussed models − but does it in a way that neutralizes their self-destructive tendencies. In a reciprocal relationship, each single case of interaction is assymetrical, yet over a long period the actions of both sides balance each other, and thus the relationship is 'equilib-rated' − it may retain its features over time without driving itself over a precipice. In simpler terms, reciprocity means a relationship in which each side has to offer something that the other side needs (for instance, the resented and discriminated minority may include the only people prepared to do badly needed, but unrewarding jobs that members of the majority avoid). The dependence on the other side's services stops each partner from demanding exaggerated rewards for its own offers. Arguably, some form of reciprocity characterizes most frameworks of interaction. At any rate, it is present, virtually by definition, in every balanced and stable framework of intercourse. It may secure the survival and reproduction of the framework over time, particularly when it assumes the form of *delayed* reciprocity (when, for instance, children 'repay' the care of their parents by caring for their own children). It ought to be noted, however, that no reciprocal framework is fully immune against the danger of sliding on occasion into a symmetrical or complementary relationship, and thereby triggering off the process of schismogenesis.

Chapter Three

Strangers

We have seen in the last chapters that 'us' and 'them' make sense only together: in their opposition to each other. We are 'us' only in so far as there are people who are not us — 'them'; and they belong together, form a group, a whole, only because each and every one of them shares the same characteristic: none of them is 'one of us'. Both concepts derive their meaning from the dividing line they service. Without such a division, without the possibility of opposing ourselves to 'them', we would be hard put to make sense of our own identity.

The 'strangers', on the other hand, defy that division; one may say that what they oppose is the opposition itself: divisions of any kind, boundaries which guard them, and thus the clarity of the social world which results from all that. Herein lie their significance, their meaning and the role they play in social life. By their sheer presence, which does not fit easily into any of the established categories, the strangers deny the very validity of the accepted oppositions. They belie the oppositions' 'natural' character, expose their arbitrariness, lay bare their fragility. They show the divisions for what they indeed are: imaginary lines which can be crossed or redrawn.

To avoid confusion, let us note from the start that the stranger is not simply an *unfamiliar* person — any person we do not know well, do not know at all or do not know of. If anything, the opposite is true: the remarkable feature of the strangers is that they are to a large extent *familiar*; to conceive of a person as a stranger, I must first know quite a few things about him or her. Above all, they are bound to come time and again, uninvited, into my field of vision — so that I must watch them at close quarters; whether I want it or not, they sit firmly inside the world which I occupy and in which I act and do not show signs of leaving. Were it not for this reason, they would not be strangers, but just 'nobodies'. They would dissolve among the many faceless, interchangeable figures who move in the background of my daily life — most often unobtrusively, without calling for my attention and fastening it on themselves — those background figures I look at, but do not see. I listen, but do not hear what they are saying. The strangers, on the contrary, are people whom I see and hear. It is precisely because I note their presence, because I cannot disregard this presence and cannot make this presence irrelevant simply by refusing to give it my attention, that I find it difficult to make sense of them. They are, as it were, neither close nor distant. Neither a part of 'us' nor a part of 'them'. Neither friends nor foes. For this reason, they cause confusion and anxiety. I do not know exactly what I should make of them, what to expect, how to behave.

Making the boundaries as exact and precise as possible, so that they can be easily noticed and once noticed understood unambiguously, seems to be a matter of supreme importance for human beings living and trained to live in a man-made world. All the acquired skills of life in society would be useless, often harmful, sometimes downright suicidal, were it not for the fact that well-marked boundaries send us an unmistakable signal as to what to expect and which of the learned patterns of conduct to employ to reach whatever happens to be our desired purpose. And yet such boundaries are always conventional. People on the opposite sides of the border do not differ so sharply from each other as to spare us mistaken classification. And so constant effort is needed to maintain 'yes—no' divisions in a reality that knows of no such sharp, unmistakable contours. For instance, drawing the all-important boundary between the field where community-like rules bind and the field where the pragmatics of warfare is called for is always an attempt to impose an artificial (and hence precarious) clarity on a situation which is much less clear-cut. Hardly ever are people 'exact and complete opposites' of each other. If they differ in one respect, they are similar in another. Their differences themselves are seldom as obvious and unconditional as the assignment to opposite categories would imply. Most traits may be shown to vary in a gradual, smooth, often imperceptible way. (Remember Schutz's image of a continuous line that has no natural divisions, so that the distance between two people plotted on the line next to each other may be infinitely small; obviously each boundary, each interruption point which attempts to assign all the people plotted to the left of the line to a sharply distinct, opposite category from the one for the people on the right will be equally random and difficult to defend.) Because of the overlap between various human attributes and the graduality of variations, each dividing line would inevitably leave on both sides of the boundary a sort of grey area, where people would not be immediately recognizable as belonging to one or other of the two opposite groups which the dividing line implies. Such an unwanted but unavoidable ambiguity is seen as threatening, since it confuses the situation and makes it exceedingly difficult to select with certainty an attitude proper for either an in-group or an out-group context — for a setting of friendly cooperation or that of a vigilant and hostile reserve. With enemies we fight, friends we like and help; but what about people who are neither? Or who can be both?

The British-American social anthropologist **Mary Douglas** pointed out that among human preoccupations quite a crucial role is played by the never ending task of making the human-made order 'stick'; most of the differences which are vital for human life do not exist naturally, by themselves; they must be introduced and vigilantly defended. (It has been said that an underground drawing was circulated in the Middle Ages: it portrayed four skulls, and contained a caption: 'Guess which one belonged to the Pope, which to the Prince, which to the peasant, which to the beggar?' Of course the skulls were identical, and their complete similarity suggested that all the by no means inconsiderable, unbridgeable differences — say between princes and beggars — were related to what one wore or did not wear on one's head, and not to the shape or size of the head itself. No wonder this was an *underground* cartoon.) To achieve this purpose, all ambiguity which blurs the boundaries and hence undermines the design, muddles the intended order, thrusts confusion where clarity should rule, needs to be suppressed or exterminated. It is my image of the order I wish to achieve, my notion of elegance and beauty, which inspires me to resent those stubbornly ambivalent bits of reality which do not fit the divisions. The rubbish which I work hard to sweep away is simply a thing 'out of place', something which has no clear place of its own in my image of the world. There is nothing wrong with the thing itself. It is only finding it where it should not be which makes it repulsive and undesirable.

Here are a few examples. What makes some plants into 'weeds', which we mercilessly poison and uproot, is their horrifying tendency to obliterate the boundary between our garden and wilderness. The 'weeds' are often quite nice looking, fragrant and pleasing; we would certainly admire them as adorable specimens of wildlife if we found them while walking through woods or a meadow. Their 'fault' is that they have come, uninvited, to a place which ought to be neatly cut into lawns, rose garden, vegetable plot and flower borders. They spoil the harmony we envisaged, they play havoc with our design. We admire a plateful of food on our dining table but would abhor the sight of the same dish splattered over a sheet or pillow — for the simple reason that its being out of place saps the design of our home, where two physically identical spaces are kept strictly distinct and dedicated to functions we keep apart — one is the dining room, another is a bedroom. Even the most elegant and shiny shoes we would proudly sport on our feet would seem like 'dirt' if put on the desk. So will hair clippings or nail-parings, though hair and nails are normally objects of our loving care and pride as long as they remain part of our bodies. It has been found that some chemical companies had to put two clearly distinct labels onto packages containing identical detergents; they learned from careful research that most people proud of their housekeeping would not dream of confusing the difference between bathroom and kitchen through using the same detergent in both places. In these as in other similar cases the intense, obsessive attention we all devote to the fighting of 'dirt', putting things in their right place (where they belong), etc. is motivated by the need to keep steady, intact and clear the boundaries between such divisions as make our world orderly and hence liveable and easy to move about in.

The borderline between the in-group and the out-group, between 'us' and 'them', belongs to the divisions most hotly defended and absorbing most attention. One can say of the out-group that it is useful, even indispensable, to the in-group, since it brings into relief the identity of the in-group and fortifies its coherence and solidarity. The same cannot be said, however, of that formless grey area which extends *between* the two groups. It can hardly perform a conceivably useful role; it is seen as being harmful, without qualification. Hence the principle favoured by any politician seeking popular support through mobilizing feelings of patriotic or partisan solidarity: 'Whoever is not with us, is against us.' In such a categorical division, no room is left for an intermediate, indecisive or natural position. If allowed, such positions would imply that the division between right and wrong was not as absolute as had been suggested. Many a political party, church or a nationalist or sectarian organization spends much more time and energy fighting its own dissidents than its declared enemies. On the whole, traitors and renegades tend to be hated much more intensely than the outright, self-acknowledged enemies. For a nationalist or a party militant, no enemy is as detestable and hateful as 'one of us' who ran to the other side, or who is not outspoken enough in condemning it; a conciliatory attitude is berated with much more vigour than outright enmity. In all religions, the heretics are abhorred more than the straightforward infidels and persecuted with much more venom. 'Breaking the ranks', 'rocking the boat', 'sitting astride the barricade' are the worst of the crimes of which leaders may accuse their followers. These charges are levied against people who think (worse still, say; worst of all, show by their deeds) that the divide between their own nation, party, church or movement and their declared enemies is not absolute, and that mutual understanding and even agreement are conceivable; or that the honour of their own group is not spotless, and the group itself is not beyond reproach, not always in the right.

The group's boundary is, however, threatened from both sides. It can be eroded from inside − by those ambivalent people who have been branded as deserters, detractors of values, enemies of unity, turncoats. But it can also be attacked and eventually pierced from the outside: by people who 'are not quite like us', but demand to be treated as if they were; people who have left the place where they could without error be identified as aliens, as 'not us', and now mill around where they can easily be mistaken for what they are not. By making this 'passage' they have shown that the boundary which was trusted as safe, impermeable, is far from being watertight. This sin alone would be enough to make one resent them and wish they would return to where they came from: their sight makes one feel insecure, there is something vaguely dangerous about them. Having lifted themselves from their old place and passed to our own, they accomplished a feat which makes us suspect they possess some awesome and mysterious power we cannot resist, a cunning we cannot match; and that they nourish ill intentions towards us and thus are likely to use their horrifying superiority to our disadvantage. We do not feel confident in their presence; we half-consciously expect the newcomers to engage in acts both dangerous and disgusting. 'Neophyte' (someone who converted to our faith), '*nouveau riche*' (someone poor only yesterday, who made a sudden fortune and today joined the rich and powerful) and 'upstart' (someone of low social standing quickly promoted to a position of power) are all terms which carry a heavy load of reprobation, loathing and contempt. They all denote people who yesterday were 'there', but now are 'here'. People who because of their very mobility, because of their uncanny talent to be both here and there at will, cannot be trusted: after all, they have broken what should be foolproof and watertight, and this original sin cannot be forgotten or repented. It will not go away.

They arouse anxiety for other reasons as well. They are, indeed, *newcomers*, new to our way of life, unfamiliar with our ways and means. For this reason, whatever is normal and natural for us — 'born' into our way of life — is bizarre and sometimes baffling to them. They do not take the wisdom of our ways for granted. They therefore ask questions which we do not know how to answer, because in the past we had no occasion and saw no reason to ask them ourselves: 'Why do you do it this way? Does it make sense? Have you tried to do it differently?' The way we have lived, the kind of life which gives us our security and makes us feel comfortable, is now challenged. It has turned into a matter we are called to argue about, explain, justify. It is not self-evident and thus does not seem secure any more. The loss of security is not something one would forgive lightly. And on the whole we are not inclined to forgive. Hence we view such questions as offences, arguments as subversion, comparisons as arrogance and spite. We wish we had closed our ranks in the 'defence of our life' against the influx of strangers whom we hold responsible for this sudden crisis of confidence. Our discomfort turns into anger against the trouble-makers.

Even if the newcomers stand mum, keep their mouths shut and respectfully refrain from asking awkward questions, the way they go about their daily business of life cannot but do the questioning for them with the same upsetting effect. The people who have come from there to here and are determined to stay will wish to learn our ways of life, imitate them, become 'like us'. If not all, then most of them will try to furnish their homes just like we do, dress like we do, copy the fashion of our work and leisure. Not only will they speak our language, but they will make an arduous effort to emulate the way we talk or address each other. However hard they try (or perhaps because they try so hard), they cannot help making mistakes, at least at the beginning. Their attempts look unconvincing. Their behaviour looks clumsy, awkward, ludicrous; it seems more like a caricature of our own conduct and hence forces us to ask what the 'real thing' is like. Their performance smacks of a satirical send-up. We disown their inept imitations by ridiculing them, laughing at them, composing and telling jokes which 'caricature the caricature'. But there is an admixture of bitterness in our laughter; anxiety masking as hilarity. Whatever we do to confine the damage, the harm has been done. Our unconscious customs and habits have been shown to us in a distorted mirror of sorts. We have been forced to look at them ironically, to stand at a critical distance from our own lives. Even without explicit questioning, therefore, our comfort has been upset.

As we can see, there are plenty reasons to watch the strangers suspiciously as a potential menace. They would be relatively innocuous were they clearly branded as 'not belonging to us' and remained aliens who accepted that our way was for us and their way was theirs and the two should not mix and be confused; if, in other words, we were allowed to disregard them even if they happened to enter our field of vision. The potential for trouble, however, grows dramatically once the distinction is not as clear as it used to be and shows a disturbing tendency to lose its remaining clarity. What was perhaps seen in the beginning as a laughing matter and gave rise to jokes and ridicule may now arouse hostility — and aggression.

The first response, therefore, is to restore the lost clarity of the division by sending the strangers back 'where they came from' (that is, if there is such a natural abode from which they originally emerged; this applies above all to ethnically alien immigrants who came with the hope of settling down in their new country). Sometimes an attempt is made to force them to emigrate, or to make their lives so miserable that they themselves would treat exodus as a lesser evil. If such a move is resisted, or massive eviction is not for one reason or another a viable proposition, genocide may follow; cruel physical destruction is charged with the task that the attempt at physical removal failed to fulfil. Genocide is the extreme and most abhorrent method of 'restoring order', and yet recent history proved in a most gruesome way that the danger of genocide is not fanciful, that eruption of genocidal action cannot be excluded as a possibility — and that despite universal condemnation and widespread resentment.

More often than not, however, other, less odious and radical solutions are chosen. One of the most commonly used is **separation**. Separation may be territorial, or spiritual, or both. Its territorial variety found its fullest expression in ghettos or ethnic reserves — parts of the towns or areas of the country reserved for the habitation of people whom the native population refused to mix with, seeing them as aliens and wishing their alien status to last for ever. Sometimes the allocated land was surrounded by walls and by even thicker layers of legally enforced prohibitions (the passbooks needed to leave black 'homelands' and the ban on purchasing estate property in the areas reserved for the whites in South Africa provide a recent yet by no means unprecedented example), and the aliens were forbidden to leave the area they were allowed to inhabit. Sometimes movement to and from the reserved space is not legally punishable and nominally free, but in practice its residents cannot or will not escape their confinement — either because the conditions 'outside' have been made intolerable for them (they are physically assaulted, ridiculed and otherwise pestered), or because the miserable standard of living in their own, usually derelict, quarters is the only one they can afford. When the physique and demeanour of the people defined as alien contained little to distinguish them from the natives, special dress or other stigmatizing signs were often prescribed to make the difference visible and reduce the danger of accidental intercourse. Thanks to the warning signs they were told to wear, the strangers carried, so to speak, their separate territory with them wherever they went — even if they were allowed to move around. And they had to be allowed to move, as they often performed perhaps menial and despised, yet vital and indispensable services for the natives (as when the Jews in medieval Europe provided most of the cash loans and banking credit).

In cases where territorial separation is incomplete or becomes altogether impracticable, spiritual separation grows in importance. Intercourse with the strangers is reduced to strictly business exchanges. Social contacts are avoided. An effort is made to prevent the unavoidable physical proximity from turning into a spiritual one. Resentment or overt hostility are the most obvious among such preventive efforts. A barrier built of prejudice and resentment frequently proved more effective than the thickest of stone walls. Active avoidance of contact is constantly boosted by the fear of contamination — in the literal or metaphorical sense: the strangers are believed to carry contagious diseases, to be infested with insects, to defy rules of hygiene and thus represent a health hazard; or to spread morbid ideas and habits, practise black arts or dismal and gory cults, disseminate moral depravity and laxity of mores. Resentment spills over everything one can associate with the strangers: their way of talking, their way of dressing, their religious rituals, the way they organize their family life, even the smell of the food they like to cook.

The practices of separation discussed so far have all assumed a simple situation: here we are, the 'us' who need to defend ourselves against 'them' who came to stay among 'us' and would not leave despite being unwelcome. Who belongs to each group has not been in dispute, as if there were just one standard for 'us' and one for 'them'; it is these well-formed and evidently different standards that have to be kept at arm's length. It is easy to see, however, that this kind of simple situation and the clear-cut task it tends to generate is hardly ever met in our type of society. The society we live in is an urban society: people live together in great density, travel a lot; in the course of their daily business they enter very diverse areas inhabited by very diverse people, move from one town to another, or from one part of town to another. In the course of one day we meet far too many people to know them all. In most cases, we cannot be sure that people we meet uphold our standards. Almost constantly we are struck by new sights and sounds we do not fully comprehend; worse still, hardly ever do we have time to pause, reflect and make an honest attempt to understand. The world we live in seems to be populated mostly by strangers; it looks like the world of *universal strangerhood*. We live among strangers, among whom we are strangers ourselves. In such a world, strangers cannot be confined or kept at bay. Strangers must be lived with.

This does not mean that the practices described above are completely abandoned in the new circumstances. If mutually estranged groups cannot on the whole be effectively separated, their intercourse can still be somewhat reduced (and made inconsequential and thus innocuous) by practices of **segregation** — which, however, need now to be modified.

Take as an example one of the methods of segregation we have encountered before: the wearing of salient, easily visible marks of group membership. Such a group-ascribed appearance may be enforced by law, so that 'passing for someone else' will be punished. But it may also be achieved without legal interference. For most of urban history, only the rich and the privileged could afford sumptuous, elaborate dresses, normally no dresses were obtainable far from where they were made (always according to local customs), and thus one could classify unknown persons by the splendour, misery or oddity of their *appearance*. This is not easy any more, however. Relatively cheap copies of admired and highly praised dresses are now produced in massive quantities, so that they can be acquired and worn by people on a relatively modest income (which, most importantly, means that wellnigh everybody can wear them). Moreover, the copies are on the whole so faithfully made that they are difficult to distinguish, particularly at a distance, from the real thing.

Because of the wide availability of any fashion, clothing has all but lost its traditional segregatory function. This, in turn, changed the 'social address' of sartorial innovations. Most of them are not now permanently bound to any particular income group or class; shortly after they have been introduced, they appear within the reach of the public at large. Fashions have also lost their local character and become truly 'exterritorial' or cosmopolitan. The same or virtually indistinguishable dresses can be and are obtained in places far away from each other. They hide now rather than disclose the territorial origin and mobility of their owners and wearers. This does not mean that appearance does not set their wearers apart; on the contrary, dress has acquired the role of one of the prime symbolic devices used by men and women to make a public statement about the reference group they have chosen as their pattern, and the capacity in which they wish to be perceived and approached. It is as if, by choosing my dress, I were telling the world, 'Look, this is where I belong, this is the kind of person I am, and please note that this is the kind of person you had better take me for and treat accordingly.' And so by the choice of dress I may deceive as much as inform; I may disguise myself as someone I otherwise would not be allowed to be, and escape (or at least make secret for a time) the socially imposed classification. My dress cannot be trusted as a reliable guide to my identity. And so I cannot trust the informative value of other people's appearance either. They may deliberately wish to mislead the onlookers. They may now put on, now take off the eminently detachable symbols they brandish. In another hour they may pass for someone quite different from the person they seem to be now.

With segregation *by appearance* losing much of its practical value, more importance is acquired by segregation *by space*. The territory of shared urban residence tends to be divided into areas in which one kind of person is more likely to be found than all the others, or some kinds of people are unlikely to be come across – and thus the probability of mistake is greatly reduced. Even in such specialized areas, areas with selective entry, one still moves among strangers, but at least one can safely assume that the strangers belong roughly to one category (or, rather, that most of the alternative categories are excluded). The orientation value of segregated areas is therefore attained by the practices of *exclusion*; of selective, and thus limited, admission.

The box office, the receptionist and security guards are all salient symbols and tools of the practices of exclusion. Their presence conveys that only selected people will be admitted to the place they protect and control. The criteria of selection vary. In the case of the box office, money is the most important criterion, though a ticket may still be refused to a person who does not meet some other demands, for instance, decent dress or the right colour of skin. Receptionists and security guards decide whether the person wishing to enter 'has the right' to do so. Whoever is allowed to enter must prove their entitlement to be inside; the burden of proof rests entirely on those who wish to enter, though the authority to decide whether the proof is satisfactory lies with the persons who control entry. The test of entitlement sets a situation in which the entry is denied to all as long as they remain total strangers, as long as they do not 'identify' themselves. The act of identification transforms a faceless member of the grey, indiscriminate category of strangers into a 'concrete person', a 'person with a face'. The disturbingly opaque shield of strangeness is thereby at least partially lifted. The restricted territory circumscribed by guarded gates is, uncharacter-istically, free from strangers. Whoever enters a place so guarded may rest assured that the others inside have been to some extent purified of the usual ambiguity of the strangers, that someone made sure that all people likely to be encountered inside are similar to each other in at least some selected aspects and hence may be treated as belonging to the same category. The uncertainty entailed in being in the presence of persons 'who can be anybody' has been thereby considerably, though only locally and temporarily, reduced.

The power to refuse entry is, in other words, deployed to secure a relative homogeneity, a non-ambivalence of selected spaces inside the densely populated anonymous world of urban living. We all practise this power on a small scale when we take care that only people whom we can in some way identify are admitted to the controlled space which we call our home; we refuse entry to the 'total strangers'. We trust, however, that other people use their powers to do a similar job for us on a grander scale. Thus we feel relatively secure whenever we enter the spaces they guard. In most of our lives, a day in the town is divided into time-spans spent in such guarded spaces, and the time devoted to travelling between such spaces (we go from home to the office where we are employed, to a college where we study, to the club or the local pub or a concert hall, and back home). Between the enclosures that practise exclusion extends the vast area with an open entry, where everyone, or almost everyone, is a stranger. On the whole we try to reduce the time spent in such intermediary areas to a minimum − if not to eliminate it altogether if we can (for instance, by travelling from one closely guarded space to another in the isolation of the hermetically sealed shell of a private car).

The most upsetting aspects of living among strangers may therefore be partly defused, even rendered less disturbing for a time, but hardly ever can they be disposed of completely. All the ingenious methods of segregation notwithstanding, we cannot avoid altogether the company of people who are physically close yet spiritually distant, who remain around not at our invitation and whose coming and going we do not control. While inside the public space (a space we cannot avoid) we cannot stop being aware of their presence for a single moment. This is a burdensome awareness: the awareness of constraints imposed on our freedom. Even if we could be certain that the presence of strangers hides no threat of aggression (something of which we can never be fully convinced), we are aware of being constantly gazed at, watched, scrutinized, evaluated; the 'privacy' of our persons has been pierced, infiltrated, violated. If not our bodies, then at any rate our dignity, self-esteem or just our self-definition are now hostages to faceless persons on whose judgement we have little, if any, influence. Whatever we do, we must worry about how our actions would affect the image of ourselves held by those who watch us. As long as we stay within the field of their vision, we have to be on guard. The most we can do is to try to remain inconspicuous, or at any rate to avoid attracting attention.

The American sociologist **Erving Goffman** found **civil inattention** to be paramount among the techniques that make life in a city, life among strangers, possible. Civil inattention consists of *pretending* that one does not look and does not listen; or at least assuming a posture suggesting that one does not see and does not hear and, above all, does not care what the others around are doing. Most conspicuously, civil inattention expresses itself in the avoidance of eye-contact. (Meeting of eyes is always an invitation to an intercourse more personal than is allowed between strangers; it means giving up one's own right to remain anonymous, and waiving or at least suspending one's assumed right and determination to remain invisible to the other person's gaze.) The studious avoidance of eye-contact is a public announcement that one does not take note even if one's eyes occasionally or accidentally 'glide' over another person (indeed, one's eyes are allowed to 'glide' only, never to stop and focus, unless personal encounter is intended). Not looking at all is not possible. Streets of any town are crowded at most times, and a simple passage from here to there requires that the road ahead and all that stands or moves on it must be carefully monitored to avoid collision. Though the job of monitoring cannot be avoided, it must be done unobtrusively, without causing disquiet and arousing the vigilance of those on whom our gaze must fall. One must see while pretending that one is not looking − this is the essence of civil inattention. Think of a common everyday experience you have while entering a crowded department store, moving through the waiting room of a railway station, or just walking down the street on the way to college; think of all those little moves you must have been making unthinkingly, to steer safely along the pavement or stroll through the aisles dividing the display stands of a department store or an exhibition; and think how few faces of the countless people you passed by you can remember, how few of the people who walked through the same store or the same street you can describe. You will be amazed how well you have learned the difficult art of 'inattending' − of treating the strangers as a faceless backcloth against which the things which truly matter happen.

The careful, elaborate inattention with which the strangers treat one another obviously has an important value in survival under urban conditions. But it also has less endearing consequences. A newcomer from a village or a small township is often struck by what he perceives as the peculiar callousness and cold indifference of the big city. People seem not to care for other humans. They walk by briskly, paying no attention to people. One can bet that they could not care less if something awful happened to you. There is a wall of reserve, perhaps even antipathy, invisibly rising between you and them — a wall which one cannot hope to scale, a distance one has little chance to bridge. People are tantalizingly close physically, and yet spiritually — mentally, morally — they manage to remain infinitely remote from each other. The silence which separates them, and the distance which is used as a clever and indispensable weapon against the danger sensed in the presence of strangers, feel like a threat. Lost in the crowd, one feels abandoned to one's own resources; one feels unimportant, lonely and disposable. Security based on the protection of privacy against intrusion rebounds as *loneliness*. Or, rather, loneliness is the price of privacy. Living with strangers is an art with a value as ambiguous as the strangers themselves.

On the one hand, 'universal strangerhood' of the big city means emancipation from the noxious and vexing surveillance and interference of the others, who in smaller and more personalized contexts would feel entitled to be curious and to meddle. Now one can remain in a public place while keeping one's privacy intact. 'Moral invisibility', attained thanks to the universal application of civil inattention, offers a scope of freedom unthinkable under different conditions. As long as the unwritten code of civil inattention is universally obeyed, one can move around the city relatively unobstructed. The volume of impressions, new, intriguing and pleasurable, is thereby expanded. With it, the sphere of experience expands. An urban setting is a fertile soil for the intellect. As the great German sociologist **Georg Simmel** pointed out, urban life and abstract thinking are resonant and develop together: abstract thought is boosted by the awesome richness of urban experience which cannot be grasped in its qualitative diversity, while the capacity for operating general concepts and categories is the skill without which survival in an urban environment is inconceivable.

These are, so to speak, the positive aspects of the matter. There is a price to be paid, however; no gains without losses. Together with the cumbersome curiosity of others, their sympathetic interest and willingness to help disappears. Through the exhilarating bustle of urban life shows cool human indifference. By and large, social intercourse is reduced to exchange, which — as we have seen before — leaves the participants, as persons, indifferent and uncommitted. The cash nexus, mutual services evaluated solely in quantities of money, closely follows the intellectual, unemotional and dispassionate urban attitude.

What is lost in the process is the *ethical* character of human relationships. A wide range of human intercourse which is devoid of **moral** significance now becomes possible; conduct exempt from being evaluated and judged by the standards of morality becomes a rule.

A human relationship is moral in so far as it stems from the feeling of responsibility for the welfare and well-being of the other person. First, moral responsibility is distinguished by being disinterested. It does not derive from fear of punishment nor from calculation of personal gain: not from the obligations contained in a contract I've signed and am legally bound to fulfil, or from my anticipation that the person in question may offer me something useful in exchange and thus make my effort to earn his or her favours worth while. Neither is it conditional on what the other person is doing or what sort of person he or she is. The responsibility is moral as long as it is totally selfless and unconditional: I am responsible for another person simply because he or she is a person, and hence commands my responsibility. Secondly, responsibility is moral in so far as I see it as mine and mine alone; it is not negotiable, it cannot be passed on to another human being. I cannot talk myself out of this responsibility and no power on earth can absolve me from carrying it. Responsibility for the other — for any other — human being simply because this is a human being, and the specifically moral impulse to give help and succour that follows from it, need no argument, legitimation or proof.

Moral proximity, unlike physical proximity pure and simple, is made precisely of this kind of responsibility. Under conditions of 'universal strangerhood', however, physical proximity has been cleansed of its moral aspect. This means that people may now live and act close to each other and affect each other's life conditions and well-being without experiencing *moral* proximity, hence remaining oblivious to the moral significance of their actions. What follows in practice is that they may refrain from actions which moral responsibility would have prompted them to take, and engage in actions which moral responsibility would have barred them from performing. Thanks to the rules of civil inattention, strangers are not treated as enemies and most of the time escape the fate which tends to befall the enemy; they are not a target of hostility and aggression. And yet, not unlike the enemies, the strangers (and this includes ourselves, inasmuch as all of us are part of the 'universal strangerhood') are deprived of that protection which only moral proximity may offer. It is but a short step from civil inattention to moral indifference, heartlessness and disregard for the needs of others.

Chapter Four

Together and Apart

It has probably occurred to you, more than once, to start your speech with the phrase 'As all of us agree ...' I am sure you have heard other people saying this. Or you will have read this expression in newspaper articles — particularly in the editorials, which are, indeed, a sort of editor's speech addressed to the newspaper's readers. But have you ever asked yourself *who* these 'all of us' who 'agree' were?

Were I to use phrases like 'As we all know ...' or 'As we all agree ...', I would refer to an unspecified collection of people who think like me. But I would imply more than this: that I have selected such people, and set them apart, from all the others who may think differently; that this selected collection is one which counts (to me, at any rate); and that it is precisely this selected group and no other that counts, that the shared opinion of its members lends authority — a sufficient, trustworthy and credible authority — to what follows. By using the phrase, I would establish an invisible link of *mutual understanding* between myself and my listeners or readers. I would suggest that we are united by the views we share, by the fact that we see the topic of our conversation in the same way and from the same angle. All these implied meanings would tacitly accompany my use of the phrase without my ever spelling them out. It is as if both the unity of 'us all' who agree, and our shared disregard for those who do not, seemed too 'natural' to me (and, so I hope or take for granted, to my audience) for me to argue about it or seek and supply the proof that it is, indeed, the case.

It is such a collection of people (not at all clearly defined or circumscribed), who agree to something that other people presumably reject, and such an authority bestowed upon the agreement in disregard and defiance of anything else, which we have in mind whenever we speak of **community**. However we try to justify or explain the 'togetherness' of the community, its unity, its genuine or merely desired persistence, it is the *spiritual* unity, subject to a shared spiritual authority, that we have in mind first and foremost. Without it, there is no community.

One shared view which underlies and conditions the sharing of all other views is the agreement that the collection under discussion is indeed a community — that is, that inside its boundaries views and attitudes are, or ought to be, shared, and that agreement can and should be achieved if any of the views (merely temporarily, one believes) differ. Agreement, or at least the readiness to agree, is assumed to be the primary, natural reality of all community members. A community is a group in which factors which unite people are stronger and more important than anything which may divide it; the differences between members are minor or secondary by comparison with their essential — one is tempted to say overwhelming — similarity. Community is thought of as a *natural* unity.

If we can get away without explaining precisely who the 'all of us' are, and without proving that the views we allegedly share are indeed true and proper and thus deserve to be treated with respect and believed, it is mostly because of that 'naturalness' of the implied bond. The community type of belonging comes about as if of itself, like other 'facts of nature'; it need not be laboriously constructed, maintained and serviced. The community type of belonging is at its strongest and most secure when we believe just this: that we have not chosen it on purpose, have done nothing to make it exist and can do nothing to undo it. For the sake of their effectiveness, their hold over reality, it is better that the images and postulates implied by the phrase 'as we all agree' are never given in detail, never come into focus, are never written down in a formal code or turn into an object of conscious effort. Their hold is all the stronger the less they are spoken about or even noticed. Only as long as they stay silent is the community what we believe it to be: 'naturally' united. Sharing of beliefs comes naturally as long as it is not argued about and thus stays unchallenged.

Ideally, such sharing would be at its fullest among isolated people who conduct all their life-business, from birth to death, in the same company, who neither venture into other places nor are visited by members of other groups who practice different styles of life. Such people would have no occasion to contemplate their own ways and means 'from outside', to see them as something strange and baffling, needing an explanation or argument. Neither would such people be pressed to justify and explain why they are living in their particular fashion, sticking to one way of life rather than another. (Note that we are considering here an ideal case. Situations that truly meet such ideal conditions hardly ever exist. It is sometimes assumed that the old-time isolated villages or far-away islands came relatively close to fulfilling such conditions, though even this supposition rarely stands up to closer scrutiny. More than often not, community is a *postulate*, an expression of desire, a clarion call to close the ranks, rather than a reality. In the memorable words of the great British scholar Raymond Williams, 'the remarkable thing about community is that it always has been'.) Even if it ever existed in the past, community certainly does not exist any more, not in its imaginary idealized form, the moment it is spoken about. People are most eager to invoke the unshakeable powers of 'natural' unity when they confront the practical task of creating unity artificially or rescuing by conscious effort the crumbling unity of the past.

When we use a phrase like 'As we all agree ...' we attempt, therefore, to bring to life, or keep alive, or resuscitate a community of meanings and beliefs which has never existed 'naturally', or is already about to fall apart, or is to rise again from the ashes. We do it under conditions admittedly unfavourable for the existence and survival of 'natural' communities — in a world in which contradictory beliefs coexist, different descriptions of reality compete with each other, and each view has to defend itself against the arguments of the other side. In practice, the idea of community as 'spiritual unity' serves as a tool for drawing as yet non-existent boundaries between 'us' and 'them'; it is an instrument of *mobilization*, of convincing the group to which the appeal is made of its common fate and shared interests, in order to solicit a unified action.

Let us repeat: the reference to the 'naturality' of community is itself a factor in making the appeal to unity effective. Most powerful (and, as it were, the most effective) community-building efforts allude paradoxically to factors seen as 'beyond human power', as things one can neither choose at will nor reject: traits like 'common blood', hereditary character and a timeless link with the land, which allegedly bind a *race* to its fate and mission; or the shared historical past, the joint record of victories and defeats, 'our common historical heritage' which made the *nation* into a separate entity bound together for ever, for better or worse; or common *religion*, which in the distant past was born of a revelation received by the forefathers, attracted persecution later, and hence made the ancestors' beliefs sacrosanct and venerable, and the survival of their heritage a sacred cause and duty of the descendants. What makes the appeal to such ostensibly objective 'facts of the case' particularly useful for community-building is that the invoked facts remain steadfastly beyond the control of the people to whom the appeal is being made. The reference to such facts effectively hides the element of choice and arbitrariness involved in the choice. To induce the targets of community-building appeals to make their choice, they are told that they find themselves in a *non-choice* situation – that the decision has already been made for them by their ancestors or by providence. Under such circumstances unwillingness to join forces cannot but be treated as an act of treason. Those who commit such an act betray their own nature, memory of the ancestors, their calling, etc.; they are renegades, or fools, arrogant enough to challenge the decision already made for them by history.

Not in all cases, however, can the community-building efforts refer to necessities beyond control and thus conceal their arbitrary character. Many political and religious movements openly proclaim their intention to create a community of beliefs or faith by converting (*proselytizing*) people to new ideas of which they have not been aware or which they used to reject at their own peril. They aim at creating a community of the faithful – people united by common attachment to the cause revealed to them by the saintly founder of the religious sect or by a perceptive, far-sighted political leader. In this kind of community-building exercise, the language used is not that of sacred tradition, historical fate or class mission, but one of good news, eye-opening, of 'being born again', and, above all, of *truth*. Appeal is made not to the allegedly non-choice situation, but, on the contrary, to the noble act of choosing truth over falsehood, of embracing the true faith while rejecting superstition, illusion or ideological distortion of reality. People are asked to join the community, rather than stay in one to which they belong 'naturally'. Joining is presented as an act of liberation and the beginning of a new life; it is spoken about as an act of free will — indeed, the first true manifestation of one's freedom. What is concealed this time is the pressure which from now on will be exerted on the converts to remain obedient to the newly embraced faith and to surrender their freedom to whatever the cause may demand. Such demands may be no less excessive than those which invoke historical tradition as their legitimation.

Communities of faith cannot limit themselves to *propaganda* — to the preaching of a new creed intended to unite the future devotees. Devotion to the articles of faith would never be really secure unless supported by *ritual*: a series of regular events (patriotic festivals, party meetings, church services) in which the faithful are called to participate as actors so that their common membership and commonality of fate may be reasserted and devotion reinforced. Communities of faith differ, however, in the stringency and volume of demands they make on their members.

Most political parties, for example (with the important exception of those which pursue radical — revolutionary or reactionary, left-wing or right-wing — ends, treat their members as fighters and thus demand unswerving loyalty and total subordination), seek no more unity of thought than is necessary to secure regular electoral support and a modicum of voluntary 'missionary' activity on behalf of the party programme. They would leave the rest of the members' lives to their own discretion and would refrain from legislating about, say, the family life or the choice of occupation.

Religious sects, on the other hand, are on the whole more demanding. They would not settle for the participation in periodic cult rituals; the *whole* of the members' lives will come into their area of concern. As the sects are, by definition, minorities exposed to outside pressure and hence constantly under siege, they need not merely an agreed set of beliefs, but a uniformity of the whole way of life. They would aspire to a complete reform of the way the faithful conduct their daily business in all its aspects. They would also command obedience in the aspects of behaviour ostensibly indifferent to the question of faith. By making the whole of life into a profession of faith and manifestation of loyalty, sectarian communities would attempt to defend their members' commitment against the scepticism or outright hostility of the environment. In extreme cases, attempts are made to cut off the community altogether from the 'ordinary' flow of social life; not only to embrace the whole of the members' lives fill all their time, cater for all their needs (or deny the worthiness of needs which are not provided for), but to isolate the members from all other, unsupervised, contacts. The creed to which the members are asked to remain loyal has the condemnation and rejection of the ways and means of the 'ordinary' society among its central tenets. 'Normal' society is censured for its unsaintliness or sinfulness, for being dominated by selfishness and greed, for substituting material concerns for spiritual ones, for trampling upon freedom of the individual, for destroying intimacy and mutual sympathy among people, for causing inequalities between people and rampant injustice, for encouraging and demanding rivalry and competition, etc.

Which of the many possible charges is used depends on the rules of life the community intends to promote. The members may be invited to run away from the abominations of mundane life to a hermit community, dedicated fully to prayer and contemplation. Or they may be enjoined to opt out from the 'rat race' and enter instead a group in which all members are equal, no one wishes to stand above the others, and relations are based solely on mutual intimacy, sincerity and trust. Members are normally also asked to turn their backs on the attractions of consumerism and reconcile themselves to a life of modesty and austerity. Communities of this type (frequently described as *communes*) confront their members with a formidable task: to sustain their shared life, in all its aspects, by the power of affection alone. Neither habit nor contractual obligation provides the second line of defence if mutual animosities or sheer lack of consensus tear the community apart. Mutual love becomes the sole adhesive — the only, and hence indispensable, condition of the commune's survival. All dissent constitutes therefore a mortal threat; tolerance is a luxury a commune can ill afford. For this reason, the more *comprehensive* are the communities, the more *oppressive* they tend to become. Oppression cannot but generate tensions which make communes the most fragile and vulnerable of communities.

Communities differ widely in the extent of the uniformity they demand (that is, in the relative size of the portion of life they ask their members to subordinate to the shared doctrine). In most cases, however, stipulations tend to be diffuse, ill defined and impossible to determine in advance. Even if the advocates of communal unity declare neutrality regarding non-spiritual aspects of members' lives, they still claim priority and supreme importance for the beliefs they advocate. Potentially, such a claim may lead to interference in matters previously declared indifferent, should they come to clash, or be seen to be at odds, with the shared creed.

Sharply different in this respect from all communities (both the ostensibly 'natural' and those admittedly 'made up') are such groups as bring their members together solely for the sake of a single, on the whole clearly defined, task. As the purposes of such groups are limited, so are their claims on their members' time, attention and discipline. By and large, such groups admit that they have been created on purpose. Here the purpose plays a role similar to the one played by tradition, common fate or truth in the case of communities. It is in terms of the purpose, or of a task to be performed, that the discipline and commitment of the members are claimed. One can therefore speak in this case of **purpose groups**, or **organizations**. A deliberate and openly declared self-limitation is perhaps the most salient and decisive distinctive feature of organizations. Most organizations have written statutes which detail the areas in which the members must abide by the organizational rules (implying by the same token that other, unnamed areas of members' lives are free from organizational interference). Note that if the presence or absence of self-limitation, rather than of consensus of beliefs, is taken as the main difference between communities and organizations, then some of the communities discussed above ought to be, contrary to their own claims, counted rather among organizations.

The partial nature of members' involvement in the organizational activity may be expressed in a different way: members do not enter an organization as 'whole persons' — they merely play *roles*. 'Role' is, of course, a word drawn from the language of the theatre. A stage play, with its plot decided in advance and written up in the scenario, which assigns different lines to every actor in the cast, offers a pattern by which the organization runs its life. The theatre may be seen as a prototype also in another respect: stage actors do not 'exhaust' themselves in the roles they have been assigned; they 'enter' the prescribed character only for the duration of the performance and are free (indeed, expected) to leave afterwards.

As the organizations are specialized from the point of view of the tasks they perform, so are their members specialized from the point of view of the contribution they are expected to make to the performance of this task. Each members' role is set apart from the roles played by other members of the same organization, as well as from other roles the same person may play in other organizations. For part of the day I am a teacher of sociology; in the school where I teach, my role is different from that of the teacher of physical education or any other teacher, for that matter, as well as from that of the headmaster, or the librarian, or the cook. But my role as teacher also calls for different skills and actions from those demanded by other roles I play at other times of the day or on other days of the week. Thus I sit on the council of the local camera club; I am a member of the tenants' committee in the block of flats in which I live; I also belong to a charity society, to an *ad hoc* committee created in the neighbourhood to fight the project of a motorway by-pass, and to the local branch of a political party. I play a number of roles, at different places and times; each role is played among somewhat different groups of people. None of those groups knows me well in any of my other roles. In most cases, none is interested in such other roles; each wants me to identify myself fully with the role in which I participate in their particular activity and contribute to the task they join forces to perform. I may risk being frowned upon, or ridiculed, or reprimanded if, for instance, I bring my photographic concerns to the 'Fight and By-pass' citizens' committee, or confuse my teaching duties with my tasks as an active member of the political party.

Let us repeat: unlike the community, which we think of as a

group to which its members belong (or ought to belong) 'body and soul', the organization absorbs only part of the persons involved; indeed, we will better understand the way it works if we think of it as consisting of roles, not persons. People involved in an organization are expected to *embrace* their roles (that is, to dedicate themselves fully to their performance while working in and for the organization, to identify themselves completely with the role they are performing at that moment), yet at the same time to *distance* themselves from them (that is, to remember all along that it is merely a role they are playing — so that they do not confuse the right and duties attached to this particular role with those belonging to another activity or place). In fact, a particular arrangement of roles is the only aspect of the organization which remains relatively stable over a period of time, and which identifies the organization as such. Incumbents of the roles may come and go, yet the roles remain. People join and leave the organization, are hired and fired, admitted and expelled; yet the organization persists, and though the specific colouring that particular persons give to the performance of the role may change over time, the organization remains basically the same. People are interchangeable and disposable; what counts is not them as persons, but the skill they have to perform the job and the will they show to perform it.

Max Weber, one of the founders of sociology, saw the proliferation of organizations in contemporary society as a sign of the continuous **rationalization** of social life. **Rational** action (as distinct from both **traditional** action — an unreflective acting out of habit or custom — and **affective** action — an uncontrolled act, triggered by a momentary emotion and perpetrated without consideration of the consequences) is one in which the *end* to be achieved is clearly spelled out, and the actors concentrate their thoughts and efforts on selecting such *means* to the end as promise to be most effective and economical. To Weber, organization (Weber himself used the term '**bureaucracy**' — 'the rule of the office') is the supreme adaptation to the requirements of rational action; it is, in fact, the most proper method to pursue ends in a rational way, that is, the way which is simultaneously the most effective and the least costly. In his famous description of the *ideal* *type* of bureaucracy (bureaucracy as it would be were it fully adjusted to its acknowledged purpose and free from any distractions), Weber listed the principles which must be observed in members' actions and in relations between them, so that an organization could indeed be such an instrument of rationality. Let us name some of these principles.

First of all, inside the organization people must act solely in their 'official capacity', which has been defined by the rules attached to the roles they perform (so that other aspects of their social identity — for instance, their family connections, business interests, private sympathies and antipathies — are not allowed to interfere with what they do, how they do it, and with the way other people treat their actions). Roles ought to be logically divided and kept separate. This means, first, that a truly rational organization should split the overall task into simple and elementary activities, so that each participant in the common effort could become an expert in doing his or her own job; second, that someone ought to be responsible for every element of the overall task, so that no part of the task remains unattended; and third, that for every part of the task it must be clear who is in charge — so that the competences do not overlap and hence the danger of confusion arising out of contradictory decisions is averted. In performing their respective roles, the officials ought to be guided by abstract rules such as bear no regard to personal peculiarities (see chapter 5 on the principles guiding impersonal relationships). The officials themselves should be appointed to their offices and promoted or demoted solely according to the estimated 'fit' of the skills they possess to the skills required by the office; all other considerations (noble or plebeian origin, political or religious beliefs, race, sex, etc.) must be emphatically declared out of court and not allowed to interfere with the personnel policy. There ought to be continuity in both the activity of the organization as a whole and in the organizational life of its members; the official must view the job done in the organization as part of a life-career, so that he or she may build up the skills and accumulate practical experience; the organization, on the other hand ought to be bound by the precedents — decisions made in the past in its name — even if the officials which made them at the time have since left or moved to other tasks.

The history of the organization is made of its files, and hence is independent from personal memories or the loyalties of individual officials.

These are not the only requirements of the organized rational action, however. Not only must the roles be divided and kept apart; they also ought to be arranged in a *hierarchy* which corresponds to the internal division of the overall task. The further down one moves in the hierarchy, the more specialized, partial, focused and minute are the tasks and the jobs; the higher up one moves, the wider becomes the vision, and more of the overall purpose comes into view. To achieve this situation, the flow of two things must be maintained: information ought to pass from the lower to the higher rungs of the hierarchical ladder, becoming on the way ever more comprehensive and synthetic, while commands should flow from the top to the bottom, becoming as they travel ever more specific and unequivocal. *Control* from the top needs to be reciprocated by *discipline* from the bottom.

What unites all the principles in the ideal model of the rational organization is the postulate that everybody's decisions and behavioural choices should be subordinated to the task the organization has been called to perform. All other considerations should be declared irrelevant, and thus not allowed to influence decisions; they are best eliminated, but in any case neutralized or disregarded. The officials should, so to speak, leave all their private concerns and outside commitments in the cloakroom, and enter their offices dressed in their official role alone. The organization as a whole should surround itself with thick and impenetrable walls with just two gates left: the 'input', through which the task the organization is expected to perform is fed in, and the 'output', which lets out the results of the organizational processing of that task: the actions aimed at the fulfilment of the task. Between the feeding in of the task and the production of results, all outside influences ought to be barred from intervening (hence the strict requirement of organizational secrecy); nothing should interfere with the strict application of organizational rules and the selection of the most effective and economical means to the declared end.

Hardly any organization meets, however, such conditions. The postulate which underlies Weber's ideal model of rational action remains by and large unfulfilled; the question is, can it *ever* be fulfilled. A person reduced to just one role is a fiction which no reality can match; and so is a single-task action unaffected by other concerns and apparently unrelated to other human bonds. Members of the organization are naturally concerned with their own well-being, which may be adversely affected by risks involved in any decision-making. Hence the widespread tendency to avoid taking decisions on dubious and controversial matters — the notorious phenomenon of the hot potato, a popular name for the tendency to elude responsibility by shifting an urgent file onto somebody else's desk. Concern with one's own well-being (self-preservation, survival in terms defined by the organization) includes also the tendency to undermine the position of potential competitors for promotion, through obstructing their work or discrediting their decisions. But a member of the organization may also find that a command received from superiors cannot be squared with his or her moral beliefs; the choice is between organizational obedience and loyalty to moral principles. Other members may believe that the requirement of secrecy put to them by superiors may endanger public welfare or some other cause they believe to be equally valid or even more important than organizational efficiency. On the other hand, members may bring into their work the prejudices they hold in their daily lives. A man, for instance, may find it difficult to accept a command coming from a woman; or someone may resent orders received from a person of a different race.

Furthermore, no impervious walls protect the organization against the pressures and influences coming from places ostensibly unrelated to its tasks and hence denied authority in organizational decision-making. Most organizations must be concerned with their public image — a consideration which may prevent them from actions that pass muster as rationality when calculated in technical terms alone, but are likely to arouse public concern and anger, particularly in the circles which wield enough influence to damage the standing of the organization. Pressures too may come from other organizations, working in apparently remote and unrelated fields, which nevertheless find certain actions inconvenient or harmful for their own area of operation; their resistance would again put a limit on the priority given to 'pure rationality' of action.

Let us suppose for a moment, however, that the postulates entailed in the ideal model have been — miraculously — met: that the persons involved in the organizational division of tasks have indeed been reduced to the roles they have been assigned, and the organization as a whole has been at the same time effectively fenced off from all concerns and influences irrelevant to its declared purpose. However improbable such conditions, would they guarantee the *rationality* of organizational activity if put in practice? Would an organization which fully conforms to the ideal model behave indeed as rationally as Weber hoped it should? There are strong arguments that this would not happen; that the ideal recipe for rational action will generate, on the contrary, numerous obstacles to rationality.

To start with: in the hierarchy of command the model suggests, equal weight has been ascribed to the authority of the office and that of the relevant technical skill — without, however, pointing out why the two differently grounded authorities should coincide and remain in harmony. In fact, it is more than likely that the two will tend to clash (for instance, the established right to the job may be threatened by novel technical skills which the current incumbents of the office do not possess, and as a result the authority of office may be deployed to arrest or at least delay the introduction of the skills which the rationality of action demands). Nor is the principle of minute division of labour beyond reproach. Allegedly a factor boosting efficiency and expertise, it tends in fact to produce the phenomenon called **trained incapacity**. Having acquired expertise in a quick and efficient performance of narrowly circumscribed tasks, members gradually lose sight of the wider ramifications of their job and will fail to note adverse consequences of the activity which in the meantime has turned into mechanical routine. Because of the narrowness of their skills, members are also ill prepared to adjust their routines to changing circumstances and to react to unfamiliar situations with the necessary speed and flexibility. The organization as a whole, in other words, falls prey to its own pursuit of perfect rationality. It becomes stiff and inflexible, and its methods of work fail to adapt quickly enough to changing circumstances. Sooner or later, it may well turn into a factory of increasingly *irrational* decisions.

Last but not least, the ideal model of action subjected to rationality as the supreme criterion contains an inherent danger of another deviation from that purpose — the danger of so-called **goal displacement**. For the sake of their effectiveness, all organizations ought to reproduce their capacity to act: come what may, an organization must be continuously ready to make decisions and take actions. Such a reproduction calls for an effective mechanism of self-perpetuation, immune to outside interference. The trouble is that eventually the goal itself tends to fall among such outside interferences. There is nothing in the ideal model to prevent that mechanism from outliving the task the organization had been called to fulfil in the first place. Everything, on the other hand, points to the likelihood (indeed, desirability) that the concern for self-preservation should prompt the endless expansion of the organizational activity, of its resources and the scope of its authority. It may happen in effect that the task originally seen as the reason to establish it is relegated to a secondary position by the all-powerful interest of the organization in self-perpetuation and self-aggrandizement. The survival of the organization, however useless it may have become in the light of its original end, becomes the purpose in its own right: the new end against which the organization tends to measure the rationality of its performance.

And so we have found both models of human groupings wanting; neither the image of community — that total union of human *persons* — nor the model of organization — that coordination of *roles* in the service of the rational pursuit of a task — describes adequately the practice of human interaction. The two models sketch artificially separated, polar models of action, with separate and often opposite motives and expectations. Real human actions, under real circumstances, resent such a radical division.

There is a permanent and ineradicable tension between the 'conceptual frameworks' of our actions and our practical performances. By representing the action 'as if' it served one cohesive need or purpose, the model frameworks display an inherent tendency to streamline the action, which in practice cannot but be complex and convoluted; there is a tendency to purify the action which in practice is always split by many needs and motives.

As 'pure' types, the models of community and organization may be seen as extreme points of a continuum on which all practical human interactions can be plotted. Real interactions are torn between two gravitational forces, each pulling in an opposite direction. Routine interactions are, unlike the extreme models, mixed: they are *heterogeneous*, that is, subject simultaneously to logically contradictory principles. For instance, the family — this epitome of the community-like interaction pattern — is hardly ever that heaven of fully personal relationships one would expect it to be; there are tasks to be performed inside the family as in any other group of cooperating people, and it is unlikely that even a modicum of explicitly impersonal, organization-like criteria of performance would not defile the purity of the 'whole-person' relations with their characteristic particularity and diffuseness. On the other hand, in every organization the members can hardly avoid developing personal links with people with whom they join forces for a protracted period. Much of their time is spent in the company of others; they exchange services, communicate, find topics of common interest, help or fight each other, come to like or dislike each other. Sooner or later an *informal* pattern of interaction would emerge — an invisible network of personal relationships which may or may not overlap with the official chart of *formal* relationships of command and subordination. People involved in such patterns would find their interest in the organization richer than the one-role and one-task principles would imply; they seek, and find, the satisfaction of such needs of personal communication as the organization is resolutely and ostentatiously unconcerned with. This tendency is more often than not deliberately used and boosted by the people in command of the organization.

Contrary to what the ideal model would suggest, it is found in practice that the task-oriented performance may considerably benefit if the interaction is *not* reduced to specialized roles only. School is, on the face of it, a typical organization — concerned with the well-defined task of imparting knowledge and skills and evaluating its effects on the learners; yet the task would certainly suffer if the school failed to develop a feeling of community and belonging among its pupils or students. Many industrial, merchandising or financial companies set about soliciting the deeper commitment of their employees through bringing more of their concerns and interests within the orbit of the organization. They offer, for example, recreation and entertainment facilities, shopping services, even living accommodation. None of these extra services is logically related to the explicit task of the organization and the one specialized role they need their employees to perform; but all of them together are hoped to generate 'community feelings' and to prompt members to identify themselves with the company. Such emotions, apparently alien to the organizational spirit, are deemed to boost the members' dedication to the ends of the organizations and thus neutralize the adverse effects of the purely impersonal setting suggested by the criteria of rationality.

Communities and organizations alike assume freedom of their members; coming together is admittedly a voluntary act, at least in the sense that it can be revoked: one can go back on one's decision. Even if in some cases (remember the so-called natural communities) joining the group was not originally the result of a free choice, members are still credited with the right to leave (though they may be pressed, as we have seen before, to refrain from exercising it). There is one case, however, when the organization explicitly denies freedom to leave, and the people are kept under its jurisdiction by force: this is the case of **total institutions** (a name coined by **Erving Goffman**). Total institutions are *enforced communities*: there the totality of members' lives is subjected to scrupulous regulation, their needs are defined and catered for by the organization, their allowed and disallowed actions are regimented by organizational rules. Boarding schools, army barracks, prisons, mental hospitals approximate in varying degrees the model of total institutions. Their inmates are kept under surveillance day and night (or at least they are put in such conditions that they cannot be sure that they are not under observation) so that all deviation from the rules can be spotted in time and punished, or better still prevented. Total institutions depart radically from the community model in that the members are actively discouraged from developing on their own a network of personal relationships. The involvement of the total personality is combined with the requirement of totally impersonal relationships. It is, arguably, the very incongruence of such a combination which explains the formidable role played in total institutions by **coercion**. Neither spiritual dedication nor the hope of material gains can be appealed to in order to elicit desirable behaviour and secure the members' will to stay together and cooperate. Hence another feature of total institutions: the strict divide between those who set the rules and those who are bound by them. The effectiveness of coercion, as the only substitute for absent emotional commitment and calculated self-interest, depends on the gap between the two sides of the division remaining unbridgeable. (Note that the practice, here as elsewhere, differs from the ideal model. Personal relationships do develop inside total institutions, often spanning the gap between the supervisors and the inmates. Again, it is in no way clear that they weaken the general performance and stability of the institution. They nevertheless make the framework of interaction no less flexible and vulnerable to change than in groups of other types.)

I suppose the most striking impression one gets from the survey of human groupings is their diversity. With all their diversity, however, they are all forms of human *interaction*. In fact, there is no more to the existence of the group than a persistent network of interdependent actions of its members. The assertion 'there is a college' refers to the fact that a number of people come together to engage in a routine called a lecture (that is, a communicative encounter, structured in such a way that one person speaks while others, facing that person, listen and take notes), or seminar (a verbal interaction which consists of a number of people sitting around a table and speaking in turn), or tutorial (an interaction which consists of one person asking questions to which others respond), and a few other, on the whole regular and periodically repeated, patterned interactions. In their interactions group members are guided by their image of what the right conduct specific to the group ought to be. Yet the image is never complete, and hardly ever provides the unambiguous prescription for any situation which may arise in the course of interaction. The ideal framework is constantly interpreted and reinterpreted, and the practical actions of the members are such interpretations. Interpretation cannot but feed back on the image itself. Ideal framework and routine practices incessantly inform and transform each other.

The self-preservation and continuity of a group as a distinct entity is hence a question identical with that of maintaining the routine actions of its members, conforming to a shared mental image of the group's patterns of the right conduct.

Chapter Five

Gift and Exchange

Reminders from my creditors pile up on my desk. Some bills are most urgent; still, there are things I must buy — my shoes are in tatters, I cannot work late without a desk lamp, and one needs to eat every day . . . What can I do?

I can go to my brother and ask him for a loan. I'll explain my situation to him. Most probably, he'll grumble a little, and preach to me about the virtue of foresight, prudence and planning, of not living above one's means; but he'll reach into his pocket in the end and count his money. If he finds some, he'll give me what I need. Or at least a part he can afford.

Alternatively, I may go to my bank manager. But it would make no sense to explain to him how dreadfully I suffer. What does he care? The only question he'll ask me is what guarantee I can offer that the loan will be repayed. He'd like to know whether I have a regular income large enough to afford the repayment of the loan together with the interest. So I'll have to show him my salary slips; if I had a property, I'd have to offer it as collateral — a second mortgage, perhaps. If the manager is satisfied that I am not too excessive a risk and that the loan is likely to be duly repaid (with handsome interest, of course), he will lend me the money.

Depending on where I turn to solve my problem, I can expect two very different kinds of treatment. Two different sets of questions, referring obviously to two different conceptions of my right (my entitlement) to receive assistance. My brother is unlikely to inquire about my solvency; for him, the loan is not a matter of choice between good and bad business. What counts for him is that I am his brother; being his brother and being in need, I have sufficient

.n to his help. My need is his obligation. The bank manager, on
: other hand, could not care less who I am and whether I need the
.oney I ask for. The one thing he would wish to know is whether
he loan is likely to be a sensible, profitable business transaction for
him or the bank he represents. In no way is he obliged, morally or
otherwise, to lend me money. Were my brother to refuse my request,
he would have to prove to *me* that he was unable to offer me the
loan. With the bank manager, it would be the other way around: if I
wanted him to offer me a loan, it is *I* who would have to prove to
him that I am capable of prompt repayment of my debts.

Human interaction succumbs to the pressure of two principles
which all too often contradict each other: the principle of **equivalent
exchange**, and the principle of the **gift**. In the case of equivalent
exchange, self-interest rules supreme. The other partner of the
interaction may be recognized as an autonomous person, a legitimate subject of needs and rights – and yet those needs and rights
are viewed first and foremost as constraints and obstacles to the full
satisfaction of one's own interests. One is guided above all by
concern with 'just' payment in exchange for the services one renders
to the needs of the other. 'How much will I be paid?' 'What is in it
for me?' 'Could I be better off doing something else?' 'Have I not
been cheated?' These and similar questions are what one asks about
the prospective action in order to evaluate its desirability and to
establish the order of preference between alternative choices. One
bargains about the meaning of *equivalence*. One deploys all the
resources one can lay one's hand on in order to obtain the best deal
possible and tilt the transaction in one's own favour. Not so in the
case of a gift. Here, the needs and the rights of others are the main –
perhaps the only – motive for action. Rewards, even if they come in
the end, are not a factor in the calculation of desirability of action.
The concept of equivalence is altogether inapplicable. The goods
are given away, the services are extended merely because the other
person needs them and, being the person it is, has the right for the
needs to be respected.

The 'gift' is a common name for a wide range of acts differing in
their purity. 'Pure gift' is, as it were, a 'liminal concept'; a sort of
benchmark against which all practical cases are measured. Such

practical cases depart from the ideal in various degrees. In the purest of forms, the gift would be totally disinterested, and offered without regard to the quality of the recipient. **Disinterestedness** means the lack of remuneration in any shape or form. Judged by the ordinary standards of ownership and exchange, the pure gift is a pure loss; it is a gain solely in *moral* terms, the very terms which the logic of gain does not recognize. Its moral value actually rises as the loss deepens. The moral value of the gift is not measured by the market price of the goods or services offered, but precisely by the subjective loss they constitute for the donor (remember the proverbial widow's farthing). The disregard for the quality of the recipient means that the only qualification of the recipient considered when the gift is offered is that the recipient belongs to the category of people in need. For this reason, generosity towards members of one's own kin or close friends, which we discussed in chapter 2, does not in fact meet the requirements of the pure gift: it sets apart the recipients as special people selected for special treatment. Being special, the recipients have the right to expect such generosity from others with whom they are bound by a network of special — personal — relationships. In its pure form, the gift is offered to anyone who may need it — just because, and only because, he or she needs it. The pure gift is the recognition of the *humanity* of the other — who otherwise remains anonymous, allocated to no particular division in the donor's cognitive map.

Gifts offer the donor that elusive, yet deeply gratifying, reward of moral satisfaction: the experience of selflessness, of self-sacrifice for the sake of another human being. In a sharp contrast to the context of exchange or gain-seeking, such moral satisfaction grows in proportion to the painfulness of self-sacrifice and the resulting loss. To qualify the purity ideal still further, most religious teachings encourage gift-giving by presenting it as an exchange of sorts: as a means to redeem one's sins and earn happiness in the after-life. Giving to the needy is stimulated as the 'way of the righteous' — as the good deeds required for one's salvation. Though undoubtedly reinforcing the inclination to compassion and gift-giving, such argumentation achieves its effect by paying lip-service to the equally strong desire of gain, and so, inadvertently, reaffirming the authority of the latter.

Research of human behaviour under extreme, cruel condition of war and foreign occupation has shown that the most heroic cases of gift-giving — sacrificing one's own life in order to save another whose life was threatened — were on the whole performed by people whose motives came very close to the ideal of pure gift: they considered helping other human beings as, purely and simply, their moral duty — one that does not call for any justification, as it is natural, self-evident and elementary. One of the most remarkable findings of this research is that the most selfless among the helpers found it difficult to understand the unique heroism of their actions. They tended to play down the courage such conduct required and the moral virtue it evidenced.

The two kinds of treatment which we discussed at the beginning of this chapter offer an example of the daily manifestations of the gift—exchange choice. As a first approximation, we may call my relationship with my brother (in which the gift motive prevailed) a *personal* one, and the relationship between myself and my bank manager (in which the exchange attitude came to the fore) *impersonal*. What happens in the framework of a personal relationship depends almost entirely on who we, the partners, are — and very little on what either of us has done, is doing or will do: on our *quality*, not *performance*. We are brothers, and hence we are obliged to assist each other in need. It does not matter (or, at least, it should not matter) whether the need in question arises from bad luck, miscalculation or improvidence. It matters even less whether the sum offered to bail me out is 'secure' — that means, whether my performance is such that it warrants the hope of repayment. In an impersonal relationship, the opposite is true. It is only performance which counts, not the quality. It does not matter who I am, only what I am likely to do. My partner will be interested in my past record, as a basis on which to judge the likelihood of my future behaviour.

Talcott Parsons, one of the most influential post-war sociologists, considered the opposition between quality and performance as one of the four major oppositions among which each conceivable pattern of human relationship must choose. He gave these oppositions the name of **pattern variables**. Another pair of opposite options to choose between is, according to Parsons, that of *universalism* and *particularism*. Pondering over my request, my brother might think of many things, yet universal principles, like legal regulations, codes of conduct or current interest rates were not, in all probability, among them. For him, I was not a 'specimen of a category', a case to which some universal rule may apply. I was a particular, unique case — his brother. Whatever he was going to do he would do because I was such a unique person, unlike any other, and hence the question 'What would he do in other similar circumstances?' simply did not arise. It was again very different with the bank manager. For him, I was just one member of a large category of past, current and prospective borrowers. Having dealt with so many others 'like me' before, the bank manager surely worked out universal rules to be applied for all similar cases in the future. The outcome of my particular application would depend therefore on whatever the universal rules say about the credibility of my case.

The next pattern variable also sets the two cases under consideration in opposition to each other. The relationship between me and my brother is *diffuse*; the relationship between me and the bank manager is *specific*. The generosity of my brother was not just a one-off whim; it was not an attitude improvised specifically for the distress I reported in this one conversation. His brotherly predisposition towards me spills over into everything which concerns me — everything is also a matter of his concern. There is nothing in the life of either of us which does not matter for the other. If my brother was inclined to be helpful in this particular case, it is because he is generally well disposed towards me and interested in everything I do and might have done. His understanding and care would not be confined to financial matters. Not so with the bank manager; his conduct was specifically geared to this application there and then; his reaction to my request and his final decision were based entirely on the facts of the case and bore no relation whatsoever to other aspects of my life or personality. Most things important to me he rightly saw as irrelevant as far as the application for the loan was concerned, and hence left them out of consideration.

The fourth opposition crowns, so to speak, the other three (though one could argue as well that it underlies them and, indeed, makes them possible). This is the opposition, in Parsons' words, between *affectivity* and *affective neutrality*. This means that some interactions are infused with emotions — compassion, sympathy or love. Some others are 'cool', detached, unemotional. Impersonal relations do not arouse in the actors any feelings other than a passionate urge to achieve a successful transaction. The actors themselves are not objects of emotions; they are neither liked nor disliked. If they strike a hard bargain, try to cheat, prevaricate or avoid commitments, some of the impatience with the unduly slow progress of the transaction may rub off on the attitude towards them; again, some affection may be born if they cooperate in the transaction with zeal and goodwill — when they are the sort of person 'it is a pleasure to do business with'. By and large, however, emotions are not an indispensable part of impersonal interactions, while they are the very factors which make personal interaction plausible.

I and my brother both feel deeply about our relationship. In all probability, we like each other. It is more than probable, however, that we empathize with each other and have a fellow-feeling for each other: we tend to put ourselves in each other's position, to understand each other's predicament, to imagine the joy or the agony of the other partner, feel good about the joy, and suffer because of the agony. This is hardly the case in my relationship with the bank manager. We meet too seldom and know each other too little to 'read out' the partner's feeling. Were we able to do so, we still wouldn't do it — unless the feelings we wished to discover or anticipate in the partner bear a direct relationship to the success of the transaction at hand (I'd try to avoid making the bank manager angry; instead, I'd wish to elicit his or her good humour through jokes or flattery, hoping to relax the defences — counting on human weaknesses). Otherwise, feelings are neither here nor there. Moreover, they might be positively harmful if allowed to interfere with judgement; if, for instance, my bank manager decides to offer me the loan because of feeling pity and compassion for my misery, and for this reason disregards my financial recklessness, which may easily cause a loss to the bank he or she represents.

While emotion is an indispensable accompaniment to personal

relations, it would be out of place in impersonal ones. In the latter, dispassion and cool calculation are the rules one may disregard only at one's own peril. The unemotional stance taken by my partners in an impersonal transaction may well hurt my feelings, particularly when the situation which prompted me to turn to them in the first place has caused me pain and anguish. Unreasonably, I'll then be inclined to blame the unemotional attitude, so jarringly at odds with my excitement, on the 'heartlessness and insensitivity of the bureaucrats'. This is not an image which will assist the success of impersonal transactions. Hence we hear time and again of 'listening banks' and 'banks who like to say yes'; banks consider it profitable to conceal the impersonality of their attitude towards clients (that is, their interest in clients' money, not in their private problems and feelings) and therefore promise what they cannot and do not intend to deliver: to conduct impersonal transactions in a mood geared to personal ones.

Perhaps the most crucial distinction between personal and impersonal contexts of interaction lies in the factors on which the actors rely for the success of their action. We all depend on the actions of so many people of whom we know, if anything, very little; much too little to base our plans and our hopes on their personal characteristics, like reliability, trustworthiness, honesty, industry and so on. With so little knowledge at our disposal, a transaction would be downright impossible were it not for the opportunity to settle the issue in an impersonal manner: the chance to appeal not to the personal traits or aptitudes of the partners (which we do not know anyhow), but to the universal rules which apply to all cases of the same category, whoever happens to be our partner at the moment. Under conditions of limited personal knowledge, appealing to rules is the only way to make communication possible. Imagine what an incredibly large, unwieldy volume of knowledge you would need to amass if all your transactions with others were based solely on your properly researched estimate of their personal qualities. The much more realistic alternative is to get hold of the few general rules that guide the interchange, and *trust* that the partner will do the same and observe the same rules.

Most things in life are indeed organized in such a way as to enable partners to interact without any or with little personal information about each other. It would be quite impossible for me, ignorant about medical science as I am, to assess the healing ability and dedication of the consultants to whom I turn for help; fortunately, however, their competence to deal with my ailment has been confirmed, testified and certified by the British Medical Association, which accepted them as members, and by the hospital management, which employed them. I can, therefore, limit myself to reporting the fact of my case and assume — trust — that in exchange I'll receive the service which the case warrants and requires. When trying to make sure that the train I have boarded is scheduled to travel to the town I wish to reach, I may safely ask people dressed in the BR uniform, without worrying about putting their love of truth to the test. I let into my house someone showing me a gas board inspector's card without going through the checks and inquiries I'd normally apply to a complete stranger. In all these and similar cases some people, personally unknown to me (like those sitting on the board of the Medical Association or the gas board), took upon themselves the task of vouching for the competent, rule-conforming conduct of people whose credentials they endorse. By so doing, they have made it possible for me to accept the services of such people on **trust** (a phenomenon analysed in depth by the British sociologist **Anthony Giddens**).

And yet it is precisely because so many of our transactions are performed in an impersonal context that the need of personal relationships becomes so poignant and acute. It has been noted repeatedly that the more we depend on people of whom we have but vague and superficial knowledge, and the more perfunctory and fleeting our encounters are, the stronger is the tendency to expand the realm of personal relations, to force the expectations that fit only personal transactions upon interactions which are best performed in an impersonal fashion. Resentment of the indifference of an impersonal world is likely to be felt most strongly by young people who are just about to leave the relatively warm, cosy and caring world of the family and youthful friendships, and enter the coarse and emotionally cool world of employment and occupational practice. Hence the attempts to opt out of the callous and heartless world where people serve (or so it seems) only as the means to some ends which bear little relation to their own needs or happiness. Some escapees try to establish commune-like, self-enclosed and self-contained little enclaves, inside which only relations of a personal type are allowed. Such attempts, however, generally lead to disenchantment and bitterness and end in failure. One thing they prove to the participants of the experiment is that the complex business of life cannot be sustained by emotional commitment alone; the magnitude of affections such a project would require must soon prove unbearable: the dreamt-of paradise of perpetual love turns, on closer inspection, into a hell of mutual acrimony. It transpires that the unrelenting effort needed to maintain a high intensity of feelings over a long period of time, and to absorb frustrations arising from the constant clashes between affections and the considerations of effectiveness, generates even more misery than could be caused by the sheer coolness of the alternative.

If the personal context cannot accommodate the whole of the life-business, it still remains an indispensable ingredient. Our craving for 'deep and wholesome' personal relationships grows in intensity the wider and less penetrable is the network of impersonal dependencies in which we are entangled. I am an employee in the company where I earn my salary, a customer in the many shops where I buy things I need or believe I need, a passenger on the bus or on the train which takes me to and from my place of work, a viewer in the theatre, a voter in the party which I support, a patient in the doctor's surgery, and so many other things in so many other places. Everywhere I feel that only a small section of my self is present. I must constantly watch myself not to allow the rest of my self to interfere, as its other aspects are irrelevant and unwelcome in this particular context. And thus nowhere do I feel truly myself; nowhere am I fully at home. All in all, I begin to feel like a collection of the many different roles I play, each one among different people and in a different place. Is there something to connect them? Who am I in the end — the true, the real 'I'?

Most of us fall shy of settling for an image of ourselves as, merely, a patchwork of roles. Sooner or later we grow to reconcile ourselves to the plurality of our 'Me's, and even to some lack of coordination between them (recall chapter 1); but the 'I' is one, or at least ought ideally to become one. As the unity is evidently missing in the world 'out there', split as it is into a multitude of partial, strictly functional transactions, it must be supplied instead by our cohesive selves. As **Georg Simmel** observed a long time ago, in the densely populated, variegated world we inhabit the individuals tend to fall back upon themselves in the never ending search for sense and unity. Once focused on ourselves rather than on the world outside, this overwhelming thirst for unity and coherence is articulated as the search for **self-identity**.

None of the many impersonal exchanges in which we are involved will suffice to supply this identity. The self-identity we seek 'sticks out' beyond any of those exchanges. No impersonal context can accommodate it in full. In each single context we are, so to speak, somewhat displaced: our real selves, we feel, are located somewhere outside the context of the interaction now taking place. Only in a personal context, with its diffuseness, particularity, emphasis on quality and the mutual affection which saturates it, can we hope to find what we are looking for.

The German sociologist **Niklas Luhmann** presented the search for self-identity as the primary and the most powerful cause of our overwhelming need of **love** − of loving and being loved. Being loved means being treated by the other person as unique, as unlike any other; it means that the loving persons accept that the loved ones need not invoke universal rules in order to justify the images they hold of themselves or their demands; it means that the loving person accepts and confirms the sovereignty of my self, my right to decide for myself and to choose my self on my own authority; it means that he or she agrees with my emphatic and stubborn statement 'Here is what I am, what I do, and where I stand.'

Being loved means, in other words, being **understood** − or at least 'understood' in the sense in which we use it whenever we say, 'I want you to understand me!', or ask with anguish, 'Do you understand me? Do you really *understand* me?' This craving for being understood is a desperate call to someone to put himself or herself in my shoes, to see things from my point of view, to accept without further proof that I indeed have such a point of view, which ought to be respected for the simple reason that it is mine. What I am after when craving to be understood is a confirmation that my own, private experience — my inner motives, my image of ideal life, my image of myself, my misery or joy — are *real*. I want a *validation* of my self-portrayal. I find such a validation in my acceptance by another person; in the other person's approval of what I would otherwise suspect of being just a figment of my imagination, my idiosyncrasy, the product of my fantasy running wild. I hope to achieve such a validation through my partner's willingness to listen seriously and with sympathy when I am talking about myself; my partner, in Luhmann's words, should 'lower the threshold of relevances': my partner ought to accept everything I say as relevant and worth listening to and thinking about.

As a matter of fact, there is a paradox in my wishes. On one hand, I want my self to be a unique whole, and not just a collection of the roles I put on when 'out there', only to take them off the moment I move from one place (or one company) to another. Thus I want to be unlike anybody else, similar to no one but myself — not to be just one of the many cogs in someone else's wheel. On the other hand, I know that nothing exists just because I have imagined it. I know the difference between fantasy and reality, and I know that whatever truly exists must surely exists for others as much as it does for me (remember the knowledge of everyday life each of us has and without which life in society is inconceivable; one of the crucial items of this knowledge is the belief that experiences are *shared*, that the world looks to others the same way as it looks to ourselves). And so the more I succeed in developing a truly unique self, in making my experience unique, the more I need a social confirmation of my experience. It seems, at least at first sight, that such a confirmation can only be had through love. The outcome of the paradox is that, in our complex society in which most human needs are attended to in an impersonal way, the need of a loving relationship is deeper than at any other time. This means also that the burden love must carry is formidable — and so are the pressures, tensions and obstacles the lovers must fight and conquer.

What makes a love relationship particularly vulnerable and fragile is the need for **reciprocity**. If I want to be loved, the partner I select will in all probability ask me to reciprocate − to respond with love. And this means, as we have already noticed, that I should return the services of my lover: act in such a way as to confirm the reality of my partner's experience; to understand at the same time as I am seeking to be understood myself. Ideally, each partner will strive to find meaning in the other partner's world. But the two realities (mine and my partner's) are surely not identical; worse still, they have but a few, if any, common points. When two people meet for the first time, both have behind them a long life of their own which was not shared with the other. Two distinct biographies would in all probability have produced two fairly distinct sets of experiences and expectations. Now they must be renegotiated. At least in some respects the two sets are likely to be found mutually contradictory. It is improbable that I and my partner will be ready to admit right away that both sets, in their entirety, are equally real and acceptable and do not need corrections and compromises. One set, or even both, will have to give way, be trimmed or even surrendered for the sake of a lasting relationship. And yet such a surrender defies the very purpose of love and the very need love is expected to satisfy. If renegotiation indeed takes place, if both partners see it through, the rewards are great. But the road to the happy end is thorny, and much patience and looking forward is needed to travel it unscathed.

The American sociologist **Richard Sennett** coined the term, '**destructive Gemeinschaft**' for a relationship in which both partners obsessively pursue the right to **intimacy**, to open oneself up to the partner, to share with the partner the whole, most private truth about one's inner life, to be absolutely sincere − that is, to hide nothing, however upsetting the information may be for the partner. In Sennett's view, stripping one's soul bare in front of the partner thrusts an enormous burden on the latter's shoulders, as the partner is asked to give agreement to things which do not necessarily arouse enthusiasm, and to be equally sincere and honest in reply. Sennett does not believe that a lasting relationship, and particularly a lasting *loving* relationship, can be erected on the wobbly ground of mutual intimacy. The odds are overwhelming that the partners will make demands of each other which they cannot meet (or, rather, do not wish to meet, considering the price); they will suffer and feel tormented and frustrated — and more often than not they will decide to call it a day, stop trying and withdraw. One or other of the partners will choose to opt out, and to seek satisfaction of his or her need of self-confirmation elsewhere.

Once again we find out, therefore, that the fragility of the love relationship — the destructiveness of the communion sought by the partners in love — is caused first and foremost by the requirement of reciprocity. Paradoxically, my love would be sustainable and safe only if I did not expect it to be reciprocated. Strange as it may seem, the least vulnerable is love as a gift: I am prepared to accept my beloved's world, to put myself in that world and try to comprehend it from inside — without expecting a similar service in exchange . . . I need no negotiation, agreement or contract. Once aimed in both directions, however, intimacy makes negotiation and compromise inevitable. And it is precisely the negotiation and compromise which one or both partners may be too impatient, or too self-concerned, to bear lightly. With love being such a difficult and costly achievement, it is no wonder one finds demand for a substitute for love: for someone who would perform the function of love (that is, supply confirmation of inner experience, having first patiently absorbed a full, intimate confession) without demanding reciprocity in exchange. Herein lies the secret of the astounding success and popularity of psychoanalytic sessions, psychological counselling, marriage guidance, etc. For the right to open oneself up, make one's innermost feelings known to another person, and in the end receive the longed-for approval of one's identity, one need only pay money. Monetary payment transforms the analyst's or the therapist's relation to their patients or clients into an impersonal one. And so one can be loved without loving. One can be concerned with oneself, and have the concerns shared, without giving a single thought to the people whose services have been bought, and who have therefore taken upon themselves the obligation of sharing as a part of a business transaction. The patient buys an *illusion* of being loved. (Let us note, however, that as the one-sided love is 'against nature', that is, in sharp disagreement with the socially accepted model of love, psychoanalytical exercise tends to be plagued with the so-called *transference*: the patient's tendency to mistake the 'as if' conduct of the analyst for an expression of love, and to respond with a behaviour which steps beyond the strictly business-like, impersonal terms of the agreement. The phenomenon of transference may be interpreted as a most powerful confirmation of therapy as a love substitute.)

Another, perhaps less vulnerable substitute for love (more precisely, for the function of identity-approval) is offered by the consumer market. The market puts on display a wide range of 'identities' from which one can select one's own. Commercial advertisements take pains to show the commodities they try to sell in their social context, that means as a part of a particular **life-style**, so that the prospective customer can consciously purchase symbols of such self-identity as he or she would wish to possess. The market also offers identity-making tools, which can be used differentially, to produce results which differ somewhat from each other and are in this way personalized. Through the market, one can put together various elements of the complete identikit of a DIY, customized self. One can learn how to express oneself as a modern, liberated, carefree woman; or as a thoughtful, reasonable, caring housewife; or as an aspiring, self-confident tycoon; or as an easy-going, likeable fellow; or as an outdoor, physically fit, macho man; or as a romantic, dreamy and love-hungry creature; or as any mixture of all these. The advantage of market-promoted identities is that they come complete with their social approval, and so the agony of seeking confirmation is spared. Identikits and life-style symbols are introduced by people with authority, and supported by the information that very many people approve of them by using them or by 'switching to them'. Social approval therefore does not need to be negotiated — it has been, so to speak, built into the marketed product from the start.

With such alternatives widely available and growing in popularity, the effort required by the drive to solve the self-identity problem through reciprocal love has an ever smaller chance of success. As we have seen before, negotiating approval is a tormenting experience for the partners in love. Success is not possible without long and dedicated effort. It needs self-sacrifice on both sides. The effort and the sacrifice would perhaps be made more frequently and with greater zeal were it not for the availability of 'easy' substitutes. With the substitutes being easy to obtain (the only sacrifice needed is to part with a quantity of money) and aggressively peddled by the sellers, there is, arguably, less motivation for a laborious, time-consuming and frequently frustrating effort. Resilience withers when confronted with alluringly 'foolproof' and less demanding marketed alternatives. Often the first hurdle, the first setback in the developing and vulnerable love partnership would be enough for one or both partners to wish to slow down, or to leave the track altogether. Often the substitutes are first sought with the intention to 'complement', and hence to strengthen or resuscitate, the failing love relationship; sooner or later, however, the substitutes unload that relationship of its original function and drain off the energy which prompted the partners to seek its resurrection in the first place.

One of the manifestations of such a devaluation of love, which has been discussed by **Richard Sennett**, is the tendency of *eroticism* to be ousted and supplanted by *sexuality*. Eroticism means the deployment of sexual desire, and ultimately of sexual intercourse itself, as a hub around which a lasting love relationship is built and maintained: a social partnership of a stable kind, bearing all the features previously ascribed to multi-sided, wholesome personal relations. Sexuality means the reduction of sexual intercourse to one function only – that of the satisfaction of sexual desire. Such a reduction is often supplemented by special precautions aimed at preventing the sexual relationship from giving rise to mutual sympathy and obligation, and thus from growing into a fully fledged personal partnership. Prised from love, sex is reduced to an unloading of tension, in which the partner is used as an essentially replaceable means to an end. Another consequence, however, is that the emancipation of sexuality from the context of eroticism leaves the love relationship considerably weakened. It now lacks (or has to share) one of the most powerful of its resources, and finds its stability still more difficult to defend.

A love relationship is thus exposed to a twofold danger. It may collapse under the pressure of inner tensions. Or it may retreat before, or turn itself into, another type of relationship – one which bears many or all the marks of an impersonal relationship: that of **exchange**.

We have observed a typical form of exchange relationship when considering bank customers' transactions with the bank manager. We have noted that the only thing which counted there was the passing of a particular object, or a service, from one side of the transaction to the other; an object was changing hands. The living persons involved in the transactions did not do much more than play the role of carriers or mediators; they prompted and facilitated the circulation of goods. Only apparently was their gaze fixed on their respective partners. In fact, they assigned relevance solely to the object of exchange, while granting the other persons a secondary, derivative importance – as holders or gatekeepers of the goods they wanted. They saw 'through' their partners, straight into the goods themselves. The last thing the partners would consider would be the tender feelings or spiritual cravings of their counterparts (that is, unless the mood of the partner should influence the successful completion of the exchange). To put it bluntly, both partners acted *selfishly*; the supreme motive of their action was to give away as little as possible and to get as much as possible; both pursued their own self-interest, concentrating their thought solely on the task at hand. Their aims were, therefore, at cross purposes. We may say that in transactions of impersonal exchange, the interests of the actors are in **conflict**.

Nothing in an exchange transaction is done simply for the sake of the other; nothing about the partner is important unless it may be used to secure a better bargain in the transaction. The actors are therefore naturally suspicious of each other's motives. They fear being cheated. They feel they need to remain wide awake, wary and vigilant. They cannot afford to look the other way, lose their attention for a single moment. They want protection against the selfishness of the other side; they would not, of course, expect the other side to act selflessly, but they insist on a fair deal – that is, on whatever they consider to be an equivalent exchange. Hence the exchange relationships call for a *binding rule*, a law, and an *authority* entrusted with the task of adjudicating the fairness of the transaction and capable of imposing its decision by force in the case of transgression. Various consumer associations, consumer watchdogs, ombudsmen, etc. are established out of this urge for protection. They take upon themselves the difficult task of monitoring the fairness of exchange. They also press the authorities for laws which would restrain the freedom of the stronger side to exploit the ignorance or naïvety of the weaker one.

Seldom are the two counterparts of a transaction in a truly equal position: those who produce or sell the goods know much more of the quality of their product than the buyers and users are ever likely to learn. They may well push the product to gullible customers under false pretences, unless constrained by a law like the Trade Descriptions Act. The more complex and technically sophisticated the goods, the less their buyers are able to judge their true quality and value. To avoid being deceived, the prospective buyers have to resort to the help of independent, that is, disinterested, authorities; they would press for a law which clearly states their rights and allows them to make up for their relatively inferior position by taking their case to court.

It is, however, precisely because the partners enter exchange relationships only as functions of exchange, as conveyers of the goods, and consequently remain 'invisible' to each other, that they feel much less overwhelmed and tied down than in the case of love relationships. They are much less involved. They do not take upon themselves cumbersome duties, or obligations other than the promise to abide by the terms of the transaction. Aspects of their selves which are not relevant to the transaction at hand are unaffected and retain their autonomy. All in all, they feel that their freedom has not been compromised, and their future choices will not be constrained by the bond they enter. Exchange is relatively 'inconsequential' as it is confined to a transaction entered into and finished here and now and restricted in time and space. Neither does it involve the whole of one's personality. (Note that the fashion in which exchange is linked to personal autonomy disqualifies the claim, often taken for granted in economic and political reasonings, that human labour is a commodity like others and can be treated as an object of exchange. Unlike exchangeable goods, labour cannot be detached from the labourer. Selling one's labour means agreeing that one's actions as a person — the whole of the person for a specific period of time — will from now on be subordinated to other people's will and decisions. The *totality* of the labourer's self, and not just a detachable object in his possession, is parted with and transferred to somebody else's control. The apparently impersonal contract reaches far beyond the limits proper for transactions of exchange.)

Love and exchange are two extremes of a continuous line along which all human relations may be plotted. In the form we have described them here they seldom appear in your or my experience. We have discussed them in a pure form, as models. Most relationships are 'impure', and mix the two models in varying proportions. Most love relationships contain elements of business-like bargaining for the fair rate of exchange in the 'I'll do this if you do that' style. Except for a chance encounter or one-off transaction, the actors in exchange relationships seldom remain indifferent to each other for long, and sooner or later more is involved than just money and goods. Each extreme model, however, retains its relative identity even if submerged in a mixed relationship. Each carries its own set of expectations, its own image of the perfect state of affairs — and hence orients the conduct of the actors in its own specific direction. Much of the ambiguity of the relationships we enter with other people can be accounted for by reference to the tensions and contradictions between the two extreme, complementary yet incompatible, sets of expectations. The model-like, pure relationships seldom appear in life, where the ambivalence of human relationships is the rule.

Our dreams and cravings seem to be torn between two needs it is well nigh impossible to gratify at the same time, yet equally difficult to satisfy when pursued separately. These are the needs of *belonging* and of *individuality*. The first need prompts us to seek strong and secure ties with others. We express this need whenever we speak or think of togetherness or of community. The second need sways us towards privacy, a state in which we are immune to pressures and free from demands, do whatever we think is worth doing, 'are ourselves'. Both needs are pressing and powerful; the pressure of each grows the less the given need is satisfied. On the other hand, the nearer one need comes to its satisfaction, the more painfully we feel the neglect of the other. We find out that community without privacy feels more like oppression than belonging. And that privacy without community feels more like loneliness than 'being oneself'.

Chapter Six

Power and Choice

Why do I do what I do? Unless I happen to be in a philosophical mood, this looks too simple a question to bother with. Is the answer not obvious? At least, so it seems. Of course, I do it *because* ... (I rush to the tutorial because I was reprimanded by the tutor for missing the last one; I stop at the lights because there the cross-traffic is heavy; I cook my dinner because I feel hungry; I wear jeans because this is the thing one wears nowadays.) What makes my explanations seem so simple — indeed, self-evident — is that they conform to a habit we all share: the habit of explaining events by pointing out that they are *effects* of a *cause*.

In most cases, when it comes to explain things we do or things that happen to us, our curiosity is by and large sated when we satisfy ourselves that provided something else has happened, the event we wish to explain must have happened; it was, in other words, inevitable, or at least highly probable. Why was there an explosion in that house down the road? Because there was a leak in the gas pipes. Well, gas is a highly inflammable substance and a spark is enough to ignite it. Why did no one hear the burglar breaking the window? Because everybody was asleep. Well, people do not normally hear sounds when they are asleep. And so on. Our search for the explanation grinds to a halt once we have found an event or a state of affairs which the event we wish to explain always follows (we speak then of a *law*, a link with no exceptions), or follows it in most cases (we speak then of a *norm*; a link will show itself in most, though not in all, cases). Explanation consists, therefore, of representing the event we want to explain as a proposition which may be deduced from another, more general proposition or set of propositions. Because we can represent the event in such a fashion, we see it as essentially predictable: given the general law or norm and the presence of certain circumstances in which the law or the norm manifest themselves, the event must have occurred and it could not be replaced with any other event. Explanation does not allow the possibility of a choice, a voluntary selection, an arbitrary sequence of events.

When applied to human conduct, however, this habitual explanation leaves something important unsaid. What it leaves out is the fact that the event we wish to explain was someone's action, and the person whose action it was had a choice. He or she could have behaved differently. There was more than one way of acting, yet only one was selected, and this is precisely what ought have been explained — but was not. This event was in no way inevitable. There is no set of general propositions from which it could be deduced — not with any certainty anyway. It was not, therefore, predictable. We can try to comprehend this event after it occurred; retrospectively, with the benefit of hindsight, we can *interpret* the event — this action — as an outcome of certain *rules* which the actors must have followed to do what they did. These rules, however, might have generated more than one kind of behaviour. And there was no need for the actor to follow them.

In the case of human conduct, explanations of the kind given above do not satisfy us as being the whole story, everything there was to know. We know from our own experience that things are done by people with a purpose. Men and women have *motives*; like myself, they do what they do *in order to* create or achieve a situation which for one reason or another seems to them preferable (thus I come to the tutorials regularly in order to avoid the tutor's reprimands or in order to follow the course in its entirety; I watch the traffic carefully in order to escape accidents and remain alive; I cook dinner in order to satisfy my hunger or to entertain my guest; I wear jeans, a thing most people around me do, in order not to stick out and be conspicuous).

And so there is nothing inevitable in my sitting in my tutor's room at the appointed hour simply because the attendance of tutorials is required by the university authorities; I am sitting there because I want to comply with the regulation — for one reason or another I consider it the right thing to do. There is nothing inevitable in my stopping and waiting for a green light to show — even if, quite sensibly, I want to avoid an accident; I obviously also believe that the system of changing lights makes sense as a means of avoiding accidents and ought to be followed for this reason. To everything I do, there is always an alternative, a choice. Plainly speaking, I could do something else instead.

Human actions could be different from what they were even if the circumstances of action, and the motives of the actors, remained the same. Circumstances could be disregarded, motives discarded, different conclusions could be drawn from both. Therefore, pointing to external circumstances, or to more general laws, does not satisfy us as fully as in the case of events which are not concerned with human actions. We know well that this man or that woman could have behaved differently in objectively identical circumstances (which would not be identical to them subjectively, since the relevance they attach to them varies, as does their very perception of them). If we wish to know why this rather than that form of action has been selected, we would therefore do better to think of the decision made by the actor. We cannot avoid thinking of the actor as a decision-maker, and the action itself as an outcome of the **decision-making process**.

We can conceive, to be sure, of a human conduct in which the decision-making does not play an important role. Some actions are virtually **unreflective** — that is, alternatives are not consciously pondered, do not become a topic for consideration. One can point out two types of such an unthinking conduct.

Habitual (sometimes, less aptly, called traditional) behaviour is one of them. I normally wake up at the same hour every day, as if I had an alarm clock built into my body ... Still half asleep, I go through the motions of my morning routine — I wash, brush my teeth, shave. I do not remember making decisions to follow that routine; as a matter of fact, I probably think of something else while following it (often I must look in the mirror to check whether I have indeed shaved, since I did it without paying any attention). Every day I feel hunger at the same regular hours, precisely at the time I usually have my meal. When I come back home in the evening, I switch on the light, so to speak, automatically. I do not notice the darkness, do not ponder the advantage of light over darkness, do not give one preference over the other; I hardly think at all about the substance and the purpose of my action. But I do start thinking if upon my return I see that the lights in my room are already on, though usually they are not ... I notice them, because they break the daily routine: something *unusual* must have happened — perhaps guests have arrived unexpectedly, or, worse still, burglars are inside ... The normal sequence of events, of which one could afford not to think at all, has been broken. The habitual actions would not do, and so I am forced to think about my next step. I have to *make decisions*. Or consider another case: I need a book which I left on the table in another room. When I go to fetch it, I find the room dark. I would naturally switch on the light, but then I notice that someone is lying asleep on the couch. Again, following the habit would not do. If I switch on the light, I might wake the sleeper. Yet if I grope for the book in the dark, I might unwittingly knock a chair or break a vase and again disturb the sleeper. Circumstances are not routine any more, and the habit is suddenly a poor guide. The situation clearly calls for a *choice*, and my decision-making process is again set in motion.

Habitual conduct is a sediment of past learning. At some point in the past, the habit has been acquired. Since then, however, thanks to regular repetition, it has absolved me from the need to think, to calculate and to make decisions; one movement follows another, in a regular and immutable sequence; that is, as long as the circumstances also remain regular. Indeed, so habitualized are my actions that I'd find it difficult, if asked, to describe them. They come into my attention — are noticed by me — only if something goes wrong. Even my seemingly automatic morning routine may grind to a halt and call for my attention if I find myself in an unfamiliar house where bathroom implements are not 'where they should be', that is, where I am used to find them; or if my toothbrush breaks, or the soap has been misplaced. The effectiveness of my habitual behaviour depends, as it were, on the regularity and orderliness of the environment in which my action occurs.

There is another type of conduct in which my thinking plays but a minor role, if any. This is an **affective** action: acting out of strong emotions — strong enough, in fact, to switch off reasoning, suspend all calculation of the purposes and possible consequences of action. Affective action is compulsive and can hardly be resisted by the actor; it does not listen to argument, is deaf to the voice of reason. It usually follows an outburst of feelings very closely. With the passage of time, the cooling off of passions would have had its effect, and I'd think twice before committing the act. Whatever I do after that will be a calculated (and hence not an affective) act. Being a temperamental person, I may hit or kick a man who has offended me or a person I love and cherish. Or I may give all the money I have to a person in need in an impulse of pity or compassion. However, if I decide to ambush a person I hate in a dark passage in order to avenge the harm for which I blame her or him, this would hardly be an affective act; the premeditation involved would suggest instead that the act was an outcome of a calculated decision. Neither would an act be affective if the help I offered people in need was a deliberate attempt to ingratiate myself in their eyes or in the eyes of God; such an offer would be, rather, a step in a calculated campaign, a means to an end — in this case, the earning of salvation and forgiveness of my sins. An action is truly affective only as long as it stays *unreflective*, spontaneous, unpremeditated, and is perpetrated before any weighing of arguments and measuring of effects has had time to take place.

Habitual and affective actions are often described as **irrational**. What is meant by this name is not that they are foolish, ineffective, wrong or damaging. Indeed, the name does not imply any evaluation of the utility of the act. Most habitualized routines are quite effective and useful. They accomplish something vital to the business of life, and in addition spare us much thinking time and make our conduct less absorbing and the tasks easier to perform. Similarly, hitting an offender may in the end prove more effective than many a calculated, 'cool' method of discouraging his abusive behaviour in the future. Action is irrational not when it lacks utility, but when the consideration of its utility did not precede it — was not a factor in the decision-making. Action is irrational if it has not been an outcome of decision-making. Conversely, the opposite, rational action may happen to be less effective (and so less reasonable) than the irrational one.

The **rational** action is one in which from among possible ways of acting the actor consciously selects one which seems to him or her best geared to the end the action is meant to achieve (this is the case of **instrumental rationality**): the means are selected according to what the given ends require. Alternatively, rational action may be **value-rational**: certain means are available to the actor that can be used for different purposes, from which the actor selects the one end he or she considers more valuable than the rest ('dear to one's heart', attractive, desirable, most closely connected to the need most poignantly felt at that moment). What unites both cases — instrumental and value-rational varieties of rationality — is that in both the means are measured against the ends, and their mutual fit, true or supposed, is seen as the ultimate criterion in the choice between the right and wrong decision. The fit may in the end prove to be illusory, the calculation may look wrong in retrospect; the only thing which makes the action rational is that a calculation was made before the action was taken. The essential idea which stands behind all this reciprocal matching, calculating, measuring and finally choosing is that action is rational as long as it is *voluntary* — as long as the actor has had, and exercised, a free choice, rather than being goaded, pulled, pushed or bullied into doing what he or she did by uncontrolled habits or a momentary outburst of passion.

Whenever we choose our actions consciously and after deliberation, we anticipate their probable outcome. This we do, first of all, by taking stock of the situation in which the action is to take place and the effects we expect to attain. More precisely, what we normally take stock of are *resources* and *values*. My resources may consist of money — in the 'liquid' form of banknotes in my pocket or an account in the bank, or in the form of valuable possessions which could be used to obtain credit. My resources also include my skills, which can be applied to create things other people need in exchange for things I demand, my 'social capital' — for instance, my access to people who are in charge of things or services I wish to obtain, and thus relevant to the task ahead. The values I hold and revere enable me to compare accessible ends with each other and determine which one seems to be the best. My resources can be turned to many uses. The alternative uses differ from each other by carrying different degrees of attractiveness and being attractive for different reasons.

They represent different values. Some seem to be more satisfying, or more indispensable, or more praiseworthy. Some may be chosen because they promise to be most useful, as they may open up the possibility of increasing the volume of resources at my disposal and thus enhance my range of freedom in the future. It is ultimately my values which preside over the decision to spend a hundred pounds of extra cash on a new turntable, or on a holiday, or on purchasing sociology books — or to keep them in my building society account. Taking stock of my resources and values shows me the degree of my freedom: what I can do and what in my case is out of the question.

Different people have different degrees of freedom. The fact that they differ in their freedom of choice, in the range of actions they may decide to take, is the essence of **social inequality** (that is, of such differences between people as are social in their origin; of such differences as have been brought into being and maintained by human interactions and which can be distributed differently or even abolished altogether with a change in that interaction). Some people are more free than others: their range of choice is wider, as they have access to more resources, and a wider range of values is within their reach (pursuit of such values is for them realistic and feasible, while remaining no more than an idle, upsetting and in the end frustrating dream for the less fortunate).

The difference in the degree of freedom is often spoken about as the difference in **power**. Power is, indeed, best understood as the ability to act — both in the sense of choosing freely the ends of any action and of commanding the means which make such ends realistic. Power is an enabling capacity. The more power people have, the wider is their range of choice, the larger the amount of decisions they can see as realistic, the broader the scope of outcomes they may realistically pursue while being reasonably certain that they would get what they want. Being less powerful, or powerless, means it is necessary to moderate one's dreams, or to abandon attempts to reach one's aims due to the absence of necessary resources.

To have power is to be able to act more freely; but having no power, or less power than others have, means having one's own freedom of choice limited by the decisions made by others. We say that A has power over B when the resources which A commands permit A to prompt such conduct of B as is necessary to achieve the ends set by A; when they allow, in other words, A to enlist B's ends as further means to A's ends; or, which means the same, to transform B's values into A's resources. We can guess that were it not for the actual or potential actions of A, B's actions would be different from what they were; as B's ends are someone else's resources and thus used as a means to someone else's ends, B's freedom of choice has been most seriously compromised. B's actions are not *autonomous* any more; they become *heteronomous* instead.

My bosses, for instance, have power over me; they can fire me if I do not conform to the rules they set and do not obey their orders, or can reward or promote me if my performance is exemplary from their point of view. But the rights to hire and fire, to reward or punish, are not among my resources, and so I cannot repay in kind. Moreover, the bosses may play their cards close to their chests. They may keep their intentions *secret* until it is too late for me to resist. They may plan a radical rearrangement of things in the office — new technical equipment, a new division of labour — which would radically worsen my situation and further diminish my freedom to manoeuvre. I cannot respond with the same weapon of secrecy, as there is little I can conspire to do which may have an impact of the same magnitude on the bosses' freedom as their clandestine designs will have on mine. My bosses' secrecy is potentially much more deadly a weapon than anything I may keep under my hat. And so we are sharply unequal in the extent to which we may affect each other's situation. In our reciprocal relation, power is unevenly distributed: this is an *asymmetrical* power relationship. My bosses can choose their actions from a much wider range of alternatives than the scope of my choice. It is because our degrees of freedom are so sharply different that I will probably do exactly what the bosses want, so that they may count on my obedience to their rules; planning their actions, they may therefore count my actions among the resources they have at their disposal. The more my range of choices is limited, the more correctly can they anticipate my conduct. I hold fewer secrets for them, I am less of an unknown quantity in their equation, and hence less a source of uncertainty in their position than they are in mine. My compliance with their ends can be safely relied upon, much like the capital or machinery they own.

To recapitulate: what power amounts to is the ability to deploy other people's actions as the means to one's own end; more generally, it is the ability to reduce the constraint imposed by other people's freedom on one's own choice of ends and the calculation of means. Such a devaluation of other people's freedom, equal to the enhancement of one's own freedom, may be achieved by two methods.

One is *coercion*, which consists of manipulating the situation of action in such a way that the resources of the other person, however large they may seem in other contexts, suddenly become inadequate or ineffective. An entirely new game is created, for which the manipulating side is much better equipped. (Whether the victim of a mugger is a rich banker, a powerful politician or a famous show-business personality, their respective resources, which assure them a large degree of freedom in other contexts, lose their 'enabling' capacity once they are confronted in a dark and deserted street with the point of a knife or sheer muscle power.) A drastic reduction of freedom may also be achieved through enforced re-evaluation of values – or, rather, through reshuffling the choice in such a fashion that the normally highly placed values abruptly lose much of their importance. In a night encounter with the mugger, a wallet full of banknotes and credit cards – usually of supreme value to a greedy person – may suddenly seem insignificant; the choice is now between life and death, not between more and less money. Under an institutionalized coercion, in prison or in a labour camp, the new values – good food, light work, permission of leave or receiving visitors, the avoidance of solitary confinement or high-security jail, or just the benevolence of a prison guard may well dwarf and make eerie or laughable the old, once cherished priorities. In the extreme conditions of concentration camps the value of self-preservation and survival may well overshadow all the prisoner's choices.

The other method is less straightforward (and more costly for the power-holder) than coercion. It consists of enlisting the values of other people as one's own resources: 'making the desires of others work for me'. More specifically, it is manipulating the situation in such way that other people may attain the values they pursue only if they follow the rules set by the power-holder. Thus the zeal and efficiency with which the enemies are killed is rewarded by enhancing the social standing of the brave soldier with medals and honourable citations (in the past, it could be rewarded with knighthoods and estates). Formal acknowledgement of skills and knowledge is made dependent upon a student's obedience to college regulations, like regular attendance of classes and the submission of essays on time. Factory workers may secure improved living standards (wage rises) on condition that they work with more dedication and intensity and comply unconditionally with the management orders. In such a way, the values of the subordinates become the resources of their superiors; their dreams and cravings are deployed in the service of ends set by the power-holders. Having no capital of my own, I depend for my living on being employed. Yet being employed means that I must act in accordance with the terms of the job; I suspend my freedom for the duration of my work-time. Having freely chosen the value of a better standard of living − or, for that matter, of simply staying alive − as my own, voluntary commitment, I now find that I have no other way of reaching the value of my choice but to surrender quite a considerable part of my freedom.

Whoever can deploy coercion, or manipulate rewards, may by the same token change my chances of attaining the values I covet. Their decisions affect the volume, or the utility of the resources which I may use in my action. They may also influence the ends of my actions, though only indirectly. I may give up the chase after some values I cherished in the past because I have now found my dream 'unrealistic'. The odds have been too overwhelming, the probability of overcoming them virtually nil; fatigue and disenchantment have taken their toll, and slowly the ends I hoped to achieve (and, indeed, my total life-project) have become sweet dreams of the sort one likes to muse on, but on which does not act. My actions change orientation; they are now directed to more 'realistic' ends, my assessment of the potency of my resources is altered, and from now on I reverse the order of calculation: I measure the ends against the means. The odds are that I'd settle eventually for much less than I dreamt of achieving at the beginning.

Where have my values come from in the first place, however? Why do I put values on some ends, and disregard or downgrade others? Are these values a matter of my free choice? Can I pick them up and drop them at will? Or are they, much like my resources, affected by actions of other people and by such elements of my situation over which I have but little, if any, control? Consider the following: I intended to go to college straight from school. My friends, however, decided otherwise. Arguing about our respective choices, they convinced me that going on with my education would not make my life much happier; it would be more fun to start enjoying life right away — have some income of my own, rather than condemn myself to three years of self-sacrifice and semi-starvation. After listening to their argument, I changed my mind, and instead of applying for a college place started looking for an instant income. Now I enjoy my regular pay-cheques; it is pleasant to have money in my pocket and use it to shop for things I would like to have. Then the union people suggested that we should strike to force the management to go back on their decision to reorganize the office so that economies can be made by making quite a few employees redundant. My own job and income were secure, prospects of promotion good, after reorganization even better. Moreover, the board has announced that in the event of a strike important orders will be lost and in the end all of us will be fired. I did not like this prospect at all; yet most of my fellow employees put solidarity above the security of their own jobs, dignity above income, and voted for the strike. I did not wish to be a black sheep, and so I joined them — though it is now likely that I'll lose my own job as a result, and with it my freedom to enjoy life as I understand it . . .

As happened in this case, the values people select to orient and guide their actions (that is, to order their ends according to their rising or diminishing importance) change in the course, and under the impact, of social interaction. It is this impact we have in mind whenever we speak of *influence*. Unlike power, influence affects the values directly: it manifests itself by shifting the relative position of various ends in the hierarchy of importance, by making some ends seem more attractive than others, and hence worthy of more effort. Selecting values, putting some ends above the others, means believing that the ends which have been assigned priority are ultimately more satisfying, they bring more pleasure, are more dignified, more morally elevated, more aesthetically pleasing — on the whole they are more attuned to one's sense of the proper and improper.

Not always are the values consciously chosen. As we saw before, many of our actions are habitual and routine, and do not involve a consideration of means and ends. As long as the actions remain habitual, we seldom pause to ask about the values they serve. Habitual action does not need justification, and we would find it hard to explain why we put them above their alternatives. If really pressed, we would perhaps come up with an answer like 'This is the way things have always been done', or 'This is how it is' — as if the very length of time for which habits have persisted lends them authority of sorts, or as if the fact that many people do it this way is in itself a value which makes the action desirable. Let us remember, however, that these are 'enforced' explanations, prompted by questioning. They were not necessarily present in the mind of the questioned person before the questioning started. As you may recall, the whole point about acting by habit, or a traditional action, is that it does not need justification. The action remains traditional as long as it is not called to *legitimize* itself; traditional action can do without *legitimation*, that is, it does not require reference to values it is supposed to serve. It goes on repeating itself, by and large according to the same pattern, on the strength of the habit alone. Many of our daily activities are traditional (habitual, routine and not reflected upon), even if most of us are most emphatically not traditionalists (that is, were we given the opportunity to think about it and express our considered views, we would deny the authority of the old and the timeless, and disagree with the intrinsic value of stability and lack of change).

The most general values which guide our lives (the values which preside over the selection of the specific ends of our actions) — such as the standards of decency or success, honesty or cleverness, hard work or enjoyment, consistency or flexibility — are established on the whole in our childhood years. More often than not they are sedimented in the subconscious level; they constitute the voice of conscience rather than a set of clearly articulated commandments we can spell out at will or need to spell out for ourselves whenever facing a decision. We hardly ever remember the influences of our childhood years; it is a measure of the success of such influences that they are forgotten and no longer perceived as outside pressures. We become aware of the outside influence only when it comes to the making of deliberate choices: when the values we obey are challenged, defied and called to legitimize themselves.

The ability of influence other people's values is an attribute of *authority*. Authority is measured by the probability that people will accept given values for the sole reason that someone else — the person or the organization endowed with authority — practises or preaches such values. A person or organization may carry authority for certain people inasmuch as the fact that they vouch for the values in question will be seen by those people as a sufficient reason for acceptance and compliance. The authority a person or an organization wields therefore boils down to the likelihood that other people will follow their example or advice. That obedience may be justified in all sorts of terms, such as wisdom, truthfulness, experience, the moral integrity of the source of guidance which has been followed. In each case, however, what is thus justified is the *trust* of the followers in the basic soundness of the guidance that comes from such a source.

The values we cherish are ultimately a matter of our choice. In the end it is we who bestow authority upon the examples we decide to follow and refuse authority to examples we do not like. Before we decide whom to trust, we may ponder the claims that various competing 'value-leaders', or others on their behalf, make for the worthiness of their example and for their ability to come forward with a good, trustworthy example. To become an authority for us, a person or an organization must produce a *legitimation*, or an argument, which demonstrates why their advice (or their hierarchy of values) ought to be followed in preference to another.

One such legitimation we have already met: let us recall that some values are presented as worthy of esteem because of the *tradition* which stands behind them. They are, so we are told, time-honoured and time-tested. One ought to remain faithful to the past; to the group with which this past has been shared; to the common heritage of which we are jointly the guardians. History, we are told, binds its heirs; what history brought together, no human presumption should dare to set apart. Old virtues are venerable just because they are old . . .

Thus goes the argument. Often it reverses the truth: rather than values being revered because of their old age, those who seek popular acceptance for the values they preach (sometimes brand new, freshly invented values) bend over backwards to dig out genuine, or putative, historical evidence of their antiquity. The image of the historical past is always selective; in this case it is put together in such a way as to give credence to the venerable age of the values on offer. The deference people feel for the past is enlisted in the service of the current contest of values. Once it has been accepted that certain values were held by our ancestors, they are less vulnerable to contemporary criticism; other values have still to prove themselves, while those of the good old days have already passed the test of time, even if not with flying colours. The traditionalist legitimation becomes particularly attractive in times of rapid change which cannot but generate uneasiness and anxiety. It helps if radical and unprecedented innovations are acclaimed as the restoration of old and tried ways; such representation may sometimes somewhat reduce uncertainty, caused by rapid social change, and seems to offer a relatively safe, less agonizing choice.

The alternative would be to defend new values as a revelation of sorts — as the result of an epoch-making discovery, a particularly profound insight into the truth of the matter, or a strong vision that pierced through the unknown and hence threatening future. This kind of argument is associated with *charismatic* legitimation. Charisma was the quality first noted in the study of the deep and unchallenged influence exerted by the Church upon the faithful. The concept of charisma referred in that case to the conviction of the faithful that the Church is endowed with a privileged access to truth: it has been, as an institution, anointed by God to guide men to a godly life and, ultimately, salvation. Charisma, however, need not be confined to religious beliefs and institutions. We can speak of charisma whenever the acceptance of certain values is motivated by the conviction that the preacher or preachers of such values have superhuman qualities (unusual wisdom, foresight, access to sources of knowledge closed to ordinary men and women) that guarantee the truth of their vision and the propriety of their choice. The ordinary reason of ordinary people has therefore no means of evaluating what charismatic people aver and thus no right to doubt the power of their perception. The stronger the charisma of the leaders, the more difficult it is to question their commands; the more comforting it is for people to follow their orders when exposed to a situation of acute uncertainty.

With rapid and profound social change fast invalidating customary patterns of acting, the demand for charismatic 'guarantees' of unerring value choices is expanding unabated. Established churches satisfy, however, only a minor part of that demand. There are numerous choice situations generated by new and unprecedented social changes for which churches have not got ready recipes, or have recipes poorly geared to the present conditions. This does not necessarily mean that the divine forms of charismatic authority fall from grace. Updated versions offered by television evangelists, religious gurus and manifold sectarian cults testify, if anything, to the widely and strongly felt need for superhuman solutions to problems which clearly transcend the human capacity of judgement.

With the demand for charismatic solutions to the problems of value growing to unprecedented proportions, some political parties and mass social movements stepped in to provide a substitute service. Among the first, the so-called totalitarian parties (parties claiming the total dedication of their followers in every aspect of their lives), like the fascists or communists, gained particular notoriety for either generating charismatic leaders credited with superhuman foresight and an unimpeachable sense of right and wrong, or turning themselves into collective carriers of charismatic authority. The latter development in particular puts the charismatic influence on an altogether new, more stable basis; the influence of a charismatic organization can in principle (and sometimes in practice) outlive the charismatic leader. More importantly, it can become relatively immune to the eroding impact of past errors for which mere individuals would be blamed, leaving the organization unscathed and its continuous authority assured. Such luxury is not, on the whole, available to loosely organized mass movements (unless, that is, they succeed in establishing a strong, party-like organization capable of self-perpetuation). Usually they share the fate of their leader who is the proper carrier of charismatic authority: his meteoric rise and his rapid fall once his popularity is undermined by setbacks and unfulfilled promises or overshadowed by more successful (not yet discredited) contenders for public attention.

The centre of charismatic authority, however, now seems to have shifted away from both the religious and the political arena. The advent of mass media — powerful technology capable of making message-senders visible and audible, yet virtually inaccessible, to millions of message-recipients — has played a major role in this shift. The psychological effect of this situation has proved shattering. The sheer mass exposure-cum-inaccessibility of TV personalities, or TV-assisted public personalities, seems to be a source of a powerful, charismatic influence. Much like the charismatic leaders of old, they are credited with a capacity for superior judgement, this time first and foremost in the field of taste — so that they may become the trend-setters of a life-style. The impression of superiority is, one may suppose, the reflection of their exposure and the massiveness of their following. The quantity itself becomes now an authority — the genuine carrier of charismatic aura. The large number of people who look to public personalities for guidance and advice on their own choices reinforces the power of charisma and adds strength to the popular trust in the validity of the source.

Another example of collective charismatic influence is provided by the professions. Their claim to pronounce and adjudicate on human choices is grounded in their expertise: in their privileged access to knowledge otherwise difficult to obtain, and for this reason superior to the untested and often erroneous beliefs of a lay person. The knowledge the professions command is normally beyond the reach and comprehension of those who are called to obey the verdicts based on that knowledge — and so the propriety of the verdicts cannot be checked. Verdicts are accepted because people who obey them assume the impeccability of the adjudicating authority; and the verdicts go on being accepted as long as people who obey them believe, first, in the collective wisdom of the profession as a whole and, secondly, in the profession's ability to monitor its individual members so that each one acts as a competent and reliable spokesperson for that wisdom. One is inclined, for instance, to forgo the pleasure of smoking or drinking once 'the doctors say' that such pleasures are harmful; or one accepts the doctors' opinion on the right body weight even at the cost of depriving oneself of one's favourite food. The charismatic authority of the professions is a special case of a wider phenomenon: our common trust in the unassailable superiority of science as a method of generating valuable and trustworthy knowledge. Whatever the substantive difference between scientific knowledge and religious revelation, the mechanisms of their acceptance by the lay public do not substantively differ. In both cases the ordinary, uninitiated people have no way of testing the truthfulness of information — they can only take it *on trust*, being confident about the wisdom and veracity of persons or organizations (the Church, the University) who collectively purvey the information complete with the guarantee of its quality.

The two legitimations which we have considered so far — the traditionalist and the charismatic — share one feature: they both imply the surrender of one's right to make value choices and ceding it to another, single or collective, actor. The ceding of choice is very often associated with the surrender of responsibility. It is now the other actors (the past generations as we imagine them, or present-day authoritative institutions) which have already made choices for us and thus bear the responsibility for the results — including *moral* responsibility for the consequences of our actions.

Legitimation of the third type, however — the *legal-rational* one — goes further still, as it apparently removes the very problem of value choice and the attendant agony of self-justification. It implies that some organizations, and the persons entitled to speak on their behalf, have the legally guaranteed right to tell us what sort of action ought to be undertaken, while it is our equally lawful duty to obey without further argument. If this is the case, the very question of the wisdom or moral quality of the advice seems to have lost its import- ance. We do not bear the responsibility (or so we are told) for choosing between competing carriers of charismatic authority. It is now the law and lawful command, and not our decision, which selects for us the authority which determines our action. The legal- rational legitimation separates action from value choice and hence makes it apparently value-free. The executors of a command need not scrutinize the morality of the action they have been ordered to perform, nor do they need to feel responsible if the action fails the moral test. Self-righteously, they would react with indignation to any reproach on this account: 'I was only carrying out the orders I received from my legal superiors.'

Whatever it gains in enhancing the potency and efficiency of human enterprise, the legal-rational legitimation is pregnant with potentially sinister consequences — and that precisely because of its tendency to absolve the actors from their responsibility for value choice and, in a sense, remove the whole issue of value choice from discussion. The mass murder and genocide of the last war provided the most conspicuous, though by no means unique and exceptional, example of such consequences: the perpetrators of murder refused to accept moral responsibility, pointing instead to the legal determination of their obedience to command; they rejected the charge that their decision to obey was, in fact, a moral choice on their part.

Removing the values which the actions serve from the sight of the actors by the simple expedient of extending the chain of command beyond the vision of the executors renders the action apparently value-free and exempt from moral judgement. The actors are offered, so to speak, escape from the burden of their freedom, which always comes complete with the responsibility for one's actions.

Chapter Seven

Self-preservation and Moral Duty

'I need it. I must have it' — all too often I say these two sentences in one breath, as if the second sentence merely put a greater emphasis on the point made in the first; or as if the second sentence clarified the meaning of the first; or the second sentence drew an obvious practical conclusion from the statement of fact made in the first. It looks like needing something means not having something that should be had: a *deprivation*. And that needing prompts the wish to have what has been missing. 'Having it' is some sort of necessity or compulsion which the need prompts. 'I *must* have it'; 'it' — something I need to possess to be happy, or to escape the present state of need which is, presumably, a state of discomfort and unease and thus restlessness and anxiety. Possessing it is a condition of my **self-preservation** or even **survival**. Without it, I cannot remain the sort of person I am. My life would be flawed or even intolerable. In an extreme case, it would not continue at all. Not just my well-being, but my very physical existence would be in danger.

It is the quality of being needed for my survival or self-preservation that makes this something I lack and miss into a *good*. The good is, as it were, the other side of the need. Since I need something, this something is a good; something is a good in so far as I need it. This something could mean many things: commodities one can buy in the shop in exchange for money; silence in the street at night or clean air and uncontaminated water, which cannot be attained but by the concerted effort of many others; the safety of one's home and safe passage through public spaces, which depends on the actions of people with power; love of another person — and the other person's will to understand and to manifest compassion which come with it.

In other words, any 'good', anything that is made an object of our concern because we need it, always brings us into a relation with other people. Our needs cannot be satisfied unless we gain access to the goods in question, either through being allowed to use them, or through owning them. But this always involves other people and their actions. However self-concerned the interest in self-preservation is, it strengthens our ties with other people; it makes us dependent on other people's actions and the motives which guide them.

This truth is not evident at a first glance. On the contrary: on the face of it, **ownership** is widely understood as a thoroughly 'private' thing; a kind of special relation between the person and the object this person owns. The image which most often comes to mind when I say, 'This is mine', or 'This belongs to me', is that of an invisible link extending between me and, say, a pen or a book or a desk which is 'mine'. It seems that the object (the property) is somehow invisibly connected to its owner; it is in such a connection that we suppose the essence of ownership rests. If I am the owner of the piece of paper on which I write these words, it is I and I alone who decide what to do with it. I can use it at will − I can write on it a part of a book, or a letter to a friend, or I can wrap a sandwich in it; what is more, I can destroy it if I wish. (It is true that for some of my possessions I am prohibited from doing so by law: I cannot, for instance, fell an old tree in my garden without permission; neither am I allowed to set my house on fire. But the fact that a special law is needed to forbid me to dispose of certain property in such a way only further underlines the general principle that it is up to *me*, and to me alone, what becomes of the things I own.) What this popular image of ownership overlooks, however, and the popular descriptions of the property relation leave unsaid, is that ownership is also, and more than anything else, a relation of **exclusion**. Think of it: whenever I say, 'This is mine', I mean also, though I do not say it out loud and often do not think of it at all, this is *not* yours. Ownership is never a private quality; it is always a social affair. Ownership conveys a special relation between an object and its owner only because it conveys at the same time a special relation between the owner and other people. Owning a thing means denying others access to it.

Ownership, therefore, establishes a mutual dependence, and hence a close relationship between me and the others, but it does not connect (things and people) as much as it divides (people). The fact of ownership sets apart, in a relation of mutual antagonism, those who own the object and all those who do not; the first can use (and abuse, unless specifically constrained by the law) the object in question, while the second are denied such a right. The fact of ownership differentiates between people (I can reach into my pocket to take out some money, but no one else is allowed to do the same). It may also (remember our discussion of power) make the relationship between people asymmetrical; those who are denied access to the object of ownership must obey the conditions set by the owner whenever they need or want to use it. Their need, therefore, and their willingness to satisfy that need, puts them in a position of **dependence** on the owner (that is, the goods necessary to satiate their needs, goods crucial to their preservation as the kind of persons they are and wish to remain, or to their continuing existence, cannot be acquired without some action being taken by their present owner).

How and for what purpose the machine plant in a factory is used by the workers who operate it is decided upon by the owner, or by the people given the right to act in the owner's name. As he or she has bought (in exchange for wages) the time of his employees, the owner considers that time as his or her property — much like the machines or the factory buildings. The owner therefore claims the right to decide what part of it, if any, is allowed to be used for rest, chats, drinking coffee, etc. It is the right to decide about the use, rather than the use itself, which is most jealously guarded as the function from which others are to be excluded. The right to decide, the freedom of choice is the true essence of the distinction between the owner and the non-owners. The difference between ownership and non-ownership here is the difference between freedom and dependence. To own things means to be free to decide about what those who do not own them must do — which, in fact, amounts to having **power** over other people. The two — ownership and power — merge in practice into one thing. A person's yearning for property in such a case becomes virtually indistinguishable from the lust for power.

All ownership divides and sets apart (that is, it excludes the non-owners from the use of someone else's property). Not in all cases, however, and not all the time does ownership give the owner power over those who have been excluded. Ownership gives power only if the needs of the excluded require the use of the objects owned. Ownership of the tools of work, of raw materials to be processed by human labour, of sites on which such processing can take place, offers such power. (In the example considered before, employees need access to the machine plant controlled by the factory owner to gain their livelihood; they need it for self-preservation, even for their very survival. Without such access, their skills and their time would be useless; they would be unable to use them gainfully, to make a living out of them.) This is not so, however, with the ownership of goods to be consumed by the owner. If I own a car or a video-recorder or a washing machine, this may make my life easier or more enjoyable than it would otherwise be. It may even add to my prestige — to the respect I enjoy among the people whose approval is important to me: I may boast of my new acquisitions, hoping that people whom I like to impress will from now on look up to me. But it does not necessarily give me power over other people. Unless, of course, they wish to use these things for their own comfort or enjoyment, in which case I'll set the conditions of use to which they must conform. Most things we own do not offer power; what they do offer, however, is independence from other people's power (I need no longer observe the conditions other people may set for the use of goods I need). The larger the part of my needs which I can satisfy directly, without asking for the right to use things other people control, the less I must conform to the rules and conditions set by other people. We may say that ownership is an *enabling* faculty. It extends one's autonomy, freedom of action and choice. It makes one independent. It allows one to act on one's own motives and pursue one's own values. The two — ownership and freedom — merge into one thing. Often the task of enlarging the scope of freedom translates into the extension of control over things — of ownership.

Both functions — that of power over others and that of autonomy — are performed by ownership only in so far as it *divides*. Indeed, in all its versions and under all circumstances ownership means differentiation and exclusion. Underlying all ownership is the principle that the rights of others are limits of my own rights (and vice versa); that the promotion of my own freedom requires that others have their freedom restricted. By this principle, enabling always comes together with some (albeit partial and relative) disabling of someone else. The principle assumes an irreparable conflict of interests between people engrossed in the pursuit of their respective purposes: what one gains, the other loses. The situation is one of the zero-sum game; nothing could be (or so it is assumed) gained by sharing and cooperation. In a situation in which ability to act depends on the exclusive control over resources, to act reasonably means to follow the commandment 'everyone for himself (herself)'. This is how the task of self-preservation appears to us; this is the logic which apparently derives from it and hence ought to be the principle of all sensible action.

Whenever human action conforms to such a principle, interaction takes the form of **competition**. Competitors are moved by the desire to exclude their actual or potential rivals from using resources they control, hope to control or dream of controlling. The goods for which the rivals compete are perceived as *scarce*: it is believed that there is not enough of them to satisfy everybody, and that some rivals must be forced to settle for less than they would wish to possess. It is an essential part of the idea of competition, and the basic assumption of competitive action, that some desires are bound to be frustrated, and hence the relations between the winners and the defeated must be permanently marked with mutual dislike or enmity. For the same reason no competitive gains are considered secure unless actively and vigilantly defended against challenge and contest. Competitive struggle never ends; its results are never final and irreversible. From this, a number of important consequences follow.

First, all competition breeds a tendency to **monopoly**. The winning side tends to make its gains secure and permanent by denying the losers the very right (or at least a realistic prospect) of challenging the gains. The ultimate, though elusive and unattainable, purpose of the competitors is to *abolish* the competition; competitive relations have an in-built tendency to self-annihilation. If left to themselves, they would eventually lead to a sharp polarization of chances. Resources would cluster and tend to become ever more abundant on one side of the relationship, while becoming increasingly scarce on the other. More often than not, such a polarization of resources would give the winning side the ability to dictate the rules of all further interaction and leave the losers in no position to contest the rules. Gains in such a case would be transformed into a monopoly; monopoly, in its turn, would allow the winning side to dictate the conditions of further competition (for example, to fix the prices of the otherwise unavailable goods), and so attract more gains still and further deepen the gap between the sides.

Secondly, the permanent polarization of chances brought about by the monopoly (that is, by the constraints imposed on competition) tends to lead in the long run to the differential treatment of winners and losers. Sooner or later winners and losers 'solidify' into 'permanent' categories. The winners blame the failure of the losers on the latter's inherent inferiority. The losers are declared responsible for their own misfortune. They are described as inept or wicked, fickle or depraved, improvident or morally contemptible: in short, lacking in the qualities seen as a necessary condition of competitive success, which also happen to be qualities commanding respect. So defined, the losers are denied the legitimacy of their grievances. Since it has been accepted that the misery they suffer has been brought about by their own defects, they have no one but themselves to blame, and no right to claim their share of the cake, particularly the part gained by the successful. The disparagement and vilification of the poor is used as a defence of the advantages enjoyed by the well-off. The poor are defiled as lazy, slovenly and negligent, as *depraved* rather than *deprived*: lacking in character, shirking hard labour and inclined to delinquency and law-breaking. Like everyone else, it is said, they are 'self-made people' — they have chosen their own fate. Their misery has been visited upon them as a consequence of their own character or conduct. The more fortunate do not owe them anything. If it happens that the better-off share part of their possessions with the poor, it is only because of the goodness of those who share, not because of the right of those they share with. Similarly, in the male-dominated society women are blamed for their oppressed state; their confinement to less prestigious and desirable functions is explained by 'inborn' inferiority: excessive emotionality, lack of competitive spirit and lesser rationality or intelligence.

Defamation of the victims of the competition is one of the most powerful means of silencing the alternative motives of human conduct: **moral duty**. Moral motives clash with the motives of gain in a number of important respects. Gain-oriented action favours self-concern and ruthlessness in treating potential competitors. Moral action, on the other hand, requires solidarity, disinterested help, willingness to assist the neighbour in need without asking for, or expecting, remuneration. A moral attitude finds its expression in the consideration of the needs of others, and more often than not would result in self-restraint and a voluntary renunciation of personal gain. If in a **gain-motivated** action my needs (however I may define them) are the sole consideration, in a **morally motivated** action the needs of others become the basic criterion of choice. In principle, self-interest and moral duty point in opposite directions.

It was first noted by **Max Weber** that the separation of business from the household is one of the most conspicuous characteristics of modern society. Such a separation is a way of avoiding the clash between the two opposite criteria of action. This effect is achieved through isolating from each other the two contexts in which the gain or the moral duty are, respectively, the dominant considerations. When engaged in a business activity, the person is prised from the network of family bonds; freed, in other words, from the pressures of moral duties. Considerations of gain may therefore be given the sole attention the successful business activity demands. Back in the family, cool calculations of business may be forgotten, and goods shared among family members according to the needs of each member. Ideally, family life (as well as the life of all those communal forms which are or aim to be patterned after the family) ought to be free from the motivations of gain. Equally ideally, business activities should not be affected by the motives prompted by moral feelings. Business and morality do not go well together. Success in business (that is, in an essentially competitive effort) depends on the *rationality* of conduct, and this in turn is equal to the stubborn subordination of all conduct to considerations of self-interest. Rationality means being guided by the head rather than by the heart. Action is considered rational only in so far as it consists of the application of the most effective and least costly means to the task at hand.

We have noted before that the **organization** (or **bureaucracy**, as it is commonly called) is an attempt to adjust human action to the ideal requirements of rationality. We see again that such an attempt must involve, more than anything else, the silencing of moral considerations (that is, of the concern for others for the others' sakes, a disinterested concern, upheld even if in conflict with the dictate of self-preservation). The task of every member of the organization is reduced to a simple choice of obeying or refusing to obey a command. It is also reduced to a small part of the overall purpose pursued by the organization as a whole, so that the wider consequences of the act are not necessarily visible to the actor. One can do things which have dire consequences one does not see and affect people one does not even know exist — and thus do even the most abominable and abhorrent things without experiencing moral conflict or a guilty conscience (as when one earns one's living, often a very decent living, by working in a weapons factory, or in an enterprise which heavily pollutes the environment or produces potentially addictive and poisonous drugs). Most importantly, the organization puts discipline in place of moral responsibility as the paramount standard of propriety ('I have just been following orders', 'I just tried to do my job well' will be the most popular, and self-evident, excuses). As long as a member of an organization strictly follows the rules and the commands of superiors, he or she is offered freedom from moral doubts. A morally reprehensible action, unthinkable under different conditions, becomes suddenly possible and relatively easy to obtain.

The potency of organizational discipline to silence or suspend moral reservations has been dramatically demonstrated in the notorious experiments of **Stanley Milgram**, in which a number of volunteers were instructed to deliver painful electric shocks to the objects of a fake 'scientific research'. Most volunteers, convinced of the noble scientific purpose of their cruelty (which they, as lay persons, could only admire and not really comprehend or judge) and relying on the admittedly superior judgement of the scientists in charge of the research project, followed the intructions faithfully — undaunted by the cries of anguish of their victims. What the experiment revealed on a small scale and in laboratory conditions was demonstrated in breath-taking dimensions by the practice of genocide during the Second World War and thereafter. The murder of millions of Jews initiated and supervised by a few thousand top Nazi leaders and officials was a gigantic bureaucratic operation which involved the cooperation of millions of 'ordinary' people — most of them, in all probability, friendly neighbours, loving spouses and caring parents. Such people drove the trains which carried the victims to gas chambers, worked in factories which produced poisonous gas or crematoria appliances, and in myriads of other small ways contributed to the overall task of annihilation. Every person had 'a job to do', a problem to be solved, the job consuming all their energy and physical strength, the problem absorbing all their thoughts. These people could do the things they did only because they were but dimly, if at all, aware of the ultimate consequences of their actions; they never saw them — just as the learned men who designed the clever tools of destruction to be visited upon the peasants of Vietnam did not see their brainchildren in action. The final results could by so remote from the simple tasks they themselves were busy with that the connections could escape their attention or be barred from consciousness.

Even if the functionaries of a complex organization are aware of the ultimate effect of the joint activity of which they are a part, that effect is often too remote to worry them. Remoteness may be a matter of mental rather than geographical distance. Because of the vertical and horizontal division of labour, the actions of any single person are as a rule *mediated* by the actions of many other people. Either one's own job is of no direct consequence, or it is sheltered from the distant targets of action by the multitude of other jobs performed by other people. There seems to be, therefore, no direct causal connection between what one is doing and what happens to the ultimate objects of action. In the end, one's own contribution pales into insignificance, and its influence on the final result seems too small to be seriously considered as a moral problem. 'I myself did not do anything wrong, there is nothing you can reproach me for' would be a normal excuse. After all, one could have been doing things as innocuous and harmless as drawing blueprints, composing reports, filing documents or switching on and off the machine which mixed two chemical compounds . . . One would not easily recognize the charred bodies in an exotic country as the effects of one's action, as one's own responsibility.

Keeping one's eyes firmly shut on the morally horrifying end-products of ostensibly innocent deeds is further helped by the notorious impersonality of organizational functions. It is an essential feature of any organization that any role can be filled by anybody with proper skills. It can be argued, therefore, that the contribution to the overall task is made by the role itself, rather than by its incumbent. If the current occupant does not perform the role properly, someone else will be put in his or her place and the task will be carried out anyway. The argument can be pushed as far as insisting that the very responsibility for making the overall task feasible rests with the role, and not its performer; and the role ought not to be confused with the personality of the performer. It should be noted that even those among the perpetrators of genocidal actions who stayed too close to the scene of the murder to claim ignorance of the real consequences of their acts could, and did, point out that in the context of bureaucratic command and division of labour moral evaluations were irrelevant. Their own feelings were 'neither here nor there'. It did not matter whether they hated their victims or felt sympathy for them. The task demanded their discipline, not their emotions. As in other routinely organized actions, they dealt with appointed targets, not fellow human beings.

Bureaucracy made to service inhuman purposes has demonstrated its ability to silence moral motivations not only in its employees, but also well beyond the boundaries of the bureaucratic organization itself; it did so through appealing to the motive of self-preservation of those whom it intended to destroy as well as of those who unwillingly witnessed the destruction. The bureaucratic management of genocide secured the cooperation of many of its victims and the moral indifference of most of the bystanders. Prospective victims had been transformed into 'psychological captives'; bewitched by the illusory prospects of benign treatment as a reward for compliance, they often played into the hands of their oppressors and facilitated their own perdition. They hoped against hope that something might still be saved, some dangers averted, if only the oppressors were not unduly aggrieved; that cooperation would be rewarded. In a great number of cases, the phenomenon called anticipatory compliance appeared: the victims went out of their way to please the oppressors by guessing their intention in advance and implementing it with zestful passion. Above all, not until the last moment were they faced with the unavoidability of their ultimate fate. Each successive step on the road to destruction had been presented to them as unpleasant, yet not terminal, and certainly not irreversible; each step confronted them with a clearly defined choice with only one rational solution — invariably the one which brought the final destruction a bit closer. The managers of genocide thus attained their ends with the minimum of disorder and virtually no resistance; very few guards were needed to supervise the long, obedient march to the gas chambers.

As for the bystanders, their compliance, or at least their silence and inactivity, were secured through setting high the price of moral behaviour and of solidarity with the victims. Choosing morally correct behaviour would have meant inviting an awesome punishment, and more often than not putting one's own physical survival at risk. Once the stakes are raised high, the interests of self-preservation push aside moral duties and *moral* compunctions tend to be quelled with *rational* arguments: 'I could not help the victims without jeopardizing my own and my family's lives; I would have saved *one* person at best, yet if I failed, *ten* would die.' Quantitative calculation of survival chances are given priority over the moral quality of action.

These have been extreme illustrations of the ultimate opposition between the motives of self-preservation and those of moral duty; admittedly, they have been drawn from rare and widely condemned situations. In a milder and for that reason less alarming form, however, the opposition leaves its imprint on the everyday human condition. By and large, in any organizational context rationality of action, hailed as the most effective tool of self-preservation, is promoted at the expense of moral obligation. Rational conduct has an apparent advantage over the action guided by moral duty in that it offers an unambiguous recipe for correct choice and appeals directly to the sense of self-preservation and self-enhancement. It is made still more alluring by its success in satisfying the desire for self-aggrandizement induced by competition. Expressed in the zero-sum competition and armed with reliable weapons of bureaucratic rationality, the motive of self-preservation turns into a formidable, perhaps invincible adversary of moral concerns.

Extinguishing moral obligations is further facilitated by statistical treatment of human objects of action, promoted by all bureaucracy. Seen as figures — pure forms which can be filled with any content — such human objects lose their individuality and are deprived of their separate existence as bearers of human rights and moral obligations. They become instead specimens of a category, fully defined by the attached assembly of organizational rules and criteria. Their personal uniqueness, and thus their unique, individual needs, lose their significance as points of orientation of bureaucratic action. What matters is solely the category to which they have been officially designated. The classification sharpens the focus on selected shared attributes of the individuals in which the organization has expressed its interest; at the same time, it licenses neglect for all the rest of the attributes, that is, for the very individual characteristics which form the individuals as moral subjects, as unique and irreplaceable human beings.

As a matter of fact, bureaucracy is not the only context in which moral motivations of action tend to be declared out of court, silenced or suspended for the duration. A very similar effect of suppressing moral drive happens in a context that in virtually all other respects is diametrically opposed to the cool, calculating rationality of a bureaucratic organization, and that is also virtually free from gain-seeking and greed-arousing competition. One particular context of this kind stands out as a most effective silencer of morality: the **crowd**.

It has been noted that people who find themselves tightly packed together in a confined space with great numbers of other people whom they do not know — whom they have not met under other circumstances, have not interacted with before, and with whom they are 'united' at present only by a temporary, accidental interest — are prone to behave in a way they would not deem plausible in 'normal' conditions. The wildest of behaviours may suddenly spread through the crowd in a fashion which can only be compared with forest fire, wind blast or contagion. In an accidental crowd, for instance in a congested market place or in a theatre in the grip of panic, people overwhelmed with the desire for self-preservation may trample over their fellow humans, push others into the fire, just to secure a breathing-space for themselves or to get out of the danger. They may on other occasions attack and kill the ostensible villain pointed out to them and denounced as the source of threat. In a crowd, people are able to commit deeds no single perpetrator would be morally capable of committing left to himself or herself. If the crowd may commit collectively an odious act which every single member abhors, it is because of the *facelessness* of the crowd. In the crowd, individuals lose their individuality and 'dissolve' in the anonymous gathering; they are no longer perceived as moral subjects, as the targets of moral duty (an effect not unlike that of the distancing attained by bureaucratic division of labour). A lynch mob or crowd of team supporters absolve their members from moral responsibility for violent acts visited upon fellow human beings, who are normally protected against violence by the moral constraints of the would-be attackers. In these and similar cases, the suspension of moral obligation is an effect of the anonymity of the crowd and of a virtual absence of any lasting bonds between the participants. The crowd dissolves as quickly as it gathers, and its collective action, however coordinated it may appear, neither follows nor generates interaction of any degree of permanence. It is precisely the momentary and inconsequential character of the crowd action which makes possible the purely *affective* conduct of its individual members. For a fleeting moment, all stops are pulled, all inhibitions removed, all obligations made void, all rules suspended.

The orderly, unemotional conduct in the context of a bureaucratic organization and the riotous eruptions of a crowd's anger or panic seem to be poles apart; and yet their effects on moral drive and inhibitions are remarkably similar. Similar effects have similar causes: **depersonalization**, 'effacing of faces', annihilation of individual autonomy. Bureaucracy — by being constructed of roles instead of persons and by reducing other human beings to the roles or to so many resources or obstacles on the road to goal-attainment or problem-solving — and the unruly, billowing crowd — by being made of indistinguishable particles rather than individual human beings, by acquiring its character from numbers, rather than individual qualities of its members — are both faceless and anonymous.

For their fellow humans, people remain moral subjects as long as they are acknowledged as *humans*: that is, as beings eligible for the treatment reserved for fellow human beings alone, and proper for every human being (a treatment which assumes that the partners of interaction possess their own unique needs, that these needs are as valid and important as one's own and ought to be paid similar attention and respect). One may even say that the concepts of a 'moral object' and 'human being' have the same referent — their respective scopes overlap. Whenever certain persons or categories of people are denied the right to our moral responsibility, they are treated as 'lesser humans', 'flawed humans', 'not fully human', or downright 'non-human'.

The **universe of moral obligations** (the collection of people embraced by moral duty) may or may not include all members of the human species. Many 'primitive' tribes gave themselves names which meant, simply, 'human beings'; the human status of other tribes, particularly those with whom no interaction except occasional outbursts of hostility had been established, was not fully recognized. The refusal to accept the humanity of strange tribes and their members lingered on in slave-owning societies, where slaves had been assigned the status of 'talking tools' and considered (at least in principle) solely in the light of their usefulness to the accredited task. The status of limited humanity meant in practice that the essential requirement of moral attitude — respect for another person's needs, which includes first and foremost the recognition of the other person's integrity and the sanctity of his or her life — was not seen as binding in relation to the bearers of such status. It looks as if history consisted of a gradual, yet relentless extension of the idea of humanity — with a pronounced tendency of the universe of obligations to become ever more inclusive and in the end co-terminous with the totality of the human species.

As we have seen, however, this process has not been straightforward. Our century has been notorious for the appearance of highly influential world-views that called for the exclusion of whole categories of the population — classes, nations, races, religions — from the universe of obligations. The perfection of the bureaucratically organized action, on the other hand, has reached a point where moral inhibitions cannot effectively interfere with considerations of efficiency any more. The combination of both factors — the possibility of suspending moral responsibility offered by bureaucratic technology of management, and the presence of world-views ready and willing to deploy such a possibility — resulted on many occasions in the successful confinement of the universe of obligations, which in its turn opened the way to such diverse consequences as the mass terror practised in communist societies against the members of hostile classes and persons classified as their helpers, persistent discrimination of racial and ethnic minorities in countries otherwise proud of their human-rights record, many overt or surreptitiously practised apartheid systems, and the numerous cases of genocide, moving from the massacre of Armenians in Turkey, through the annihilation of millions of Jews, gypsies and Slavs by Nazi Germany, to the gassing of Kurds or the mass murders of Cambodia. The boundaries of the universe of obligations remain to this day a contentious issue. One may suspect that the development of the bureaucratic technology adept at the task of silencing moral motivation (as much an achievement of modern society as the extension of moral sensitivity to all members of the human species) has made them more contentious than before — in practice, if not in theory.

Inside the universe of obligations, the authority of other people's needs is recognized. It is accepted that the needs of others are legitimate reasons for their demands; if the demands are not met, the failure always calls for explanation and often for some sort of apology. The life of others ought to be preserved, whatever the costs. Everything possible ought to be done to secure their welfare, expand their life chances, open their access to the amenities society has to offer. Their poverty, ill health, dreariness of daily life constitute a challenge and an admonition to all other members of the same universe of obligations. Faced with such a challenge, we feel obliged to excuse ourselves — to supply a convincing explanation why so little has been done to alleviate their lot and why not much more can be done; we also feel obliged to prove that everything that could be done was done. Not that the explanations provided must of necessity be true. We hear, for instance, that the health service offered to the population at large cannot be improved because 'money cannot be spent until it is earned'. What such an explanation conceals, however, is that the profits made by private medicine used by well-off patients are classified as 'earnings', while the services provided for those who cannot afford private fees are counted among 'expenditures'; such an explanation hides the differential treatment of needs depending on people's ability to pay. The very fact, however, that the explanation is offered at all, and that those who give it feel obliged to provide one, testifies to the recognition that the people whose health needs are neglected remain nevertheless inside the universe of obligations.

The fact that the needs of others remain unsatisfied would not be felt as our failure, and the inner compulsion to explain it would lose much of its urgency, only if the neglected 'others' were evicted altogether from the universe of obligations; or, at least, if it was demonstrated that their presence inside the universe of obligations was doubtful or 'undeserved'. Such a situation is not at all fanciful. It tends to be produced through casting those 'others' in a relatively subhuman situation, and then blaming the misfortune on their inability to act like 'humans do'. From this there is just one step to the decision that the others in question cannot be treated as human beings are, since their failings are beyond cure and nothing can bring them back into the fold of mankind. They will, for instance, for ever remain 'an alien race' that cannot be accommodated in the 'native' moral order, as they themselves would not be able to abide by it.

Self-preservation and moral duty stand in opposition to each other. Neither of them can claim to be 'more natural' than the other, better attuned to the inherent predisposition of human nature. If one gains an upper hand over the other and becomes a dominant motive of human action, the cause of imbalance can usually be traced back to the socially determined context of interaction – to the way the stakes are defined and given prominence. Self-interested and moral motives become prevalent depending on circumstances over which the people who are guided by them have only a limited control. It has been observed, however, that the power of circumstances is never absolute, and the choice between the two contradictory motives remains open even under the most extreme conditions. Moral responsibility of the human person, or its renouncement, cannot be explained away in the end by reference to external powers and pressures.

Chapter Eight

Nature and Culture

'Look, what a short man. Poor fellow, nature was not generous,' we say with pity and compassion. We do not blame the man for his unimpressive height. He strikes us as shorter than most people we know; certainly shorter than 'normal'. And yet it does not occur to us that someone, somewhere, neglected to do something to make the man taller. As far as we know, one cannot manipulate one's height; the height is, so to speak, a verdict of nature from which there is no appeal. There are no known means of rescinding or quashing the verdict. One has no choice but to accept it and live with it as well as one can. 'Look, what a fat man,' we say the next moment, and laugh. 'He must be a glutton or a beer-swiller. Shame on him. He really should do something about it.' Unlike height, the width of the human body – or so we believe – is normally under human control. It can be made larger or smaller. There is nothing irrevocable about it. Human weight can and ought to be regulated and brought to the required standard by human effort. Humans are in charge of their own weight, they carry obligations towards it and should be ashamed of themselves if they neglect them.

How do the two cases differ from each other? Why do we react to them in such strikingly different ways? The answer to these questions can be found in our knowledge of what people *can* do and our belief in what people *should* do. First, the question is whether doing something is 'within human power' (whether knowledge, skills or technology exist, are available and can be used by men and women to make a fragment or an aspect of the world more to their liking). Second, there is the question of whether there is a standard, a *norm*, to which that 'something' *should* submit. In other words, there are things which may be changed by people, made different from what they are. They are to be treated differently from other things, which stay beyond human power. The first we call **culture**, the second **nature**. If, therefore, we think of something as being a matter of culture, rather than nature, what we imply is that the thing in question is manipulable, and that there is a desirable, 'proper' end-state for such a manipulation.

Indeed, if you think about it, the very word 'culture' suggests that much. It calls to mind the labours of a farmer or a gardener, who carefully design the plots won from the wilderness and brought under cultivation, select the seeds to be sown and the seedlings to be planted, choose and supply their nourishment, trim the growing plants to give them the right shape — that is, the shape they consider proper for the plants in question. But the farmer and the gardener do more than that. They also weed out the unwelcome guests, the 'uninvited' plants which have grown 'on their own initiative', and therefore spoiled the neat design of the plot, diminished the planned profitability of the field, or detracted from the aesthetic ideal of the garden. It was the calculation of profitability or the idea of order and beauty which divided the plants in the first place — into useful ones, seen as proper objects calling for loving care, and weeds to be ripped out, poisoned or otherwise destroyed. It is the farmer and the gardener who conjure up the vision of the 'order of things', and then deploy their skills and tools to implement that vision, to make reality itself 'orderly', that is, more akin to their vision of order (note that in most cases the skills and the tools they already possess set the limits to farmers' and gardeners' imaginations; only such visions of order are likely to be conceived as are already feasible given the current state of the art). By the same token, they offer the criteria to distinguish between *order* and *disorder*, between the *norm* and the *deviation from the norm*.

Farmers' and gardeners' jobs are prime examples of culture, as an activity with a purpose, and a special kind of purpose at that: the imposition on a certain section of reality of a form which would not be there otherwise, and which certainly would not emerge without the effort to bring it about. Culture is about making things different from what they are and otherwise would be — and about keeping them in this made-up, artificial shape. Culture is about introducing and keeping an order and fighting everything that departs from it and that from the point of view of this order looks like *chaos*. Culture is about supplanting or supplementing the 'order of nature' (that is, the state of things as they are without human interference) with an artificial, designed one. Culture not only *promotes* such an artificial order, it also *evaluates* it. Culture means a preference. It lauds one order as the best, perhaps even as the only good one. It denigrates all alternatives as inferior, or altogether disorderly.

Where exactly the dividing line between nature and culture falls depends, of course, on what skills and knowledge are available, and on whether there is an ambition to deploy them for purposes previously untried. On the whole, the development of science and technology widens the scope of possible manipulation of heretofore 'natural' phenomena, and thus extends the realm of culture. To return to our original example, the know-how and the practice of genetic engineering and chemical industry together with the medical profession may well transfer the height of humans from the natural to the cultural sphere: sooner or later, the technology of manipulating the genes or drugs influencing the growth of tissues and organs of the body may be capable of preventing any individual from falling below the desired standard height, which would then become a norm. The proper height, like the proper weight today, would become a matter of collective concern and personal responsibility.

Let us pause, however, a little longer over our imaginary example, as it illustrates another important feature of all culture. If the genetical control is applied to the regulation of height, it will be the parents who will decide how tall their offspring will be; or the law passed and enforced by the state authority which will decide the proper height of the citizens; or the judgement of the medical profession which will recommend the 'normal', as distinct from the 'abnormal', size of the human body. Whichever is the case, the owner of the body will have to accept the pronouncement of others, or (as in the case of genetic engineering) his or her acceptance or non-acceptance will be simply irrelevant. Culture, which manifests the growing might of mankind as a whole (we may say: the growing independence, freedom of the human species regarding nature), may itself appear to the individual, much like the laws of nature, as a fate against which one cannot rebel.

As our example shows, culture is indeed a human activity — but an activity which some people perform on some others. Like in the case of the garden, in any cultural process the roles of the cultivating gardener and the cultivated plants are clearly distinguished and kept apart. The reason why such division is less immediately evident in the case of 'human plants' is that more often than not it is not clear who the 'gardener' is. The authority that stands behind the norm which individuals are either shaped by or bound to observe is as a rule diffuse, often anonymous. It is impossible to tell exactly where it resides. The awesome and overwhelming authority which shapes human bodies and thoughts appears in the form of 'public opinion', fashion, 'common consent', 'expert view' or even such an elusive entity as common sense — which is a sense of all, but of nobody in particular. It may seem, therefore, that it is the evasive, intangible, abstract culture itself which makes people do things — for instance, paint their lips rather than their ears, or urinate in private while they drink in public. Culture acquires an illusory 'substance'; it seems solid, heavy, pressing and irresistible. From the vantage point of the person who finds all resistance to the dominant forms of life risky and unrewarding, it may well appear indistinguishable from the rest of reality 'out there'. It does not seem less 'natural' than nature itself. Certainly, there is little that is *artificial* about it, if artificial means being made by humans and thus having nothing but someone's decision, convention and tacit agreement to support it. Despite its apparently human origin, culture like nature looms high above the reach of the individual, tough and unassailable. Like nature, it stands for 'how things are'. While no one doubts that agriculture or horticulture are human doings, a similar truth is hidden or at least veiled in the case of '*homini*-culture'. It is, however, no less a truth here than in previous cases.

Once you take a closer look at the 'human-made elements' in your own life, you will probably note that they enter your situation in a twofold way; or, to put it in a different fashion, you may say that actions entailed in the introduction and sustenance of the artificial, 'man-made' order are of two types. The first is aimed at the environment, the second at the individual. The first regulates, makes orderly the context in which individual life-processes are conducted. The second shapes the motives and purposes of the life-process itself. The first makes the world of one's life less random, more regular — so that certain kinds of behaviour become more sensible, reasonable, and in the end more probable than any other kind of conduct. The second makes one more inclined to select certain motives and purposes from innumerable others that could be imagined. Let us note that the two analytically distinct types are not mutually exclusive in their application and effects; neither are they independent from each other. The environment of my and anybody else's individual life-processes consists in no small measure of other individuals with motives and purposes of their own — and thus the 'normative regulation' of individual motives and patterns of conduct is an important factor in the overall regularity and predictability of the environment.

Order is distinguished from randomness or chaos by the fact that in an orderly situation not everything may happen: not everything is possible. Out of a virtually infinite set of conceivable events, only a finite number may take place. Different events carry different degrees of probability: some events are more likely to occur than others. An artificial order is successfully established once what used to be improbable has been transformed into the necessary or inevitable (like, for instance, making the thoroughly unlikely event of meeting between eggs and bacon into a regular morning occurrence). To design an order means, therefore, to manipulate the probability of events. Some events which otherwise would occur at random are made more probable — 'normal' — while obstacles are mounted to prevent other events from happening. To design an order means to select, to choose — and to establish preferences and priorities, to *evaluate*. The **values** stand behind and are eventually incorporated into all artificial orders. No description of an artificial order can be truly value-free. Each such order represents just one of many ways in which probabilities could be slanted: one way which had been selected in preference to all the others. Once this order has become well entrenched, solid and secure, we naturally 'forget' this truth; we perceive the order as the only one thinkable. It seems now that while there could be one and only one order, the variety of *dis*order is infinite. A specific, given order is then perceived as synonymous with order as such; all alternatives are uniformly classified as varieties of disorder or chaos.

As human beings, we all have a vested interest in creating and maintaining an orderly environment. This is because of the fact most of our behaviour is *learned*. We memorize those of our past actions which proved successful: brought the desired effect, the pleasure, approval and praise of people around us. Thanks to the precious gift of memory and learning capacity, we are able to acquire ever more effective life-skills; we *accumulate* knowledge, skills, experience. But memory and learning bring beneficial results only as long as the context of our action stays by and large unchanged. It is thanks to the constancy of the world around us that the actions which were successful before are likely to remain so if repeated today and tomorrow. Just imagine what havoc would occur, if, for instance, the meaning of the colours of traffic lights were changed without warning. In a randomly mutable world, memory and learning would turn from blessing into a curse. To learn, to go by past experience, would be truly suicidal.

The *orderly* world — that regular and thus comfortably predictable environment in which we conduct our life-business most of the time — is a product of cultural design and selection. When properly designed and executed, buildings radically limit the amplitude of possible temperatures, totally excluding the unbearable extremes. Splitting the road into pedestrian and vehicle lanes considerably diminishes the probability of a deadly encounter between a moving vehicle and a pedestrian. A bridge spanning two banks of a river reduces the likelihood of getting wet while crossing the river. The division of the city into quarters with different levels of rate values and rents and different qualities of amenities limits the range of people one can meet as passers-by or neighbours. The division of the train or plane into first and second class, with sharply different fare prices, similarly limits the range of likely travelling companions.

The order of the world around us has its counterpart in the orderliness of our own behaviour. On the whole, we choose different lanes for walking and driving. We do not behave at a drinks party in the same fashion as we do at a college seminar or business meeting. We conduct ourselves differently at our parental home during the holidays and at a formal visit among people whom we do not know. We use a different tone of voice and different words, depending on whether we address our boss or chat to our friends. There are words we say on one occasion but avoid on another. There are things we do in public, but also 'private' things which we do only when we are sure that we are not being watched. The remarkable thing is that while choosing a conduct 'proper' for the occasion, we find ourselves in the company of others behaving exactly like us; departures from what apparently is a *rule* happen but seldom — as if a sort of invisible string pulled all of us in a similar fashion.

If I confuse things, and behave in a way suitable for one context in circumstances which this conduct does not fit, I am likely to feel embarrassed or guilty. I regret committing an error which may cost me dearly — for instance, in losing a job or promotion, compromising my reputation, failing to earn or losing the sympathy of a person dear to me. On other occasions I may feel ashamed — as if I've let out some secret truth about my 'real self' which I wished to keep under cover or even wished was not true in the first place. Unlike the case of regretting a move that brought unpleasant results, there is nothing calculated or, indeed, rational in my feeling of shame. The feeling has been triggered off without much thinking. Shame is an automatic reaction to the mix-up, to the confusion of what should have been kept apart, to violating a distinction which should have been observed and kept intact. We can say that shame is a (culturally trained) defence against such a mix-up — against neglecting *differences*. It can be thought of as a device to keep our conduct on the right (that is, culturally prescribed) track.

It must have become clear by now that culture — this labour of artificial order — is performed mostly by making distinctions, setting apart, segregating, discriminating between things or acts which otherwise would barely have been separated from one another. In a desert, untouched by human activity and indifferent to human purpose, there are neither signposts nor fences making one stretch of land different from another; one dune is exactly like another, devoid of a meaning of its own, carrying nothing to distinguish it from the next one. Uninhabited desert is, it seems, formless. In an environment subjected to the work of culture, on the other hand, a uniform, flat surface is divided into areas which draw some people but repel others, or into strips fit only for driven vehicles and those that are suitable solely for walkers; the world acquires a **structure**. People are divided into superiors and inferiors, agents of authority and lay persons, those who speak and those who listen and take notice – and all this without reference to, or in defiance of, the 'natural' differences or similarities of their physical build or mental constitution. A uniform flow of time is divided into breakfast-time, coffee break, lunchtime, afternoon tea or dinner. Gatherings similar or even identical in their 'physical' composition are nevertheless discriminated between – being once a seminar, a conference at some other time, a wine-and-cheese party on yet another occasion. The intake of food differentiates into events as distinct as teas, TV suppers or candlelit dinners.

These and similar distinctions seem to be drawn simultaneously on two planes. One is the 'shape of the world' in which the action takes place. The other is the action itself. Parts of the world are made different from each other as well as different in themselves depending on the periods distinguished in the flow of time (the same building may be a school in the morning and a ballroom in the evening, while a bedsitter is a study room during day and a bedroom at night; both change their character in the process). The actions are equally differentiated. Conduct at the table differs sharply depending on what has been put on the table and who is sitting around it. Even table manners – the way we behave while eating – differ depending on whether the meal is formal, a routine family supper or just a friendly get-together.

Let us note again that the setting apart of the two planes (context and action, external and internal, objective and subjective) is a product of abstraction. The two theoretically separated planes are not really independent from each other. There would be no formal dinner without the diners behaving in the formal way, or a ball without the dancers being in the ball-like mood, any more than there could be a river without flowing, or wind without blowing. It is a certain conduct of teachers and students which makes a seminar a seminar. The two theoretically distinct planes are in practice inextricably linked — more like two faces of the same coin than two separate entities. One cannot exist without the other. They may be brought into being and maintained only simultaneously, and together. The *distinctions* which are the substance of the culturally produced order affect simultaneously, and in a parallel, coordinated, synchronized way, the context of action and the action itself. One may say that the oppositions drawn in the world around are replicated in the differentiation of the actors' behaviour; and that deployment of opposite patterns of conduct is reflected in the internal divisions of the world around. One can even go a step further and say that the differentiation of behaviour is the substance, or meaning, of the differentiation of the environment — and vice versa.

The other way of expressing this coordination is to say that both the culturally organized social world and the behaviour of culturally trained individuals are *structured* — that is, 'articulated', with the help of oppositions, into separate social contexts calling for distinctive conduct and separate patterns of behaviour suitable for distinctive social contexts — and that the two articulations 'correspond' to each other (or, to use the technical term, they are isomorphic). Whenever we notice an opposition in the modes of conduct (for example, the previously mentioned juxtaposition of formal and informal behaviour), we may safely guess the presence of a similar opposition in the social context in which these distinct modes would be deployed — and vice versa.

The device which secures this amazing 'overlap', the correspondence between structures of social reality and of culturally regulated behaviour, is called the **cultural code**. As you have probably guessed by now, the code is first and foremost a system of oppositions. Indeed, what is opposed in this system are **signs** — visible, audible, tactile, olfactory objects or events like lights of different colours, elements of dress, inscriptions, oral statements, tones of voice, gestures, facial expressions, scents, etc. — which link actors' behaviour and the social figuration sustained by this behaviour. The signs, as it were, point in two directions at the same time: towards the intentions of the actors and towards the given segment of social reality in which they act. Neither of the two is just a reflection of the other. Neither is primary or secondary. Both, let us repeat, exist only together, grounded in the same facility of the cultural code.

Think, for instance, of 'no entry' notice nailed to the door in an office building. You must have observed that such a notice appears, as a rule, on one side of the door only, and that the door on which it appears is usually unlocked (were the door impossible to open, there would hardly be a need for the notice). The notice is not, therefore, giving information of the 'objective state of the door'. It is, rather, an instruction, meant to create and sustain a situation which otherwise would not occur. What the words 'no entry' do, in fact, is to distinguish between the two sides of the door, between the two kinds of people who approach the door from the opposite sides, and the two kinds of conduct in which those people are expected or permitted to engage. The space behind the marked side of the door is barred to those who approach it from the side of the notice, but for the people on the other side, on the contrary, no such restriction has been imposed. The sign stands precisely for this distinction. Its achievement is to make a discrimination in an otherwise uniform space among equally uniform people.

The 'homini-culture', the training of human individuals, consists of imparting the knowledge of the cultural code: teaching the ability to read the signs and the skill to select and display them. All properly cultured persons can faultlessly determine the demands and expectations inherent in the context they enter; and respond to it by selecting the appropriate pattern of their own conduct. Conversely, all culturally trained persons are able to pick up, without error, a mode of behaviour likely to result in the type of situation they intend to evoke. Whoever 'knows' the code, is addressed in both directions at the same time. Traffic lights at a crossroads offer a good example of this two-sidedness. A red light *informs* the drivers that the road ahead is closed. It also *induces* them to stop the car, thereby making the road ahead truly closed to the traffic from that direction and making true the information conveyed by the green light which opens the road going across.

The code works, of course, only if all the persons participating in a given figuration have undergone a similar cultural training. All of them must have learned to read the cultural code and use it in a similar way. Otherwise, the signs will not be seen as signs — will fail to send the reader to the objects or conduct they were meant to stand for; or will be read, if at all, in different, perhaps contradictory, ways. The intended coordination will not occur, as the actions of various readers will be out of line (just imagine what would happen at the crossroads if some of the drivers read the red light wrongly; or if some drivers fixed red lights at the front of their cars and white lights at the rear). Whoever has entered a college or an office for the first time, or whoever has visited a faraway country on holidays, must surely have learned this unpleasant truth from experience. The comfortable feeling of security which is associated with familiar surroundings, with being at home, stems precisely from the thorough knowledge of the locally used cultural code, coupled with a reassuring and well-grounded expectation that this knowledge is shared by everybody around.

To know the code is therefore to *understand* the meaning of signs; to understand the meaning of signs, in its turn, means knowing how to go on in a situation in which such signs appear, and how to use them to make such a situation appear. To understand is to be able to act effectively, and thereby sustain the coordination between the structures of the situation and one's own behaviour. Understanding stands for a double selection. The sign sends the person who is able to read it to the bond between a particular kind of setting and a particular kind of conduct.

It is often said that to uderstand a sign is to grasp its meaning. It would be false, however, to think of that 'grasping of meaning' as evoking a thought, a mental image in one's mind. A thought (the verbal 'unravelling' of the content of the sign: a sort of 'reading aloud' of the sign in your head — for instance, this is a red light, and it means a command to stop) may indeed accompany the sight or the sound of the sign — but it is neither necessary nor sufficient for the understanding. To grasp the meaning, like understanding itself, means no more and no less than to know how to go on. What follows is that the meaning of a sign resides, so to speak, in the difference its presence or absence makes. To put this in another way — the meaning resides in its relation — opposition — to other signs. The meaning of a sign is the *distinction* between the situation here and now and other situations which could have taken its place but did not; to put it plainly, the distinction between this one situation and all the others.

More often than not — in fact in any but the simplest of cases — one sign is insufficient to make this distinction clear and, above all, to make it 'stick'. We may say that one sign sometimes does not carry enough information to single the situation out, to bring it to the attention of all involved, to force them to select the right behaviour, and thus to ensure that the intended situation indeed takes place. One sign may be read incorrectly, and if such an erroneous reading does happen, there will be nothing to correct the mistake. For instance, the sight of a military uniform tells us in unambiguous terms that the person in front of us is a member of the armed forces; for most civilians this information would be quite sufficient to 'structure' the encounter. For other members of the armed forces, with their complex hierarchy of power and division of duties, the information conveyed by the uniform would not be enough (one relates to a corporal and a colonel in very different ways). Other rank-showing signs are therefore 'piled up' on the primary and general sign, which is the military uniform itself, to offer the missing information. This is not the only remarkable thing we note, however: on military uniforms the signs that signal a given rank generally appear in greater quantity than would be absolutely necessary to convey all the information one needs to pinpoint unambiguously a given situation. More than one pair of opposed signs sets apart the corporal from the colonel: the uniforms are differently cut and made of different kinds of cloth, the buttons are made of different metals, there are signs of sharply different shapes on the shoulders, and also on the sleeves. This excess of signs, this adding of further oppositions which merely replicate the information already conveyed by other signs, we may describe as **redundancy**.

Redundancy seems to be quite essential to the proper functioning of any cultural code. It is, one may say, an insurance against mistakes; a device required to make sure that ambivalence is thoroughly eliminated and no misreading occurs. Were it not for redundancy, the accidental distortion or overlooking of just one sign could prompt the wrong kind of behaviour. The more important for the overall order the information conveyed by a given opposition of signs is, the more redundancy one can expect. Redundancy is in no way a waste. On the contrary, it is an indispensable factor in the order-producing activity of culture. It reduces the danger of mistake, of *mis*understanding; it ensures that the meaning is read exactly as it has been intended. In other words, it makes possible the use of the cultural code as a means of **communication** − that is, mutual coordination of behaviour.

Let us repeat: it is the *opposition* between signs which is *meaningful*, not a single sign taken apart. Which implies in turn that the meanings to be 'read out' and understood reside in the system of signs − in the cultural code as a whole, in the distinctions it makes, not in the assumed special link between the sign and its referent. As a matter of fact, such a special link does not exist at all (the impression that there is a natural bond between a sign and the thing it stands for is in itself a product of culture, the result of learning the code). In relation to the fragments of the world or of our actions which they evoke, the signs are *arbitrary*. They are unmotivated by those fragments, unconnected with them in any way but through the signifying function assigned to the signs by the cultural code. This quality of arbitrariness sets the culturally produced signs (the whole human-made system of signification) apart from anything one can find in nature; the cultural code is truly unprecedented.

Speaking of the way in which we gain our knowledge of natural phenomena, we often refer to 'signs' through which nature 'informs' us of itself, and which have to be read in order to extricate the information they contain. Thus we look at the drops of water flowing down the window pane and say, 'It is raining'; we speak of these drops as signs of rain. Or we note a wet pavement and we conclude that it must have been raining. I put my hand on my child's head, note its being unusually hot, and say, 'She must be ill, let us call the doctor.' On my walk through the countryside, I note tracks of a peculiar shape across the path and think, hares are back this spring, and in big numbers. In all these cases, what I have seen or felt gives me information about something I cannot see − and this is exactly what signs usually do. What is characteristic about signs like those, however, is that unlike the cultural signs we discussed before they are all *determined*: that is, they are effects of their respective causes. It is these causes that I 'read out' as the information they contain. Rain sends drops of water down the window pane and leaves the roads wet; illness changes the temperature of the body and makes the head feel hot; hares running across a sandy path leave footprints of a specific shape. Once I know of such causal connections, I can reconstruct the 'invisible' cause from the effects I observe. To avoid confusion, it would perhaps be better to speak of **indices** or symptoms, rather than signs, when referring to causally determined (as distinct from the arbitrary) clues in our reasoning (and so a raindrop is an index of rain, a hot head a symptom of illness).

In the case of the cultural signs, however, no such causal connection exists. The signs are arbitrary or conventional. Rain cannot cause footprints to appear on the path, nor can the hares cause water to flow down the window: there is a one-to-one relation between an effect and its cause. But various culturally determined distinctions can be signified by all sorts of signs of all kinds of shapes. There is neither a causal link nor a similarity between the signs and what they stand for. If within a given culture emphasis is put on the distinction between sexes, this may be signified in a countless number of ways. The sex-specific fashions (that is, the shape and look of the clothes worn, of make-up, gait, vocabulary, general demeanour) may radically change over time and from one place to another, provided that the difference between male and female versions is maintained. The same applies to the discrimination between generations (which, paradoxically, can sometimes be expressed in one generation's rejection of differentiating between sexes in their dress or hairstyles), formal and informal contexts, sad occasions (like funerals) and joyful ones (like weddings). Cultural signs do change their visible form freely, but the contrast between them and the signs they stand in opposition to is maintained and reconstituted with every change, so that the job of discrimination − their only job − can be properly performed again and again.

Arbitrariness, however, is not always equal to complete freedom of choice. The most free are signs that perform none but their cultural discriminatory function and serve no other need but that of human communication. These are, first and foremost, the signs of

language. Language is a sign-system specialized in the function of communication. In language (and in language only), therefore, the arbitrariness of signs has no constraints. Vocal sounds all humans are capable of producing can be modulated in an infinite number of utterly arbitrary ways, provided there is enough of them to produce the required oppositions. The same opposition, in various languages, may be construed with the help of pairs as dissimilar to each other as boy and girl, *garçon* and *fille*, *Knabe* and *Mädchen*.

But freedom (the degree of permissible arbitrariness) is not as complete in most other sign-systems. While performing the communicative function, all systems, except for language, are also closely related to other human needs and thus tied down by other functions. Dress, for instance, is fraught with arbitrary signs, yet it also offers shelter from the vagaries of an inclement climate, protects the body heat, offers an additional protection to vulnerable parts of the skin, and upholds the binding standards of decency. Most of these other functions are also culturally regulated (for instance, it is to a large extent a matter of culture which sections of the skin are considered 'vulnerable' and in need of protection; the need to wear shoes is the result of culture, as is the need to cover breasts but not legs, or vice versa), but they serve other than purely communicative needs; skirts and trousers cover the body in addition to being signifiers. Similarly, however rich and precise are the signifying distinctions impressed upon various kind of food and meals, there are limits to the material in which cultural discriminations may be expressed, as not every stuff can be made edible given the peculiarities of the human digestive system. Besides, tea or dinner, formal or informal, must, apart from signifying the specific nature of the occasion, provide nourishing substances; it is, after all, also a food intake. While the human speech capacity is utilized solely for communicative purposes, other media of communication share their **semiotic** (meaning-carrying and transferring) function with servicing other needs. Their code is carved, as it were, on the surface of other, not primarily communicative, functions.

In their communicative function (as meaningful objects or events that structure the situation in which they appear) signs are always arbitrary. The curious thing, though, is that to 'properly cultured' people – to people who can move with facility and without error through the world shaped by a given cultural code – they do not seem to be arbitrary at all. For everyone brought up in a particular language there seems to be a sort of natural, necessary bond between the sound of a word and the object this word refers to – as if the names naturally belonged to the objects, and could be listed among their attributes alongside their size, colour or resilience. The arbitrary aspect of forms carved in other media may altogether escape our attention: dress is there to dress, food to be eaten, the car to get from here to there. It is difficult to realize that in addition to being worn or consumed dress or food also distinguish between different people and different roles they currently play: that 'things to be eaten' or 'things to be worn' also serve the creation and the reproduction of a particular, 'made-up' and artificial, social order. This sort of blindness is, in fact, part of the cultural game. The less we are aware of the non-substantive (that is, unrelated to the ostensible content of a given activity), order-making function of culturally shaped actions, the more secure is the order these actions maintain. Culture is most effective when it is disguised as nature. What is artificial then appears to be rooted in the very 'nature of things', necessary and irreplaceable; something no human decision may possibly change. Sharply distinct social placement and social treatment of men and women (culturally inspired and sustained from the moment of birth and through the whole of life by differences in dress, toys, games played, the company kept, encouraged and discouraged interests or pastimes, etc.) become truly well established and secure once the trainees accept that social discrimination between sexes is somehow predetermined, entailed in the physiological constitution of the human body, 'natural' – and so *demands* to be obeyed, outwardly expressed in virtually everything one does, be it the manner of speaking and walking, the vocabulary used or the way of expressing (or not expressing) emotions. Culturally produced, social differences between men and women appear as natural as the biological difference between the male and female sexual organs and procreative functions.

Culture may pass for nature most successfully, without questions being asked, as long as the artificiality, the conventional character of the norms it propagates (the fact that these norms could be different from what they are) is not exposed. And the artificiality is unlikely to be revealed if anyone within sight has been subjected to the same type of cultural training; if everybody has internalized and retained loyalty to the same norms and values and goes on manifesting this loyalty, albeit unknowingly, in daily conduct. In other words, culture looks and acts like nature as long as no alternative conventions are seen and known. In our kind of world, however, this hardly ever happens. The contrary is the rule. Virtually everyone of us knows that there are many different ways of life. We look around us at people who dress, talk, behave differently from ourselves, and obviously (or so we assume) abide by norms different from ours. And so we are fully aware that any way of life is ultimately a matter of choice. There is more than one way of being human. Practically everything can be done in a different way from the one in which we do it — no single way is really inevitable. Even if each one of these requires a culture, a training, it is not immediately clear that the training should necessarily be pointed in this rather than that direction, that this rather than that choice should be made. We know that there are *cultures* rather than one single culture. And if culture can be thought of in the plural, it cannot be conceived of as nature is. No culture can claim such unconditional obedience as nature does.

While conducting its business in the company of many other, sometimes sharply distinct, ways of life, culture is unable to hold the same firm grip on human conduct and thought as it could if it were truly universal and free from competition. The order at which culture is aimed (that ultimate 'purpose' of any culture) cannot be really secure. Neither are we, the objects of cultural training; we, the 'cultured' people. The order conjured up by our cultural training seems disturbingly fragile and vulnerable. This is just one of many possible orders. We cannot be certain that it is the right one. We cannot even be sure that it is better than any of its many alternatives. We do not know why we should give it preference over other orders vying for our attention. We look at the way we live our lives as if from the outside, as if we were strangers in our own home. We doubt and ask questions. We need explanations and reassurance — and demand them.

Uncertainty is seldom a pleasant condition. Hence the attempts to escape it are fairly common. The pressure to conform to the norms promoted by cultural training is therefore usually accompanied by efforts to discredit and denigrate the norms of other cultures, as well as their products: the alternative orders. Other cultures are represented as showing an *absence* of culture — as the 'uncivilized', coarse, uncouth and brutal way of being, more animal than human. Alternatively, they are depicted as a product of degeneration: morbid, often pathological, departure from the 'normal'; a distortion, deviation or anomaly. If other ways of life are acknowledged as cultures in their own right, complete and viable, they tend to be portrayed as bizarre, inferior and vaguely threatening: acceptable perhaps for other, less demanding people, but certainly not for *us*, people of distinction. All such reactions are various forms of *xenophobia* (dread of the alien), or *heterophobia* (dread of the different). They are various methods of defence of that frail and unsteady order which is sustained solely by the shared cultural code: of fighting *ambivalence*.

One may say that the distinctions between 'us' and 'them', 'here' and 'there', 'inside' and 'outside', 'native' and 'foreign' are among the most crucial differences cultures establish and promote. With these distinctions, they draw the boundary of the territory they claim for their own undivided rule and intend to guard against all competition. Cultures tend to be tolerant towards other cultures only at a distance — that is, only on condition of barring all exchange or limiting it to a strictly controlled field and ritualized form (for instance, trade transactions with 'foreign' shopkeepers and restaurateurs; deploying 'foreigners' in admittedly menial jobs which involve but a minimum of interaction and are not allowed to spill over into other areas of life; admiring 'foreign' cultural products in the safe enclosure of a museum, a stage, a screen or a bandstand, as recreation or entertainment: a pastime separate and held at a distance from 'normal' daily life).

The other way of describing this tendency of cultural activity is to say that cultures aim, as a rule, at **hegemony** — at the monopoly of the norms and values on which their own peculiar orders are erected. Cultures aim at uniformity in the realm subjected to their hegemony, while at the same time sharply differentiating between this realm and the rest of the human world. They are, therefore, inherently against the equality of the forms of life, promoting as they do one choice over all others. Culture is, by and large, a *proselytizing* (missionary) activity. It aims at *conversion*, at inducing its objects to abandon their old habits and beliefs and embrace others instead. Its cutting edge is turned against *heresy* — seen as the impact of 'foreign influences'. It is resented because it exposes the inside order as arbitrary and a matter of choice, and thus weakens the grip of the dominant norms by undermining their monopolistic authority. When several cultural designs coexist without clear demarcation lines separating their fields of influence (that is, under conditions of cultural pluralism), *mutual tolerance* (mutual acknowledgement of the other side's worthiness and validity) is an attitude badly needed for co-existence, but one that does not come easily.

Chapter Nine

State and Nation

You will probably have been required on various occasions to fill in forms which asked you to give some information about your identity. It is more than likely that the very first instruction in each form was to write down your name. It was your *personal* name (your surname — the name you share with other members of your family — and all other names, given only to you, to distinguish you from the rest of your kin) you were asked to write down; the one that would set you apart from all other form-fillers, point to you alone, as an individual, that unique, unrepeatable person unlike any other. Once your unique identity had been established, other questions followed which, on the contrary, attempted to establish features which you shared with others: to locate you in certain wider categories. Whoever composed the form must have hoped that by learning of your membership of such categories (like sex, age, education, occupation, place of residence) they would obtain information about such attributes of your person as may have some predictive value regarding your present standing or prospective behaviour. The authors of the form were, of course, concerned mostly with that part of your conduct which had been or might become relevant to the purpose of the organization that designed the form and for whose use the form has been completed (if, for instance, this was an application form for a credit card or a bank loan, such information would have been collected as would allow the bank manager to assess just to what extent you are credit-worthy, and how much risk offering you a loan would entail).

On many forms a question about your **nationality** would appear. To this question you may answer 'British'. But you may also answer

'English' (or 'Welsh', or 'Scottish', or 'Jewish', or 'Greek'). As it happens, both answers are proper responses to the question of nationality. But they refer to different things. When answering 'British', you indicate that you are a 'British subject', that is, a citizen of the **state** called Great Britain or the United Kingdom. When answering 'English', you report the fact that you belong to the English **nation**. The question about nationality makes both answers possible and acceptable; this shows that in practice the two memberships are not clearly distinguished from each other and tend to overlap — and because of this tendency may well be confused. And yet, when you answer the question of nationality by writing 'British', you refer to a quite different aspect of your identity from when you write 'English'. State and nation may be confused — but they are quite different things, and your membership of each involves you in very different kinds of relationships.

To start with, there is no state without a specific territory held together by a centre of power. Every resident of the area over which the authority of the state extends belongs to the state. Belonging in this case has first of all a legal meaning. 'Authority of the state' means the ability to declare, and to enforce, the 'law of the land' — the rules which must be observed by all subjects of this authority (unless the state itself exempts them from such an obedience), by everyone who just happens to be physically there. If the laws are not observed, the culprits are liable to be punished. They will be forced to obey, whether they like it or not. In fact the state claims the sole right to apply coercive force (to use weapons in defence of the law, to deprive the law-breaker of freedom through imprisonment, and ultimately to kill if the prospect of reform is nil or if the breach of the law was of the kind considered too grave to be forgiven or punished with anything less than death; when executed by the order of the state, and only then, the killing is permissible, seen not as a murder but as a form of punishment and itself unpunishable). The other side of the state monopoly of physical coercion is that any use of force which has not been authorized by the state, or committed by anyone other than its authorized agents, is condemned as an act of violence (and thus a 'crime', unlike the state-initiated 'law enforcement'), and hence invites persecution and punishment.

The laws announced and guarded by the state determine the duties and the rights of the state subjects. The most important of the duties is the payment of taxes — giving away a part of one's income to the state, which takes it over and puts it to uses it itself determines. The rights, on the other hand, may be *personal* (like the protection of one's own body and one's possessions, unless ruled otherwise by the decision of authorized state organs; or the right to profess one's own opinions and beliefs), *political* (influencing the composition and the policy of state organs, for example by taking part in the election of the body of representatives who then become rulers or administrators of the state institutions) or *social* (the guarantee by the state of a basic livelihood and essential needs such as cannot be attained individually, or cannot be attained by the effort of a given individual). It is the combination of such rights and duties that makes the individual a subject of the state. The first thing we know about being state subjects is that however much we dislike it, we have to pay income tax, or value-added tax, or poll tax; on the other hand, we can complain to the authorities and seek their assistance if our bodies or possessions have been assaulted, and demand redress; we consider it proper to blame the state organs (government, parliament, the police, etc.) if some of our paramount needs are in danger (if the air or water has been polluted, health or education facilities are missing or inadequate, etc.).

The fact that being a subject of the state is a combination of rights and duties makes us feel simultaneously protected and oppressed. We enjoy the relative peacefulness of life which we know we owe to the awesome force always waiting somewhere in the wings to be deployed against the breakers of peace. We do not lightly contemplate the alternative. As the state is the only power permitted to set apart the permissible from the impermissible and as law enforcement by the state organs is the only method of keeping this distinction permanent and secure, we believe that if the state withdrew its punishing fist, universal violence and the 'law of the jungle' would rule instead. We believe that we owe our security and peace of mind to the power of the state, and that there would be no security or peace of mind without it. On many occasions, however, we resent the obtrusive interference of the state into our private lives. The state-imposed rules often seem too numerous and too pernickety for comfort; we feel that they constrain our freedom. If the *protective* care of the state enables us to do things — to plan our actions in the belief that the plans may be executed without obstacle — the *oppressive* function of the state feels more like disablement; because of it, many an option is rendered unrealistic. Our experience of the state is therefore inherently ambiguous. It may happen that we like it and dislike at the same time.

Just how the two feelings are balanced and which one prevails depends on circumstances. If I am well off and money is not a problem, I'd relish the prospect of securing for my children better educational credentials than those offered to the average person, and so I'd probably resent the fact that the state runs the schools and decrees which children (because of their place of residence) ought to attend which schools. If my income, on the other hand, is too modest to buy exclusive educational services, I'd be inclined to welcome the same educational monopoly of the state as protective and enabling. I'd then probably resent the call of better-off people to relax the hold of the state over the schools. I'd suspect that once the children of the rich and the influential are transferred to private schools, the state-run education, now catering only for children of poorer and less influential families, will be less well provided for than in the past and thus will lose much of its enabling power.

If I managed a factory, I'd perhaps be pleased that the state imposed severe restrictions on my employees' right to strike. I'd feel that this restriction was a manifestation of the enabling function of the state, not of its oppressive role. As far as I am concerned, it enhances my freedom; it allows me to do things unpopular with my workers, make moves to which the workers would surely respond with the withdrawal of their labour, if they were only allowed to. I see the restriction of the right to strike as an order-keeping facility, making the world around me more predictable and amenable to control; in such an 'improved' world, my freedom to manoeuvre will be extended. If, however, I happened to be a worker in the same factory, the limits imposed on strikes would feel, unambiguously, like an act of oppression. My freedom would have shrunk. The most efficient methods of resistance to the bosses would now be beyond my reach. As my employers were fully aware of my new handicap, they would not consider the possibility of my retaliation as a factor limiting their freedom when developing their plans: I would have lost a good deal of my bargaining power. I would not know how many unpleasant and damaging decisions of my employers I'd have to resign myself to. All in all, my world will become less predictable, and I myself will fall victim to other people's whims. I will feel in control of things less than ever before. In other words, what looks to my employers like an *enabling* action of the state seems more like an *oppression* to me.

And so we see that — depending on their situation and the tissue in question — some people may experience as an increase of freedom such actions of the state as others see as oppression, and may feel oppressed by the measures which others view as enabling, widening their range of choice. On the whole, however, everybody is likely to be interested in changing the proportion between the two functions of the state. Everybody would prefer as much enabling as possible and as little oppression as is truly necessary. What is perceived as enabling, and what as oppressive, differs — but the urge to control or at least to influence the composition of the mixture does not. The greater the part of our lives that depends on what the state is doing, the more widespread and intense is this urge.

As they wish to change the balance between enabling and oppressive functions, the subjects of the state demand more influence on running the affairs of the state, on the laws which the state declares and enforces; they demand to exercise their citizens' rights. To be a **citizen** means, in addition to being a subject (a bearer of the rights and duties as the state has defined them), having a say in determining the state policy (that is, in defining such rights and duties). In other words, to be a citizen means having the capacity to influence the activity of the state and thus to participate in the definition and management of that 'law and order' which the state is bent on protecting. To exercise such influence in practice, the citizens must enjoy a degree of autonomy regarding the state regulation. There must be limits to the state interference with the subject's ability to act. Here again we confront the controversy between the enabling and oppressive aspects of state activity. This time, however, enabling and oppression relate to the general capacity to influence the state policy and put a brake on excessive ambitions of the state, were such to appear. Citizenship demands that the state itself is constrained in its ability to constrain; that nothing is done by the state to prevent the citizens' ability to control, evaluate and influence its policy; and that, on the contrary, the state is obliged to render such control and influence feasible and effective. For instance, citizens' rights cannot be exercised fully if the state activity is surrounded by secrecy, if the 'ordinary people' have no insight into the intentions and the doings of their rulers, if they are denied access to the facts which allow them to evaluate the real consequences of the state's action.

The relations between the state and its subjects are often strained, as the subjects find themselves obliged to struggle to become citizens or to protect their citizen status threatened by the growing ambitions of the state. The main obstacles they encounter in this struggle are what may be called the tutelage complex and the therapeutic attitude of the state. The first refers to the tendency to treat the subjects as not fully grown-up, unable to determine what is good for them and what truly serves their interests, and so inclined to misunderstand and activities of the state and make all the wrong decisions which the state must subsequently correct and rectify if unable to nip in the bud. The second refers to the inclination of the state authorities to treat the subjects in the way doctors treat their patients — as individuals burdened with problems which they cannot resolve on their own, without expert guidance and surveillance; the problems which, as it were, 'reside inside' the patients, in body and soul, and therefore require that the patients be instructed and supervised so that they work on their bodies in accordance with the doctors' orders.

From the state's point of view, the subjects are first and foremost objects of state regulation. Their conduct is seen as something that ought to be strictly defined by the rights and duties determined by the state; if the state neglects such a defining, the subjects will determine their actions themselves — very often to their own and their fellows disadvantage, as they pursue selfish ends, making living together uncomfortable or downright impossible. The subjects' conduct, it seems, is in constant need of proscriptions and prescriptions. The state, like the doctor, is there to guide the subjects towards health and protect them against illness. If the conduct is not what it should be, it always means that — as in the case of the disease — there is something wrong with the subject himself. The inner, personal causes of ailment ought to be disclosed so that action can be taken by the warden (by the state, as by the doctor) to prompt behaviour leading to a cure. As in the doctor–patient relationship, relations between the state and its subjects are *asymmetrical*. Even if patients are allowed to choose their doctors, once the doctor has been chosen, the patient is expected to listen and to obey. It is now the doctor who tells the patient what to do. The doctor expects discipline, not discussion. After all, the patient lacks knowledge of the causes of disease and the road to health, and lacks the strength of character needed to act on this knowledge (on the whole the doctors, hiding behind specialist knowledge, see to it that such ignorance, and the resulting dependence, continue). When demanding submission and unconditional subordination, the doctor explains that he does it for the patient's own good. The state justifies its own call for the uncontested implementation of its instructions in the same terms. Its is a **pastoral power** — power exercised 'in the best interests' of the subjects who need to be protected against their own morbid inclinations.

The asymmetry of the relationship is manifested most conspicuously in the flow of information. The doctors, as we know, demand from the patients a full confession. They ask the patients to open themselves up, to report every detail of their lives the doctors may think relevant to the case in hand, to confide their innermost secrets, however intimate, and however closely guarded from all other people, including friends and kin. This sincerity is not, however, reciprocated by the doctors. The files in which the information about patients are held are secret. So is the doctors' opinion and the conclusions they draw from the data obtained from or about the patient. The doctors decide how much of this ought to be divulged to the patient. The withholding of information is again justified as being for the patient's own good: too much information may be harmful — making the patient either depressed or desperate, reckless and otherwise disobedient. A similar strategy of **secrecy** is practised by the state. Quite detailed information about its subjects is gathered, processed and stored by the state institutions, while the data about the state's own actions are classified as 'official secrets', whose betrayal is prosecuted. As most subjects of the state are denied access to such secrets, those few who are allowed access gain a distinct advantage over the rest. State freedom to collect information, coupled with the state's practice of secrecy, further deepens the asymmetry of the mutual relations. The chances of influencing each other are sharply unequal.

Citizenship therefore also carries a tendency to resist the commanding position aspired to by the state; an effort to roll back the state power, to free important areas of human life from state control and interference and to subject them instead to self-management. Such efforts go in two related, but different directions. One is *regionalism*: state power is a natural adversary of local autonomy — in fact of every intermediate power standing between the state organs and each and every subject; it is this exclusivity of the state power that is challenged. The specifity of local interests and problems is singled out as a sufficient reason for the self-management of local affairs; and representative local institutions are demanded that will stand closer to the people in the area and be more sensitive and responsive to their specific regional concerns. The second is *deterritorialization*: state power always has a territorial basis — all inhabitants of a certain territory, regardless of their other distinctive features, are subjects of the state power and the state power only; it is this principle that is now challenged. Other traits are promoted as more significant than the mere place of residence. Race, ethnicity, religion, language may be singled out as human aspects more important, with a heavier bearing on the totality of human life, than commonality of residence. Their right to autonomy, to separate management is demanded, and aimed against the pressure for uniformity from the unitary territorial power.

Even under the best of circumstances, therefore, there is always at least a residue of tension and distrust between the state and its subjects. To secure the discipline of its subjects under such conditions, the state, like all power, seeking and demanding the discipline which secures the regularity of its subjects' behaviour, needs **legitimation**: it needs to convince the subjects that there are valid reasons why they should obey commands of the state even if they are denied insight into all the facts of the case; why they should obey commands simply because they are commands of the state. Legitimation is meant to secure the subjects' trust that whatever comes from the state and bears the stamp of the appropriate authorities *deserves* to be obeyed; and the conviction that it also *must* be obeyed. One is called to follow the law even if one is not sure that it is a sensible law, even if one dislikes what the law tells one to do. One should follow the law just because it is supported by legitimate authority; because, as one is told, this is the 'law of the land'.

Legitimation is aimed at developing unconditional allegiance to the state, which is at its most secure when based on a 'this is my homeland' feeling, a 'my homeland, good or bad' feeling. If this is my homeland, I can only benefit from its wealth and might. As this wealth and might depend on universal agreement and cooperation, on protecting the order and peaceful cohabitation of all the residents, I believe that this home we share will grow in strength once we all act in unison and consent to whatever serves our common good. Our actions ought to be guided by **patriotism** − love of the homeland, the will to keep it strong and happy and to do everything its strength and happiness require. The paramount duty of the patriot is discipline; obedience to the state is, indeed, the most conspicuous sign of patriotism. Any challenge to the law of the state breeds discord, and for this very reason (regardless of the substance of the matter) is 'unpatriotic'. Legitimation aims at securing obedience through reasoning and calculation: it is better for everybody if everybody is obedient. Consensus and discipline make us all better off. All in all, a concerted action is more beneficial to everybody, therefore also to myself, than rift − even if this requires that I submit to a policy I do not approve of.

All calculation, however, invites a counter-calculation. If patriotic obedience is demanded in the name of reason, one may well be tempted to subject the argument to a test of reason. One may count the costs of obedience to a resented policy against the gains which an active resistance may bring. One may find out, or at least convince oneself, that in the end resistance is less costly and damaging than obedience, and so it pays to refuse to consent. Efforts to legitimize the need of obedience by reference to the benefits which the unity may bring are therefore hardly ever conclusive and will never end. Precisely because it presents itself as a product of rational calculation, and as long as it presents itself as such, legitimation is vulnerable and precarious, in need of constant reiteration and defence.

Loyalty to the nation, on the other hand, is free from the inner contradictions which burden discipline towards the state. **National-ism**, which calls for unconditional loyalty to the nation and its welfare, does not need to appeal to reason or calculation. It may, but it can afford not to promise that gain or welfare will be derived from service loyal to the national cause. It appeals instead to obedience as a value in its own right and its own purpose. Membership of a nation is understood as a fate more powerful than any individual — as a quality that cannot be put on or taken off at will. Nationalism implies that it is the nation that gives the individual member his identity. Unlike the state, the nation is not an association entered into in order to promote common interests. On the contrary, it is the unity of the nation, its common fate, that precedes all consideration of interests and, indeed, gives the interests their meaning.

A state which can fully identify itself with one nation (clearly not the case in the multi-national British state) — a **national state** — can therefore exploit the potential of nationalism instead of trying, less reliably, to legitimatize itself by reference to the calculation of benefits. The national state demands obedience on the grounds that it speaks in the name of the nation, and hence discipline towards the state, like obedience to one's national fate, is a value which does not serve any other objective, being as it is its own purpose. To disobey the state — a punishable crime — becomes then something much worse than a breach of the law: it turns into the betrayal of the national cause — a heinous, immoral act which strips the culprits of dignity and casts them outside the human community. It is perhaps for the reasons of legitimation and, more generally, of securing the unity of conduct that there is a sort of mutual attraction between the state and the nation. The state tends to enlist the authority of the nation to strengthen its own demand for discipline, while nations tend to constitute themselves into states to harness the enforcing potential of the state to the support of their claim to loyalty. And yet, not all states are national, and not all nations have states of their own.

What is a nation? This is a notoriously difficult question, without a single answer likely to satisfy everybody. The nation is not a 'reality' in the same way the state is. The state is 'real' in the sense of having clearly drawn boundaries, both on the map and on the land. The boundaries are on the whole guarded by force, so that random passing from one state to another, entering and leaving the state, encounters very real, tangible resistance which makes the state itself feel 'real'. Inside the boundaries of the state, a set of laws is binding which, again, is 'real' in the sense that disregarding its presence, behaving as if it did not exist, may 'bruise' and 'hurt' the sinner in much the same way as disregarding any other material object would. And so there is a clearly defined territory and a clearly defined supreme authority which make the state itself 'real' and clearly defined: a tough, stubborn, resistant object one cannot wish out of existence. The same cannot be said, however, about the nation. A nation is from start to finish an **imagined community**; it exists as an entity in so far as its members mentally and emotionally 'identify themselves' with a collective body most of whose other members they will never confront face to face. The nation becomes a mental reality as it is *imagined* as such. True, nations usually occupy a continuous territory to which, as they may credibly claim, they give a special colouring and flavour. Seldom, however, does this national colouring give the territory a uniformity comparable with that imposed by the unity of the state-sponsored 'law of the land'. Hardly ever can the nations boast monopoly of residence on any territory. Within virtually any territory there are people living side by side who define themselves as belonging to different nations, and whose loyalty is claimed by different nationalisms. In many territories no nation can really claim a majority, much less a position sufficiently dominating to define the 'national character' of the land.

It is also true that nations are usually distinguished and united by a common language. But what is deemed a common and distinct language is to a large extent a matter of a nationalist (and often contested) decision. Frequently regional dialects are so idiosyncratic in their vocabulary, syntax and idioms as to be almost mutually incomprehensible, and yet their identities are denied or actively suppressed, and they are not recognized as separate languages for fear of disrupting national unity. On the other hand, even comparatively minor local differences may well be played up, their distinctiveness exaggerated, so that a dialect may be elevated to the rank of a separate language and of a distinctive feature of a separate nation (the differences between, say, the Norwegian and Swedish, Dutch and Flemish, Ukrainian and Russian languages are, arguably, not much more conspicuous than the differences between many 'internal' dialects which are represented — if at all acknowledged — as varieties of the same national language). Besides, groups of people may admit to sharing the same language and still consider themselves separate nations (think of the English-speaking Welsh or Scots people, the sharing of English by many nations of the former Commonwealth, the sharing of German by Austrians and Swiss as well as Germans). Or, like the Swiss, they may gloss over the evident differences in the languages they use.

Territory and language are insufficient as the factors of the 'reality' of the nation for one more, and decisive, reason: one can, so to speak, move in and out of them. One can, in principle, declare a change of national allegiance. One can move home and acquire residence among a nation to which one does not belong. One can master the language of another nation. If the territory of residence (remember, this is not a territory with guarded borders) and participation in a linguistic community (remember, one is not obliged to use a national language by the fact that no other languages are admitted by power-holders) were the only constituting features of the nation, the nation would be too 'porous' and 'underdefined' to claim the absolute, unconditional and exclusive allegiance that all nationalisms demand.

Such a demand is most persuasive if the nation is conceived of as the *fate* rather than a *choice*; as a 'fact' so firmly established in the past that no human power may change it now; a 'reality' which can be tinkered with only at the tinkerer's peril. Nationalisms try on the whole to achieve just this. The *myth of origin* is their major instrument.

What this myth suggests is that, even if originally a cultural creation, in the course of its history the nation has become a truly 'natural' phenomenon, something beyond human control. The present members of the nation — so the myth says — are tied together by their common past. The national spirit is their shared and exclusive property. It unites them — and at the same time sets them apart from all other nations and all individuals who may aspire to enter their community without, however, being either entitled or able to participate in that national spirit which one can collectively inherit, but never privately acquire.

The myth-supported claim to the 'naturalness' of nations and the 'ascribed' and inherited nature of national membership cannot but embroil nationalism in a contradiction. On the one hand, it is said that the nation is a verdict of history and a reality as objective and solid as any natural phenomenon. On the other hand, however, it is precarious: its unity and coherence is constantly under threat, as other nations attempt to poach or kidnap its members and intruders try to sneak into its ranks. The nation must defend its existence; natural as it might be, it still cannot survive without constant vigilance and effort. Thus nationalisms normally demand power — the right to use coercion — in order to secure the preservation and continuity of the nation. The *state* power fits the bill best. State power, as we have seen, means monopoly over the instruments of coercion; only the state power is capable of enforcing uniform rules of conduct and promulgating laws which everybody must obey. Thus, as much as the state needs nationalism for its legitimation, nationalism needs the state for its effectiveness. The *national state* is the product of this mutual attraction.

Once the state has been identified with the nation (represented as the organ of self-government of the nation), the prospects of nationalist success grow considerably. Nationalism need no longer rely solely on the persuasiveness and cogency of its arguments, on the willingness of the members to accept them. It now has other, more efficient means at its disposal. State power means the chance of enforcing the sole use of the national language in public offices, courts and representative bodies. It means the possibility of mobilizing public resources to boost the competitive chances of the preferred national culture in general, and national literature and arts in particular. It also means, above all, control over education, which is made simultaneously free and obligatory, so that no one is excluded and no one is allowed to escape its influence. Universal education permits all inhabitants of the state territory to be trained in the values of the nation which dominates the state: to make them 'born' patriots, and so to accomplish in practice what has been claimed in theory, namely the 'naturalness' of nationality.

The combined effect of education, of ubiquitous though diffuse cultural pressure, and of the state-enforced rules of conduct is the attachment to the way of life associated with the 'national membership'. This spiritual bond sometimes manifests itself in a conscious and explicit **ethnocentrism**: in the conviction that one's own nation, and everything which relates to it, is right, morally praiseworthy and beautiful — and vastly superior to anything that may be offered as an alternative; and that what is good for one's own nation should be given precedence over the interests of anybody else. Even if such an overtly ethnocentric — 'group-selfish' — philosophy is not preached, the simple fact still remains that, having been brought up in a specific, culturally shaped environment, people tend to feel at home and secure in it, and in it alone. Conditions that deviate from the familiar devalue the acquired skills and thereby cause a feeling of unease, of vague resentment, even of hostility focused on the 'aliens' responsible for the confusion. The ways of the aliens are seen as evidence of their backwardness or arrogance, and the aliens themselves are perceived as intruders. One wishes them to be segregated or removed.

Nationalism inspires a tendency to cultural crusades: efforts to change the alien ways, to convert them, to force them to submit to the cultural authority of the dominant nation. The purpose of cultural crusade is **assimilation**. (The term 'assimilation' was originally borrowed from biology; in order to feed itself, a living organism assimilates elements of the environment — that is, it transforms 'foreign' substances into the cells and tissues of its own body. By so doing it makes them 'similar' to itself; what used to be different becomes alike.) To be sure, all nationalism is always about assimilation, as the nation which the nationalism declares as having a 'natural unity' has first to be created by rallying an often indifferent and diversified population around the myth and symbols of national distinctiveness. Assimilatory efforts become most conspicuous and most fully expose their inner contradictions when a triumphant nationalism, which has achieved state domination over a certain territory, meets among the residents some 'foreign' groups – such as either declare their distinct national identity, or are treated as distinct and nationally alien by the population that has already gone through the process of cultural unification. In such cases assimilation is often presented as a proselytizing mission – much like converting the heathen to a true religion.

Paradoxically, the converting efforts tend to be half-hearted – as if afraid of too much success. They bear the mark of the inner contradiction always present in the nationalist vision. On the one hand, nationalism claims the superiority of its own nation, of its national culture and character. The attractiveness of such a superior nation to the surrounding peoples is therefore something to be expected; indeed, the wish and the efforts of the others to join in the glory of the nation are a tribute to, and an extra confirmation of, the superiority the nation claims. Moreover, in the case of a national state it also mobilizes the popular support for state authority and undermines all other sources of authority resistant to the state-promoted uniformity. On the other hand, the influx of foreign elements into the nation, particularly when made easy by the 'open arms', hospitable attitude of the host nation, casts doubt on the 'naturalness' of national membership and thus saps the very foundation of national unity. People are seen to change places at will. Yesterday 'them' turn into 'us' under our very eyes. It looks, therefore, as if nationality were simply a matter of choice; an outcome of a decision, which – like all decisions – could, in principle, be different from what it was and even revoked. Assimilation, if effective, brings into relief the precarious, voluntary character of the nation and national membership – something the nationalism tried hard to hide.

Hence assimilation breeds resentment against the very people the cultural crusade aimed to attract and convert. They seem to be a threat to order and security: they have accomplished what in theory should be impossible; they performed by human effort something which is believed to be outside human power and control. They have thus shown that the allegedly natural boundary is in fact artificial and — worse still — passable. It is hard to admit, therefore, that their assimilation — the declared aim of the nationalist policy — has indeed been successful and complete. In the eyes of the suspicious, the ostensibly assimilated persons look more like turncoats: duplicitous, potentially treacherous people who — either for personal gain or with a still more sinister purpose in mind — pretend to be what they are not. Paradoxically, the very success of assimilation gives credence to the idea that division is permanent and is there to stay, that 'true assimilation' is not, in fact, possible and that nation-building through cultural conversion is not a viable project.

Nationalism may then retreat to a tougher and less vulnerable, racist line of defence. Unlike the nation, **race** is perceived overtly and unambiguously as a thing of nature — unambiguously beyond human influence and control. The idea of race stands for such distinctions between people as are thought of as neither human-made nor subject to change by human efforts. Often race is given a purely biological meaning (that is, it conveys the idea that the individual character, ability and inclination are closely related to observable, extrinsic characteristics, like the shape and size of skull or other parts of the body, or once and for all determined by the quality of the genes). In all cases, however, its concept refers to *hereditary* qualities, passed from one generation to another through the process of sexual reproduction. When confronted with race education must surrender. What nature has decided, no human instruction may change. Unlike the nation, race cannot be assimilated it may only 'pollute' the purity of another race and undermine its quality. To stave off such a morbid event alien races must be segregated, isolated and, best of all, removed to a safe distance to make mixing impossible and thus protect one's own race from pollution.

Assimilation and racism seem to be radically opposed. And yet they stem from the same source — the *boundary-building* concerns inherent in the nationalist tendency. Each one emphasizes one of the poles of the inner contradiction. Depending on circumstances, one or other side can be deployed as weapons in the pursuit of nationalist objectives. Yet both are constantly potentially present in any nationalist campaign — waiting for their chance. Rather than excluding, they may mutually boost and reinforce each other.

The strength of nationalism derives from the connecting role it plays in the promotion and perpetuation of the social order as defined by the authority of the state. Nationalism 'sequestrates' the diffuse heterophobia (that resentment of the different which we discussed in the chapter devoted to the phenomenon of the stranger) and mobilizes this sentiment in the service of loyalty and support for the state and discipline towards state authority. It therefore makes the state authority more effective. At the same time it deploys the resource of state power in shaping the social reality in such a way that new supplies of heterophobia, and hence new mobilizing opportunities, may be generated. As the state jealously guards its monopoly of coercion, it prohibits, as a rule, all private settling of accounts, like ethnic and racial violence. In most cases, it would also disallow and even punish private initiative in petty discrimination. Like all the rest of its resources, it would deploy nationalism as a vehicle of the one and only social order (that is, the one defined, sustained and enforced by the state), while simultaneously persecuting its diffuse, spontaneous and thus potentially disorderly manifestations. The mobilizing potential of nationalism will then be harnessed to the appropriate state policy — beefing up nationalist sentiments and patriotic identification with the state through preferably inexpensive yet prestigious military, economic or sporting victories, as well as through restrictive immigration laws, enforced repatriation and other measures ostensibly reflecting, while certainly reinforcing, the popular heterophobia.

In a large part of the world, the state and the nation historically merged; the states have been using national sentiments to reinforce their hold over society and strengthen the order they promoted, while nation-building efforts resorted to state power to enforce the unity that was allegedly natural, and hence did not need enforcement. Let us note, however, that the fact that the merger of state and nation did occur historically is not proof ot its inevitability. Ethnic loyalty and the attachment to native language and customs are not reducible to the political function to which they have been put by their alliance with state power. The marriage between state and nation is not in any way preordained; it is one of convenience.

Chapter Ten

Order and Chaos

I wonder whether you have ever had enough patience to stay in your cinema seat long after the last images of the film have faded and the credits and acknowledgements have appeared on the screen. If you have, you were no doubt astonished at the interminable length of the list of people whose names – or just the functions – the producers of the film felt obliged to mention. You would have learned from the list that the number of people who worked behind the scenes was many times larger than that of the people whose faces you watched in the film. There were many more names of invisible helpers than of actors. Moreover, only names of companies were credited for some aspects of the collective effort; each such company surely employed many more people than any list of credits could possibly name. This is not all, however. Quite a few people whose work was no less indispensable and without whom you would not see the film did not get a mention at all. For example, the company that took care of the sound processing was named, but not the company which supplied the sound-processing equipment; nor the company which produced the parts later assembled in such equipment; nor the factories which supplied the raw materials for such parts; nor the innumerable people whose work was necessary so that the people who made those raw materials or the finished parts could be fed, shod, sheltered, remain healthy, obtain the skills their work required...

To name them all, or even mention them indirectly, would be an utterly impossible task. Someone therefore must have decided where to cut the list of credits and acknowledgements; and whatever the decision was, it must have been arbitrary. The cut-off point could have been made elsewhere, with equal ease (and with equal justification or lack of justification). Each point, however carefully selected, would need to be random, contingent, and for this reason an object of contention. Contention will be as vehement as it is bound to remain inconclusive — for the sheer fact that no boundary, however painstakingly drawn, reflects an 'objective truth' (objectively existing divisions which it purports merely to report). No collection of people contained inside such a boundary could truly be considered self-contained — sufficient to produce the film; its 'reality' as a complete, self-enclosed collective is itself a product of the cutting-off operation. The collection of people who were operative in making just one single film has in fact no boundary (more precisely, it would have no boundary but for the fact that the cut-off point has been arbitrarily selected and used to perform the cutting operation). To add more complexity still to the task of boundary-drawing, what those people have done for the film cannot be clearly separated from the rest of their lives; their contribution to film-making was no more than one aspect of their life activity, which covers many other concerns and interests only loosely if at all related to their part in making the film. When deciding where to stop acknowledging the debt, one therefore made an artificial division in a double sense. From a dense web of intercrossing lives of interdependent human beings a thin layer was sliced off which, because it has been sliced off and separated from the rest, seemed to have a 'reality of its own': it seemed to be on the one hand self-contained and on the other hand internally unified by common purpose and function. In fact, it was neither.

The point is that all allegedly independent or autonomous units, all the ostensibly 'self-managing', viable subdivisions of the human world are of such a precarious, vulnerable nature; all result from the keen attempts to cut clearly marked, manageable little worlds out of a boundless and boundary-less, continuous and non-discrete reality. In the case of the credits listed at the end of the film, the cutting operation was of relatively little consequence. At most, it may lead to litigations, as the omitted collaborators demand that justice is done and the importance of their services publicly confirmed. The case offers, however, an example of a much more general predicament, known for its by no means innocuous manifestations. Think of the efforts to draw clear-cut state boundaries which would force a wedge between people closely tied together by economic and cultural bonds while they would also cast into identical conditions people who otherwise have little in common. Think also of the measures taken to salvage a marriage while leaving out of focus the manifold interdependencies in which each partner is entangled and of which the marital relationship is but one, in no way independent or even the most decisive, aspect.

As one might expect, such attempts to draw, mark and guard artificial boundaries become an object of ever growing concern — indeed, turn into a feverish obsession — as the 'natural' (that is, well-entrenched, resistant and immune to change) divisions and distances melt and dissolve, and human lives (even those lived at an enormous geographical or spiritual distance from each other) tie themselves together ever more tightly. The less 'natural' a boundary, the more flagrantly it violates complex reality, the more attention and conscious effort its defence demands, the more coercion and violence it attracts. The most peaceful and least guarded state boundaries are on the whole the ones that happen to overlap with the territorial limits of settlement of 'inward-looking', internally unified populations. Such boundaries as cut across the areas of frequent and intense economic and cultural interchange are all too often an object of contention and armed struggle. To take another example: as sexual intercourse became increasingly separated from erotic love and from the stable, multi-sided relations of cohabitation to which they 'naturally' belonged, it also became a focus of ever growing anxiety, increased urge of technical inventiveness and a psychic tension that occasionally spills into violence.

One can say that the importance of a division, the forcefulness with which it is drawn and defended, grows together with its brittleness and the extent of damage it does to the complex human reality. Divisions are fought for tooth and nail when they are unlikely to be faithfully obeyed; the struggle to keep divisions watertight turns ever more ferocious the less likely it is to achieve its purpose.

This is a situation many consider to be a conspicuous mark of what is called **modern** society: a kind of society which established itself in our part of the world about three centuries ago and in which we still live today. Under the conditions prevalent before (which, to distinguish them from present conditions, are often talked about as 'pre-modern'), the maintenace of distinctions and divisions between categories tended to attract less attention and trigger less activity than it does today — precisely because the differences seemed to come naturally, without any conscious effort on the part of people. They appeared self-evident, timeless and immutable, immune to human intervention. Indeed, they did not look at all human-made. Instead, they were perceived as parts of the 'Divine Cosmos', in which the place of everything and of everybody had been preordained and destined to stay as it was for ever. A noble was a noble from the moment of birth and almost nothing nobles did could deprive them of that quality or make them into someone else. The same applied to the peasant serfs, and by and large to the townsfolk as well (the only narrow outlet for mobility between otherwise impenetrable divisions was offered by warfare and piety; this circumstance contributed heavily to the extraordinary attention paid to the professions of clergyman and soldier, and to the construction, protection and per-petuation of church and army hierarchies). Indeed, the human con-dition seemed solidly built and settled the same way the rest of the world was: there was no reason, therefore, to distinguish between 'nature' and 'culture', between 'natural and 'man-made' laws, natural and human orders. They both seemed to be hewn from the same tough and unshakeable rock.

It was roughly towards the end of the sixteenth century that in parts of Western Europe this harmonious and monolithic picture of the world began to fall apart (in Britain, this happened just after the reign of Elizabeth I). As the number and visibility of people who did not fit neatly into any of the established partitions of the 'divine chain of being' (and thus the volume of worries generated by assigning them to a well-defined and closely supervised location) rose sharply, the pace of legislative activity quickened; statutes were introduced to regulate the areas of life which since time immemorial had been left to their own course; specialized agencies were created to survey, monitor and protect the observation of the rules and to disarm and disempower the recalcitrant. Social distinctions and discriminations had become a matter of examination, aforethought, design, planning and, above all, of conscious, organized and specialized effort. Slowly it became evident that *social* order, unlike that of the forest, the sea or the meadow, was a *human* product; that it would not last unless constantly supported by measures only human agents could and should undertake and see through. Human divisions did not seem 'natural' any more. Being a human product, they could be improved or made worse. Whatever the case, they were and would stay *arbitrary* and *artificial*. Human order was a subject of art, knowledge and technology.

This new image set nature and society sharply apart. One can say that nature and society were 'discovered' simultaneously. What was in fact discovered was neither nature nor society, but the *distinction* between them, and especially the distinction between the practices each one enabled or called for. As human conditions appeared more and more to be products of legislation, management and deliberate manipulation, 'nature' assumed the role of a huge depository for everything which human powers could not yet or had no ambition to mould; everything, that is, which was seen as being ruled by its own logic and left by humans to its own devices. Philosophers began to talk about 'laws of nature' by analogy with the laws promulgated by kings or parliaments, but also to distinguish them from the latter. 'Natural laws' were like the laws of the kings (that is, obligatory and armed with punitive sanctions), but unlike the royal decrees they had no conceivable human author (their force was therefore *super-*human, whether they had been established by God's will and inscrutable purpose or were causally determined, with an unassailable necessity, directly by the way cosmic matters were arranged).

The idea of order as a regular sequence of events, as a harmonious assembly of well-geared parts, as a situation in which things are likely to remain as they are expected to be, was not born with modern times. Distinctly modern, however, is the *concern* with order, the urgency of doing something about it, the fear that unless something is done the order will dissipate into chaos. (Chaos is imagined as a failed attempt to order things; a state of affairs different from the envisaged and attempted order is not, therefore, perceived as an alternative order, but as an absence of all order. What makes it so disorderly is the observers' inability to control the flow of events, to obtain the desired response from the environment, to prevent or eliminate happenings they did not plan and did not wish to occur. In short, *uncertainty*.) In a modern society, only the vigilant management of human affairs seems to stand between order and chaos.

And yet, as we have seen above, the boundaries of any sector of the web of dependencies, or of any composite yet partial action cut out from the universe of life activities, are arbitrary and therefore porous, easily permeable and contentious. The management of an (always partial) order is, therefore, always incomplete, less than perfect and bound to remain so. There are many outer dependencies and unaccounted-for human purposes and drives which tear the artificially drawn boundaries apart and interfere with the designs of the managers. The planned and managed sector remains no more than a shack erected on moving sands; or a tent blown through by crosswinds; or, more to the point, an eddy on a rapidly flowing river, one that keeps its shape while constantly changing its content.

At best, we can speak of islands of (temporary and fragile) order scattered over the vast sea of chaos (that is, the unplanned and undesigned flow of events). The most the order-building efforts may achieve are **relatively autonomous subtotalities** (marked by a somewhat stronger than average prevalence of centripetal over centrifugal forces, by a somewhat higher intensity of inner connections and somewhat less consequential external bonds). The advantage of the inner hold over outer pulls is always relative, near complete. Which means that the victory of order over chaos is never total or final. The struggle never stops, as its ostensible target is never reached.

Saying this, we have done no more than draw general conclusions from observations made on a number of occasions in previous chapters. Remember the trouble with forcing all the people coming within the orbit of a territorial unit or an organization into neat and clearly separate categories; classifying them as either 'us' or 'them', either insiders or outsiders, either friends or enemies. We have found as well that the most earnest of efforts to attain clarity in such divisions ends in failure, as there always remains a large number of people who are neither in nor out — the strangers whose presence spoils the purity of the picture and undermines the clarity of behav-

ioural guidance. Just because all *dichotomy* − any two-part classification − is ill suited to the complexity of the human situation, the
very effort to impose it on manifold reality creates much *ambivalence*,
which keeps the danger of chaos alive and puts off for ever the
completion of the designed order. Or recall the trouble each
bureaucratic organization faces when trying to subordinate the conduct of its members to the sole purpose set by the managers, and
strip them of all other motives and desires which the members might
have brought from other groupings in which they live outside office
hours; or the hopeless struggle to reduce all human relations inside
the organization itself to exchanges relevant to the completion of the
organizational task − so that personal ambitions, jealousies, sympathies, enmities or moral impulses are not allowed to interfere with
the exclusive concentration on the one and only purpose as defined
from the top of bureaucratic hierarchy. We have found that the most
vigorous efforts in this respect could not but fail to implement that
lucid, harmonious image which had been sketched originally on the
chart of organizational structure. Hence the constant complaints
about disloyalty, double-dealing, insubordination, betrayal.

Efforts to construe an artificial order are bound to fall short of
their ideal target. They conjure up islands of relative autonomy, but
at the same time they transform the territory adjacent to the artificially
cut island into a grey area of ambivalence. For that reason they are
bound to go on and unlikely ever to stop. Ambivalence (which is the
essence of disorder, or chaos) is the inevitable outcome of all projects
of clear-cut, exceptionless classification − that is, of the handling of
elements of reality as if they were truly separate and distinct, as if
they did not spill over any boundary; as if they belonged to one
division and one division only. Ambivalence results from the assumption that people or their many traits may be neatly divided into
the inside and to the outside, beneficial and harmful, relevant and
irrelevant − or at least that they should be divided. Each dichotomy
spawns ambivalence; there would be no ambivalence were it not for
the dichotomous vision entailed necessarily in every search for order.

The dichotomous, 'either-or' vision is itself the product of a drive
towards the relatively autonomous enclave over which a total and
ubiquitous control may be extenced. As all power has its limits, as

control over the universe as a whole is beyond human potential and eludes even the most audacious of human dreams, the creation of order always means in practice the setting apart of the orderly area from the disorderly rest, the wilderness; drawing the boundary of the island of order amidst the boundless sea of chaos. The question is how to make this setting apart, this fencing off, effective; how to build a tight dam preventing the sea from flooding the island, how to stem the tide of ambivalence. The order-building requires the use of the art of warfare against ambivalence. To build order means to wage war against ambiguity.

Within each relatively autonomous island of order, care is taken to make everything straightforward (that is, to reach situation in which there is a clear-cut type of object answering to every name, and each object bears a name that is recognizable at first sight and difficult to confuse). This requires, of course, that all other meanings, 'other capacities', unplanned traits and things and words be prohibited, suppressed or declared irrelevant and left out of sight. In order to achieve this double purpose, the criteria of classification must be such as can be fully controlled and decided upon from one place — that from which the enclave as a whole is ruled and administered (note that the monopoly of rulers — their exclusive right to decide where to draw the boundary between the inside and the outside, their sole competence to define everything that falls within their realm — is the necessary precondition of maintaining order and avoiding ambivalence; perhaps it is also its motive). Criteria which elude such a central control tend therefore to be declared unlawful; efforts are made to banish them in practice, suppress or otherwise render them ineffective. Ambivalence is the enemy against which all means of coercion and all symbolic powers are enlisted. Remember the struggle waged by the guardians of any orthodoxy against heretics and dissidents! And remember that it tended to be more fierce and merciless than the war against the declared enemies — heathen or infidels!

An imaginary line is drawn on the map. It is then called 'the state frontier'. People with arms are posted along it to ward off 'un-authorized' movement across it. These people are dressed in uniforms which allow everybody to identify them as persons in authority:

persons who have the right to decide who is and who is not allowed to cross the line. They are not the real gatekeepers, though. They act as middlemen, as agents of another authority, sitting somewhere in the capital of the state whose frontiers they guard. It is that distant authority which decides who is entitled to cross the border at will and who should be stopped and sent back. That authority issues passports to people cast in the first category, and composes lists of prohibited persons which defines the other. That authority does what all authorities do: it tries to split neatly, into two mutually exclusive sets, great numbers of people whose own traits are in no way mutually exclusive and who differ from each other (and resemble each other) in an infinite multitude of ways. It is thanks to the constant vigilance of such authority and the many middlemen busy executing its will that the precarious identity of the state as the body of people united in their capacity as state subjects is maintained. One either does or does not belong to this body; there is no third possibility, no intermediate status, no ambiguity.

The same pattern is repeated endlessly. Whenever you see uniformed or armed people at the gate, you will find it operating. Sometimes, to be admitted inside, you must display an identity card which sets you, as a confirmed and approved fan of a given football team, apart from all the unauthorized followers of the game. Or an invitation testifying that the hosts have classified you as a guest at the party. Or a membership card which defines you as 'one of us', the club insiders. Or a student card, which confirms that your reading of books in the library is legal, unlike the reading of impostors or accidental visitors merely attracted by interesting books ... If you cannot show such a card, or a passport, or an invitation, you will in all probability be turned away at the gate. If you somehow make your way inside and are spotted, you will be, at best, asked to leave. The space has been reserved for a special kind of people, expected to obey the same rules, to surrender to the same discipline defined and executed by the same authority. Were your presence uninvited, it would weaken the hold of that authority. The relative autonomy of the enclave that authority controls might be compromised and corroded by untamed ambivalence, as it was thrown open to forces and influences that made interaction random and therefore detracted from regularity and order. Generally speaking, a state or other organizations may protect and preserve their peculiar, always precarious kinds of order (and hence their identity, or relative autonomy) over a protracted stretch of time only as long as the gatekeepers stay on guard: as long as some people, or some aspects of people personalities, are safely shut out at the gates.

The closing of physical gates or physical borders is not easy, but at least it is a technically straightforward matter. On the other hand, the splitting of a human personality into parts which are allowed in and the parts which must be kept outside, and barring communication between the two, is a much more complex matter. Loyalty to the organization (which means the rejection or suspension of all other loyalties) is notoriously difficult to achieve and usually inspires the application of most ingenious and imaginative expedients. Employees of a company or an office may be prohibited from belonging to trade unions or political movements. Or they may be forbidden to talk and think and discuss organizational matters with people who do not belong to the organization (if they break this rule, they may compare opinions and judgements of such 'outsiders' with the official view of the organizational authorities and find the latter not as unimpeachable as they were told). Recall the notorious Official Secrets Act, which forbids state employees to divulge information concerning the activities and intentions of state organs, even if making this information available to all citizens could be in the public interest, that is, by definition, in the interests of other people than the insiders of the state organs themselves. It is because the organizations tend to stem the flow of information that the unity of personality and personal bonds that extends over the artificially drawn borders is construed as dangerous ambiguity and so — from the point of view of the organizations and their managers — becomes a most serious threat to order. It is the guarding of secrets that creates spies and traitors; or, rather, it labels some otherwise innocuous and 'natural' human acts as treacherous an subversive.

The area of ambivalence that inevitably surrounds all artificially drawn frontiers and the range of elaborate strategies aimed to defuse or suppress it are not the only consequences of the territorial or functional (always relative and precarious) autonomy. Natural networks of bonds and dependencies are severed and cut in pieces, communication over artificially erected borders grinds to a halt — and thus the boundary-drawing results also in numerous side-effects that no one predicts, calculates or desires. What seems to be a proper, rational solution to the problem confronted from within one relatively autonomous unit, itself becomes a problem for another unit. As the units, contrary to their pretences, are closely interdependent, the problem-solving activity rebounds eventually on the very agency which has undertaken it in the first palce. It leads to an unplanned and unpredicted shift in the overall balance of the situation that makes the continuous resolution of the original problem more costly than expected or even altogether impossible. The most notorious case of such side-effects is the destruction of the ecological and climatic equilibrium of the planet, which it is feared will endanger the existence of any land and people, whether close to or remote from the limited territory the solution-seekers covered in their practices and their imagination. The natural resources of the earth are depleted, making the problems ever more formidable and the continuous problem solving ever more difficult. Industrial organizations pollute air and water, thus creating many new awesome problems for those in charge of human health and urban development. In their efforts to improve the organization of their own activity, companies rationalize the use of labour, by the same token declaring many of their workers redundant and adding to the problems born of chronic unemployment, pockets of poverty and depressed areas. The mushrooming of private cars and motorways, of airports and aircraft, once hoped to resolve the problem of mobility and transportation, creates traffic jams, air and noise pollution, destroys whole areas of human settlement, and leads to such a centralization of cultural life and supply of services as renders many local settlements uninhabitable; travelling therefore becomes more necessary (the work place is now more distant from the place of residence) or alluring ('running away from it all', even for a few days' holiday) than ever before, while becoming at the same time more difficult and exhausting. All in all, cars and aircraft have inadvertently magnified and exacerbated the very problem they were intended to solve; they have added to its magnitude and diminished the feasibility of its future solution.

If anything, they constrained the collective freedom which they promised to expand.

This quandary seems to be universal and to offer no obvious escape. Its roots lie in the very *relativity* of the autonomy of any entity artificially prised from the whole which cannot but embrace the totality of the human species together with the world we inhabit. Autonomy is at best partial, at worst purely imaginary: often autonomy seems to be the case only because we are blind or deliberately close our eyes (this does not concern me; this is not my responsibility; am I my brother's keeper? everybody for himself, and the devil take the hindmost) to the manifold and far-reaching connections between all actors and between everything each actor is doing. The number of factors which are taken into account in the planning and implementing of the solution of any problem is always smaller than the sum total of factors which influence, or depend on, the situation in which the given problem has arisen. One may even say that power — that capacity to design, enforce and preserve order — consists precisely of the ability to disregard, neglect, push aside many factors which — if not so neglected — would make the order impossible. To have power means, among other things, to be able to decide what is important and what is not; what is relevant to the struggle for order and what is not a matter for concern. The trouble is, however, that it does not mean conjuring such irrelevant factors out of existence.

As the assignment of relevance and irrelevance is always *contingent* (that is, there is no overwhelming reason why the line of relevance should be drawn in any particular way; it could be drawn in many different ways), the decision may be, and often is, hotly contested. History is full of examples of such contests. At the threshold of the modern era one of the most seminal power struggles developed around the passage from *patronage* to what was bewailed by some modern thinkers and objected to by some modern protest movements — the *cash nexus*. Faced with the callous indifference of factory owners to the fate of the 'factory hands' (the very name given to the workers conveyed the message that it was their hands, and their hands alone, in which their employers were interested), the critics of the nascent factory system recalled the practices of artisan workshops, or even country manors, which behaved like 'one big family' that included everyone from the top to the bottom. The master of the workshop and country squire could be a ruthless, autocratic boss and unscrupulously exploit the drudgery of his workers; but the workers also expected him to care about their needs and — if it came to the worst — bail them out from impending disaster. They could hope to be provided with a place to live, assistance in the case of illness or natural calamity, even some provision for old age and invalidity. In sharp opposition to the old habits, no such expectations were accepted as legitimate by the owners of factories. They paid their employees for the labour performed in factory hours, and the rest — they insisted — was the workers' own responsibility. The critics and the people speaking for the factory workers resented such 'washing of hands'. They pointed out that the protracted, stultifying, exhausting day-to-day effort demanded by factory discipline left the workers physically exhausted and spiritually worn out, and so deeply affected the self-same individuals and their family lives for which the factory bosses renounced all responsibility; that when the factory hands emerged from the grinding administered by the factory regime, they turned into a 'human waste' (like the other parts of the factory product classified as waste, they were considered useless from the point of view of the productive plan; that unavoidable part of the final product which because of its lack of profitable use is left out of focus, uncared for and in the end simply thrown away). The critics pointed out as well that the relationship between the factory owners and the factory hands is not in fact limited to a simple exchange of labour for wages: labour cannot be cut out and isolated from the person of the worker in the same way as a cash sum is separated from the person of the boss. 'To give away labour' means to subject the whole person, body and soul, to the task set by the boss and the rhythm of exertion decided by the boss. Although the bosses, with their eyes targeted on the 'useful' product only, would be loath to admit it, the worker is asked to give in exchange for wages the whole of his or her personality and freedom. The power of the factory owners over the workers they hired expressed itself precisely in getting away with this asymmetry in their ostensibly equivalent exchange. The employers defined the meaning of employment, and reserved the right to decide what was and what was not a matter for their concern — the very right they denied their employees. By the same token, the workers' fight for batter labour conditions and more say in the running of the productive process and in defining their own roles and duties in it had to turn into the struggle against the employer's right to define the limits and the contents of the factory order.

The conflict between workers and factory owners about the definition of the boundaries of the factory system is just one example of the kind of contention that all definitions of order must necessarily trigger off. Since any definition is contingent and in the last account rests solely on someone's power to enforce it, it remains in principle *contestable*, and indeed it tends to be contested by those who fall victim to its damaging effects. Time and again you hear a heated debate about who should pay for, say, polluting the supplies of fresh water, disposing of toxic waste, or the damage caused to the landscape by a new mine or a new motorway. Debates of this kind may in principle go on for ever, as they have no impartial, objective solutions and are resolved solely through power struggle. Someone's waste may well become an important element of someone else's life condition. The objects of dispute look different depending on the relatively autonomous entity from which they are contemplated, and their meanings derive entirely from the places they occupy in those partial orders. Buffeted by many often cotradictory pressures, they assume in the end a shape no one planned in advance and no one finds agreeable. Affected by many partial orders, they are accepted as 'my responsibility' by none.

In modern times the problem has tended to become ever more acute as the power of technological instruments of human action has grown and with it the consequences of their application. As each island of order gets more streamlined, rationalized, better supervised and more effective in its performances, the multitude of such perfected partial orders results in overall chaos. Distant outcomes of planned, purposeful, rationally designed and tightly monitored actions hit back as unpredictable, uncontrollable catastrophes. Think of the terrifying prospect of the greenhouse effect — that unanticipated summary product of numerous efforts to harness ever more energy in the name of more efficiency and increased production (each effort, singly, being ever better serviced scientifically and always well justified in terms of the task at hand); or think of the yet unimaginable consequences of the release into the environment of the new genetically engineered brands of living organisms, each one separately serving its specific purpose well, but among themselves bound to change the ecological balance in a way no one is able to predict. After all, any discharge of toxic substances into the atmosphere is merely a side-effect of a quite sensible, earnest search for the best, the most rational (the most productive and the least costly) solution to a specific task faced by this or that relatively autonomous organization. Each newly engineered virus or bacteria has a clearly defined purpose and a concrete useful job to perform − like, for instance, the destruction of a particularly noxious parasite threatening the profits of wheat or barley farmers. Manipulation of human genes, if it is ever allowed to be conducted, will be similarly aimed at such evidently desirable, immediate targets − like, say, the prevention of a particular deformity, or vulnerability to a specific disease. In all such cases, however, changes in the situation 'in focus' cannot but affect many other things left 'out of focus'; those unplanned and unanticipated influences may prove more damaging than the original, once vexing, but now successfully resolved problem. Artificial fertilizers used to enhance agricultural crops illustrate the issue very vividly. Nitrates fed into soil achieve their declared effect: they multiply the crops. Rainfall, however, washes away a good portion of the fertilizers into the underground supplies of water, thereby creating a new and no less sinister problem: that of cleaning up the contents of water reservoirs to make the water suitable for consumption. The new problem calls for the construction of processing plants, which will most certainly use new chemical reactions to undo the consequences of the old ones. Sooner or later it will be discovered that the new processes have polluting effects of their own: they provide a lush feeding ground for toxic algae, which now fill the water reservoirs.

Thus the struggle against chaos will go on with no end in sight. To an increasing extent, however, the chaos that waits to be contained and conquered will be a product of purposeful, order-constructing human activity, as the problem-solving leads to the creation of new problems and every new problem cannot be handled in the same old fashion: by appointing a team charged with the task of finding the shortest, the cheapest, the 'most reasonable' way of disposing of the current trouble. The more other factors are left out of account in the process, the shorter, cheaper and thus more rational will be the recommendation they provide.

We can sum up what we have found out so far in the following way: the struggle to replace chaos with order, to make the part of the world in our immediate vicinity rule-abiding, predictable and controllable, is bound to remain inconclusive, because this struggle is itself the most important obstacle to its own success: most of the disorderly (rule-violating, unpredictable and uncontrolled) phenomena result precisely from the narrowly focused, targeted, task-oriented, single-problem-solving actions. Each new attempt to make a part of the human world, or a specific area of human activity, orderly creates new problems even if it removes the old ones. Each such attempt brings forth new types of ambivalence, and thus makes further attempts necessary — with similar results.

To put this in a different way: the very success of the modern search for artificial order is the cause of its deepest, most worrying ailments. Splitting the unmanageable totality of the human condition into a multitude of small, immediate tasks, which because of being small and confined in time can be fully scanned, monitored and managed, has rendered human action more efficient than ever before. The more precise, limited, clearly defined is the task at hand, the better it may be performed. Indeed, the specifically modern way of doing things is strikingly superior to any other — as long as it is measured in terms of value for money (that is, in terms of direct effects obtained for given costs). This is precisely what is meant when the modern way of acting is described as *rational*: dictated by instrumental reason, which measures the actual results against the intended end and calculates the expenditure of resources and labour. The catch, however, is that not all costs are included in the calculation — only those that are born by the actors themselves; and not all results are monitored — only those that are relevant to the set task as defined by or for the actors. If, on the other hand, all losses and gains were taken into account (if such an extraordinarily ambitious enterprise were feasible in the first place), the superiority of the modern way of doing things would look less certain. It might well transpire that the ultimate outcome of the multitude of partial and separate rational actions is more, not less, overall *irrationality*. And that the most spectacular achievements in problem-solving do not detract but add to the sum total of problems requiring solutions. This is, perhaps, the most irksome yet inescapable inner contradiction of that search for order and struggle against ambivalence which has been the most conspicuous mark of modern society all along.

We are all trained to think of our lives as a collection of tasks to be performed and problems to be solved. We are used to thinking that once a problem has been spotted, the task is to define it precisely, in a way which shows clearly how to deal with it (our first reaction to feeling blue, down or depressed is to ask, 'What is my problem?' — and to seek expert advice on how to handle it). We assume that once this has been done, doing away with the irritating problem is just a matter of finding the right resources and applying oneself diligently to the task. If nothing happens and the problem does not go away, we blame ourselves for ignorance, neglect, laziness or ineptitude (if the low spirits continue, we explain it either by our own lack of resolve in fighting the blues, or by wrongly defining their cause — the 'problem' to be handled). No amount of disappointment and frustration, however, is likely to undermine our belief that each situation, however complex, may be disassembled into a finite set of problems, and that any of those problems can be effectively dealt with (made innocuous or eliminated), given the proper knowledge, skill and effort. In brief, we believe that the business of life may be split up into single problems, for every problem there is a solution, and for every solution there is, or should be found, a specific tool and method.

This is the belief responsible both for the spectacular achievements of modern times and for the mounting worries of present-day society, which is now beginning to count the total cost of scientific and technological progress as it finds itself confronted with the dangers and frustrations these achievements could not but bring in their wake. As we shall see shortly, this innate ambiguity of the modern condition finds its exact replica in the way we all plan and live our lives.

Chapter Eleven

Going About the Business of Life

Like you (I hope), I am quite a resourceful and skilful person. I can do quite a lot about my home. For instance, I can repair an electric switch, connect a plug or a socket. I even keep a supply of screwdrivers, fuses, wires of various diameters for this purpose. It so happens that I do not find the right thing in the box, though; I need to put my table lamp in a different corner of the room, and so I need an extension cable, but there is no wire of sufficient length. But I know where to get it; there are special shops which keep in stock all the materials an electrician may need. There are also do-it-yourself shops that keep everything one may need to do the jobs about the house. Once I went to one of these shops; I found the nails I needed to fasten the cable to the floor, but while looking for the nails I noticed quite a few other things I had not seen before: tools, implements, gadgets. Each one could, if properly used, add something to the way I lived. An ingenious graduated switch, for example, would allow me to modify the intensity of the lighting. Another electronic switch would switch the light on and off on its own at sunset or sunrise, or would do it at the times I programmed in advance. I had never used these gadgets before, but they struck me as a good idea. I read with interest the booklets which explained their uses and described exactly how to make them work. I bought them, fixed them in my house. They have proved more difficult to repair, though, than the old switches. When they go wrong, the screwdriver is not much help. They are sealed once and for all, and not meant to be opened by a non-specialist tinkerer like me. I have to buy another gadget and replace the old one. Some of the gadgets come with spare parts, so that I can replace just one element without throwing away the whole thing.

All this to avail myself of the many uses to which electricity may be put. I use electricity to avoid sitting in the dark at night, of course. But there are many other uses as well, and over the years they have grown in number considerably. I can still remember, for example, washing my shirts in the tub. I now put them in an electric washing machine. Several years ago I purchased an automatic washing machine; since then, I have bought a special powder meant for such machines (I do not remember such a powder being available before the machines became automatic). Last year I stopped washing dishes by hand in the kitchen sink. I have an electric dishwasher instead, and a bottle of special liquid made especially for using in dishwashers. A few days ago something went wrong with my dishwasher. I found myself in quite a quandary. Washing dishes after a small party — something I did in the past many times — seemed to me an impossible chore ... There was greater trouble still when my electric razor went bust. I had really forgotten how to shave without it. I went unshaved for two whole days; just as well I found a repair shop that stored all the necessary spare parts for razors of that make.

And, of course, there was that memorable national strike, when power cuts were imposed for a few hours at a stretch. This was truly a nightmare. My radio went silent, the television blank. I did not know how to fill my evenings. Books? I found my eyes were not fit for reading in candlelight. And then, with the power cuts at their most severe, telephones went dead as well. Suddenly my friends and business associates seemed infinitely remote and unreachable. My world, virtually, fell apart ... I remember the awful feeling of being left alone in the world, and the simple things I used to do day by day without a second thought suddenly turning into formidable tasks I had no idea how to cope with.

Now that I've spelled it all out, I am beginning to think again about what I said at the start: about being a resourceful and skilful person, about being able to do all sorts of things I need in my daily life. The matters do not seem as simple now as they did. My skills, which I thought made me such a smart, self-reliant person, do not make me independent at all. If anything, they make me a hostage: of shops, of electricity plants and boards, of countless inventions made by many experts and designers, of gadgets they produce, of recipes and instructions they compose. I cannot live my life without them.

Looking back, I can see that my dependence on them has grown over the years. A long time ago I used an ordinary razor to shave myself. I could not make the razor, of course, but once I had got one (it was my father, as a matter of fact, who gave me my first razor — one of the two he used daily for most of his life), I could easily sharpen it up and keep it in shape, constantly ready for service. Then safety razors became the rage and suddenly my old reliable tool seemed clumsy, not at all as convenient to use as I'd been accustomed to think, and even somewhat undignified; as if using it made me an old-fashioned, backward person. Well, safety razors became blunt after use and could not be sharpened — not by me, at any rate. So I had to remember to buy new ones all the time. In the shops I found many brands of safety razors, and I had to exercise my wits to choose the best one. I had, I felt, a growing freedom of choice; and yet what I could not do was not buy any of the brands on display. I had to go on shaving every day, after all. Later on, electric shavers came, and the old story repeated itself. Almost overnight the safety razors lost much of their glamour; it seemed they could not really offer much, compared with the smart new gadget. And I found myself asked again and again what make of electric shaver I had bought; I had not got one yet? Why? Did I indeed intend to stick to those obsolete things? In the end, I succumbed and bought one. Now I cannot shave without access to the mains. And I can neither repair my shaver nor restore its shaving power if something goes wrong. I now need an expert mechanic to help me out of trouble.

With each step, I had to acquire new skills, and I successfully acquired them. I can now pride myself, so to speak, in being an artful operator of the most up-to-date technology. And yet with each step I needed a more complex 'technological object' with which to apply my skills. Less and less could I understand how it worked. Less and less did I know what was inside. Less and less could I force it to work properly if something went wrong. To do the same things I had done before I needed ever more sophisticated tools;

they stood now between my intention and its fulfilment. I could not now act without such tools. I forgot how to do things without them. My new skills, focused on new tools, chased away my old abilities. Together with the simpler implements of yore, off went the old skills. As far as I can remember, the way of doing things which I could practise once but now forgot required more training, experience, attention and care than the switching on and off of the button of the electric shaver does. It seems that the difficult part has been taken over by the tools. It is as if part of my past skills has moved into the tools I use and been 'locked in' there; and this is, perhaps, why am I so firmly dependent on them.

In the now distant times of my youth shaving was something everyone did routinely. It did require learning (just to avoid wounding oneself), but it hardly occurred to anybody that this was a special skill requiring a specialist knowledge. Everything required for shaving was everybody's skill; it was because of such a universal distribution of shaving skills that there was no obvious room for shaving experts and shaving technology. It has all changed now. The process of shaving has been subjected to careful scientific study. It was first split into its elementary parts and each one was examined in detail: sensitivity of various kinds of skin, the angle under which hair grows on different sections of the face, the relation between the way the blade may move and the speed with which the hair is cut, and so on. Every analysed part was then represented as a problem with its own intrinsic requirements which had to be met; each problem therefore required a solution. Then various solutions were designed, experimented with, compared; in the end one solution was selected from many, considered the best (because the most efficient, or because the most attractive and hence potentially most saleable), and then assembled together with the solutions to the remaining problems into the final gadget. Dozens of specialists, each representing a highly specific field of expert knowledge, participated in the ultimate product; they worked in research teams concerned solely with one issue — shaving — and therefore capable of examining it in a depth not attainable for ordinary people like you and me who just want their faces neat and clean when we go about our daily business.

And it has been like this with everything else: sweeping the floor, mowing the lawn, cutting the hedge, cooking a meal or washing the dishes. In all these functions expertise, locked in technological implements and gadgets, took over, polished and sharpened the skills once in everyone's possession. We now need that expertise and that technology to do the job. We also need new skills to replace the old, obsolete and forgotten ones: this time we need the skills of finding and operating the right technological instruments.

Not all the technology we use and cannot live without simply took over a spot already prepared by jobs we used to do before it was invented and made available. There are many things, quite central to our lives, which we would never do without the technology that makes them possible. Think of radios, music centres, TV sets, personal computers. Their introduction opened new possibilities which previously did not exist at all. As spending our evenings watching sitcoms or drama serials was not a feasible idea, we did not seem to have a need for it; now we feel deprived and upset if the TV set goes bust. We seem to have developed a *need* for it. Neither did we have a need for computer games before having a computer at home became a possibility. Nor a need of music as a constant background noise to everything before the arrival of the hi-fi and personal stereo. In such cases, technology seems to have created its own need. A new type of need, as a matter of fact. These new technological objects did not replace old ways of doing things; they induced us to do things we never did before, and made us feel unhappy if we did not do them.

It is not true, therefore, that expertise and technology come as a response to the need we have. Often the people who offer us their expertise and products must at first bend over backwards to convince us that we indeed have a need for the things they offer. Even in cases, however, where new products are addressed to well-established, unquestionable needs (like the shavers we discussed before), we could go on satisfying them in the way we had grown used to, if we were not tempted to change it by the allurements of the new gadget. Thus even in such cases new technology is not simply a response to a need. In no way has its appearance been determined by popular demand. It is rather the demand that has been determined by the availability of new technology. Whether the need did or did not exist before, the *demand* for new products comes *after* their introduction.

So what causes ever new, deeper, more focused, more specialized expertise and ever more sophisticated technological implements to appear? The probable answer is that the development of expertise and technology is a self-propelling, self-reinforcing process which does not need any extra causes. Given a team of experts supplied with research facilities and equipment, we can be pretty sure that they will come up with new products and propositions, guided simply by the logic of activity in an organization — the need to excel, to prove one's superiority over competitors, or just the all-too-human interest and excitement in one's job. Products usually become scientifically or technologically feasible before their uses have been ascertained: we have this technology, how can we use it? And since we have it, wouldn't it be unforgivable not to use it? Solutions come before problems; solutions seek the problems they might be able to solve. To put it in a different way: more often than not an aspect of life is not perceived as a *problem*, as something that cries for a solution, until expert advice or technological objects appear claiming to be the *solution*. Only then comes the task of persuading the prospective users that the object in question indeed has its use value. And they must be convinced of that, otherwise they would not consider the object worth spending money on. They would not decide to buy it.

You and I are *consumers* of expertise, be it in the form of verbal instruction or locked inside the technological implement we use. In fact, everyone is, including the experts themselves in each of the countless aspects of their lives outside the narrow field of their own specialism. Much of the expertise enters our lives uninvited, without asking our permission. Think, for instance, of the increasingly sophisticated technology used by the police to spot drivers exceeding the speed limit, or to disperse riots, or to identify the person they are chasing, or to infiltrate a group whose activity is seen as undesirable. Or think of the use various state and private institutions make of information technology; the mind-boggling volume of data they may now collect about you and store just in case they need to use it — not necessarily in your favour — at some undefined future date. These and similar uses of expertise and technology quite clearly constrain our freedom; they make certain choices less profitable or downright impossible. They increase the hold of whoever has access to them over our freedom of movement. In extreme cases, they may even make us helpless victims of someone else's arbitrary decisions. Yet much technology is meant for our personal use; it promises to enhance, not to limit our range of choices, to make us more free, more in control of our lives. In such cases, while embracing new technology we also become dependent on it, this is much less straightforward. By and large, we welcome new technological offers as liberating or making life richer; they allow us to do old things faster and with less fatigue, or enable us to do things we never did before. We welcome them because we believe they can really do it — and so we need to be persuaded that the belief is well placed and well founded.

We need to be persuaded — told in such a way as to trust what we hear — because on our own we have no way of knowing. I do not know, and certainly not in advance, whether the new technological offer can indeed satisfy my need. (Is this really the kind of drink that, if I serve it, will make the party I give a success? Is this indeed the scent that will make beautiful young men or women notice me — just me — in the street crowd? Is this indeed the washing powder that will make the white really white and everything truly spotless, so that everyone will notice? And will it make the people I'd particularly want to notice what I am doing for them grateful and friendly?) Sometimes I do not even know that I have the need the technological invention on offer is meant to satisfy (I do not know that washing myself with soap will not remove the 'deep dirt' I cannot see in my skin unless I rub my skin with a special liquid; I do not know that awful and nauseating bugs thrive in my carpet, which my vacuum cleaner can do little about, so that I need a special anti-carpet-bug powder in addition; I do not know that an off-putting, unappetizing substance will accumulate on my teeth if I do not wash my mouth with the contents of that bottle before brushing them; I do not know that my faithful old camera is laughably primitive and inept, until I am shown a new fully automatic one that will do the focusing for me, select the exposure time, move the film — and will thus, I am told, also make a better photographer out of me).

Once I have been told all those things, perhaps I'll wish to obtain the products I have been told about to satisfy the needs I have been told I possess which urgently demand satisfaction. Once it has dawned on me that I truly have those needs, doing nothing about them seems wrong. If I go on doing nothing — now that I know — I won't be able to excuse myself by pointing to my ignorance. From now on, doing nothing will be evidence of negligence, lack of concern, pig-headedness or ineptitude; in each case, it will somehow detract from my value and deprive me of the right to other people's and my own respect. I'll feel that I am not caring, or am unable to provide for my family, or people I love, or my body that has been entrusted to my wardenship; I'll feel that I neglect, or cannot fulfil, my duty. I'll feel guilty, or ashamed, or deprived. Suddenly, what I had and did before and the way I was doing it does not seem satisfying any more; most certainly, it does not seem worth boasting about, feeling proud of. To restore my own and other people's respect, I truly must obtain the skilful and powerful objects which will allow me to do things properly and give me the power to do them.

Very often, obtaining means purchasing. Those wonderful, skilful and powerful things come mostly as *commodities*; that is, they are marketed — produced for sale, sold, paid for with money. Someone wants to sell them to me to get that money; to make profit. But to achieve this purpose, he or she first has to convince me that parting with my money for the sake of possessing the commodity they offer is worth my while: that the commodity indeed has the *use value* which justifies its *exchange value*, the price I am going to pay for it (that it offers, as we often hear, good value for money). People who want to sell their products (make their products into saleable commodities) must make room for them in the already overcrowded market. They must make the old products seem out of date, obsolete, inferior (who dares to use a typewriter when there are word-processors around?). And, having thus prepared the ground, they must do the job of persuading: they must beef up my desire for the use their products promise, and thus my readiness to sacrifice (to work harder in order to earn, save and spend my money) in the name of possessing them. They do it, most conspicuously, with the help of *advertising* (for example, TV commercials). Advertising must achieve two effects: first, it must point out to me that my own understanding of my needs and the skills that satisfy them is inadequate, that I am not a good judge of what I truly need and what I should really do; secondly, that there are reliable ways to make up for my ignorance or poor judgement — by listening to those who know better. In most commercials, people who do the things the old way are ridiculed as being old-fashioned or ignoramuses; and they are confronted with a trustworthy authority which testifies to their ignorance while showing the way out of it. Such an authority is embodied in the image of a scientist, or a high-class expert in car technology, banking or insurance, or an avuncular, well-wishing character, or a caring and experienced mother, or an acknowledged, seasoned master of the kind of job the product is meant to serve, or just a famous person people watch with awe while knowing that millions of other people like them watch at the same time. The last example shows that the numbers themselves may carry the requisite authority (we believe, after all, that the 'great numbers of people cannot be wrong', and that 'one cannot fool all the people all the time'); some commercials inform us simply that most people do it, that more and more people switch to it, that most cats prefer it.

Each advertising copy and commercial is meant to encourage us and prompt us to buy a specific product. Between them, however, they promote our interest in commodities, in the market place (department stores, shopping malls) where commodities may be found, and in possessing them. A single commercial message would hardly have an effect on our conduct if general interest were not already well entrenched and shopping turned into a daily fact of life. In other words, the 'persuading efforts' of advertising agencies appeal to the already established **consumer attitude** — and in turn reinforce it.

What does it mean to have and to display a consumer attitude? It means, first, perceiving life as a series of problems, which can be specified, more or less clearly defined, singled out and dealt with. It means, secondly, believing that dealing with such problems, solving them, is one's duty, which one cannot neglect without incurring guilt or shame. It means, thirdly, trusting that for every problem, already known or such as may still arise in the future, there is a solution — a special object, or recipe, prepared by the specialists, by people with superior know-how, and one's task is to find it. It means, fourthly, assuming that such objects or recipes are essentially available; they may be obtained in exchange for money, and shopping is the way of obtaining them. It means, fifthly, translating the task of learning the art of living as the effort to acquire the skill of finding such objects and recipes, and gaining the power to possess them once found: shopping skills and purchasing power (it is the cunning needed to locate the best washing powder and the best washing machine, and your ability to afford them, that lead to the 'solution of the laundry problem', not the nimbleness of hands and the love of hard work your grandmother might have been proud of).

Bit by bit, problem by problem, the consumer attitude refers the whole of life to the market; it orients every desire and each effort in the search for a tool or an expertise one can buy. It dissolves the problem of control over the wider setting of life (something most people will never achieve) in the multitude of small purchasing acts that are — at least in principle — within your reach. It *privatizes*, so to speak, issues so that they are not perceived as *public*; it *individualizes* tasks so that they are not seen as *social*. It now becomes my duty (and, as I am encouraged to hope, also a task I can perform) to improve myself and my life, to culture and refine, to overcome my own shortcomings and the other vexing drawbacks to the way I live. Thus the unbearable din of the heavy traffic is translated into the urge to instal double glazing. Polluted urban air is dealt with by the purchase of eye drops. The oppressed condition of an over-worked wife and mother is coped with the help of a packet of painkillers and fast-acting headache pills. The dilapidation of the public transport facilities is responded to by purchasing a car and thereby adding to the noise, the air pollution and the painful effects of the nervous tension — as well as to the further disintegration of public transport . . .

Indeed, it is the consumer attitude which makes my life into my *individual* affair; and it is the consumer activity which makes me into the individual (people almost always create, produce, in the company of other people; most things they consume, however, they consume singly, for personal pleasure). It seems in the end as if I were made up of the many things I buy and own: tell me what you buy, in what shops you buy it, and I'll tell you who you are. It seems that with the help of carefully selected purchases I can make of myself anything I may wish, anything I believe it is worth becoming. Just as dealing with my problems is my duty and my responsibility, so the shaping of my personal **identity**, my self-assertion, making myself into a concrete someone, is my task and mine alone: it will always be a testimony to my intentions, diligence and persistence, and I'll be held to answer for whatever comes out of it in the end.

The various models for what I can make of myself are all on the market: there are plenty to choose from those that are the rage today, still more to arrive tomorrow and the day after tomorrow. The models come complete with all the bits and pieces one needs to assemble them, and with point-by-point instructions on how to put them together: genuine DIY 'identitykits'. Even when the admen offer us single, specific products ostensibly addressed to a single, specific need, they are on the whole shown to us against a clearly portrayed background of the life-style to which they (so it is suggested) naturally belong. Just compare the dress and the language and the pastimes and even the physical shape of the people in the ads meant to encourage us to drink a given brand of beer with the equivalent features of those who appear in the commercials selling an exquisite brand of perfume, or small cars, or prestigious cars, or cat food, or dog food. You will surely find out that each product comes with an 'address'. What is being sold is not just the direct use value of the product itself, but its symbolic significance as a building block of a particular cohesive life-style — as its indispensable ingredient.

The models vary in popularity over time: they come in and out of **fashion**. To keep the wheel of production and consumption rotating, the buying zeal cannot ever be allowed to relent. Were we to keep the products as long as they served their ostensible uses, the market activity would soon grind to a halt. The phenomenon of fashion prevents this from happening. Things are discarded and replaced not because they have lost their usefulness, but because they went out of fashion; that is, they are easily recognizable, from their looks, as goods chosen and obtained by the consumers of *yesterday*, and thus their presence casts suspicion on the current status of their owner as a fully-fledged, respectable consumer of today. To retain this status, one must keep up with the changing offers of the market. To obtain them means to reconfirm one's social capacity; but only until many other consumers do the same, as the fashionable items that originally bestowed distinction thus become 'common' or 'vulgar' and are ready to go out of fashion, to be eagerly replaced by something else.

The models vary also in the degree of popularity they enjoy in this or that social circle and the amount of respect that circle is likely to bestow upon their practitioners. They are, therefore, *differently* attractive. By selecting a given model, purchasing all its necessary accoutrements and diligently practising it, I make myself into a member of a group which approves of such a model and adopts it as its trade mark, a visible sign of its membership. There is no more, or almost no more, to my making myself a member of that group than sporting such signs: wearing the group-specific dress, buying the group-specific records and listening to the group-specific music, watching and discussing the group-specific TV programmes and films, embellishing the walls of my room with group-specific adornments, spending my evenings in the group-specific way and at group-specific places and so on. I may 'join the tribe' by buying and displaying the tribe-specific paraphernalia.

That means that the 'tribes' I join in search of my identity are very unlike the tribes the explorers have found in distant lands (as a matter of fact, they are unlike any groups that are constituted by a clearly defined membership, by the care to admit or expel members, to control their conduct and keep it in line with the group standards, to press the members into conformity). What makes the 'tribes' one joins by purchasing their symbols superficially similar to the real tribes is that both set themselves apart from other groups and make a lot of fuss about underlining their separate identity and avoiding confusion; both cede their own identity to their members − define them by proxy. But here the similarity ends and a decisive difference begins: the 'tribes' (let us call them henceforth **neo-tribes** to prevent misunderstanding) could not care less about who proclaim themselves members. They have no councils of elders or boards or admission committees to decide who has the right to be in and who ought to be kept out. They employ no gatekeepers and no border guards. They have no institution of authority, no supreme court which may pronounce on the correctness of members' behaviour. They, in short, do not control the members and do not undertake to monitor the degree of their conformity. Thus, as far as the neo-tribes are concerned, one can join and leave them at will. It seems that one can wander freely from one neo-tribe to another (that is, put on and take off the identity the tribe is all about) simply by changing one's dress, refurnishing one's flat and spending one's free time at different places. Neo-tribes keep their doors (if there are doors) wide open.

Or so it seems. If the neo-tribes themselves do not care to guard their entry, there is someone else who does: *the market*. Neo-tribes are in essence *life-styles*, and life-styles, as we have seen, boil down almost entirely to **styles of consumption**. Access to consumption — any consumption of any style — leads through the market, through the act of purchasing the marketed commodities. There are very few things one can consume without first buying them — and such consumer goods as come free, such goods as have not been obtained as commodities, are not in most cases deployed as the building blocks of recognizable life-styles. If some of them do contribute to a specific life-style, such a style is normally looked down on, deprived of glamour and prestige, disdained, considered unattractive, even degrading for the people who practise it (as is the lot of those who through lack of means are confined in their freedom of choice, who cannot be choosy, who are doomed to limit their consumption to what they do not pay for, who therefore do not act as consumers should and are excluded from the market place: those people whose condition is described as that of **poverty**. In a society of consumers, poverty means the limitation or absence of consumer choice).

The apparent availability of a wide and growing range of neo-tribes, each sporting a different life-style, has a powerful yet ambiguous effect on our lives. On the one hand, we experience it as the dismantling of all limitations to our freedom. We are now free to move from one personal quality to another, choose what we want to be and what we want to make of ourselves. No force seems to hold us back, no dream seems to be improper, at odds with 'our station'.

This feels, and rightly so, like liberation: an exhilarating experience of not being tied down by any constraints, of everything being in principle within our reach or at least the realm of our dreams, of no condition being final and irrevocable. As, however, each point of our arrival, lasting or temporary, seems fully a matter of our choice and the result of the way in which we have exercised our freedom in the past, it is us and us alone who can be blamed for it (or praised, depending on the degree of our satisfaction). We are all 'self-made persons', and repeatedly we are reminded of it: there is no justification for cutting our ambitions short. Every life-style of however remote a neo-tribe is a challenge. If we find it attractive, if it is more vaunted than ours, proclaimed more enjoyable or respectable than our own, we feel somewhat *deprived*. We feel seduced by it, drawn to it, prompted to do our best in order to join it. Our present life-style loses much of its allurement. It no longer brings us the satisfaction it once did. There is therefore no stop to our efforts. At no point can we say, 'I have arrived, I have done it, now I can relax and take it easy.' Just when I was ready to celebrate the fruits of a long-term effort, a new attraction appears on the horizon, and I do not feel like celebrating anymore. One result of my freedom (that is, freedom of consumer choice, freedom to make myself into someone else through adopting or rejecting different styles of consumption) is that I seem to be condemned to remain for ever in the state of deprivation. The sheer availability of ever new temptations and their apparent accessibility take the joy off any achievement. When the sky is the limit, no earthly destination seems pleasant enough to satisfy us. Publicly flaunted life-styles are not only numerous and varied: they are also often represented as differing in value, in the distinction that they bestow on their practitioners. We are all cultivating ourselves, but there is more and less refined culture − high-brow, middle-brow, low-brow. When we settle for less than the best, we are to believe from then on that our not very prestigious social standing is a natural effect of a half-hearted self-cultivating diligence.

And the story does not end here. What makes the other people's life-styles − even the most refined ones − so temptingly close and within reach is that they are not practised in secrecy. On the contrary, they appear so seductively open and inviting; indeed, the neo-tribes do not live within fortresses guarded by thick walls, moats and turrets, and each determined walker may reach them and enter. And yet, as we saw a moment ago, entry is not as free as it seems; what makes this particular unfreedom so vicious and upsetting is that the real gatekeepers are invisible. The real gatekeepers — the market forces — do not wear uniforms, and they deny all responsibility for the final success or failure of the escapade (unlike state regulation of needs and their satisfaction, which cannot but stay visible and is thus vulnerable to public protest and an easy target for collective efforts of reform). In the case of defeat the hapless walkers must believe that it was their own fault, pure and simple. They risk losing faith in themselves, in the strength of their character, intelligence, talents, motivation, stamina. There is something wrong with me, they will conclude, and perhaps seek the services of an expert, of a specialist in psychological analysis, to repair their faulty personality. The expert will confirm their suspicions: yes, there was nothing wrong with the conditions, it was rather some inner flaw, something hidden in the broken selves of the defeated, that prevented them from availing themselves of the opportunities which were undoubtedly there all along. The expert will help to reproject frustration upon the frustrated person. The anger born of frustration will not then spill over and be directed at the outside world. The invisible gatekeepers barring the intended way will remain invisible and more secure than ever. And the dream-states they so alluringly paint will not be discredited either. They will retain their attraction and seductive power: they are worth your effort, only you for one reason of another cannot force yourself to make such an effort. The unsuccessful are thus also denied the tempting consolation of decrying in retrospect the value of the life-styles they sought to adopt in vain (the proverbial 'sour grapes' consolation: I did not get them, but they were not worth getting in the first place, so I did not lose much anyway. It has been noted that frequently the failure to reach the goals advertised as superior and richly satisfying results in a feeling of resentment, or rancour and spite, aimed against the goals themselves, but tending to spread over the people who boast of having attained them).

However plausible it seems under the circumstances, more often than not the failure to acquire a particularly coveted life-style is not the fault of the people who attempted it. Even the most elaborate life-styles must be represented as universally available if they are to be successfully marketed: their alleged accessibility is the necessary condition of their seductiveness. They inspire the shopping motivation and interest of the consumers because the prospective buyers believe that the models they seek can be *obtained* in addition to being awed and *admired*, that the models are legitimate objects of practical action, and not merely of respectful contemplation. It is such a presentation (one that the market can ill afford to abandon) that suggests the **equality** of consumers, in their capacity as free choosers who themselves determine their social standing. In the light of such assumed equality, the failure to obtain goods which others enjoy feels offensive and offending.

But the failure is in fact unavoidable. The genuine accessibility of the alternative life-styles is determined by the prospective practitioners' ability to afford them; simply speaking, by the sum of money they are able to spend. The plain truth is that some people have more money than others, and thus more practical freedom of choice. In particular, those with the largest amount of money (the true entry ticket to the market and true passport to the wonders the market offers) can afford the most lauded, coveted and hence most prestigious and admired styles. As a matter of fact, what you have read just now is a tautology — a statement which *defines* the things it speaks about while pretending to *explain* them: the styles which can be obtained only by relatively few people with particularly large wealth are by the same token seen as the most distinguished and worthy of marvel. It is their rarity that is admired, their practical inaccessibility that makes them wonderful. Once acquired, they are therefore worn with pride, as distinctive marks of exclusive, exceptional social position. They are the signs of the 'best people'; they are the 'best life-styles' because they are practised by the 'best people'. Both the commodities and the people who use them (display being one of the main uses, perhaps *the* main use) derive the high esteem they enjoy precisely from this 'marriage' to each other.

All commodities have a price-tag attached to them. These tags select the pool of potential customers. They do not directly determine the decisions the consumers will eventually make; those remain free. But they draw the boundary between the realistic and feasible; the boundary which a given consumer cannot overstep. Behind the ostensible equality of chances the market promotes and advertises hides the practical **inequality** of consumers — that is, the sharply differentiated degrees of practical freedom of choice. This inequality is felt as an oppression and a stimulus at the same time. It generates the painful experience of deprivation, with all the morbid consequences for self-esteem which we have surveyed before. It also triggers off zealous efforts to enhance one's consumer capacity — efforts that secure an unabating demand for market offers.

Thus, its championship of equality notwithstanding, the market produces and reinstates inequality in a society made of consumers. The typically market-induced or market-serviced kind of inequality is kept alive and perpetually reproduced through price mechanism. The marketed life-styles bestow the sought-after distinction because their price-tags put them out of reach of the less well-off consumers; and this distinction-bestowing function adds to their attraction and in turn supports the high price attached to them. At the end of the day, it transpires that with all the alleged freedom of consumer choice the marketed life-styles are not distributed evenly or randomly; each tends to concentrate in a particular part of society and thus acquires the role of a sign of social standing. Life-styles tend to become, one may say, class-specific. The fact that they are assembled from items that are all available in shops does not make them a vehicle of equality, though it does turn them into a factor constantly sapping the acceptability of real inequality. The latter becomes less bearable, more difficult to endure for the relatively poor and deprived, than it was when possessions were overtly ascribed to the already occupied, often inherited and immutable, social rank.

It is against such an *ascribed* inequality that the market-prompted and sustained inequality of consumers truly militates. The market thrives on the inequality of income and wealth, but it does not recognize ranks. It devalues all vehicles of inequality but the price-tags. Goods must be accessible to everybody who can afford to pay their price. Life-styles — *all* life-styles — are up for grabs. The purchasing ability is the only entitlement the market would recognize.

It is for this reason that in a market-dominated consumer society the resistance to all other, ascribed inequality grows to unprecedented proportion. Exclusive clubs that do not accept members from certain races or ethnic groups, restaurants or hotels that bar access to customers because they have the 'wrong colour of skin', estate developers who won't sell property for a similar reason – all come under fierce attack. The overwhelming power of market-supported criteria of social differentiation seemingly invalidates all its competitors: there should be no goods that money cannot buy.

Very often the market-oriented and the race- or ethnicity-grounded deprivations overlap. The groups that are held in an inferior position by 'ascriptive' restrictions are usually also employed in poorly paid jobs, so that they cannot afford the life-styles destined for the 'better people'. In this case, the ascriptive character of the deprivation remains hidden. Visible inequalities are explained away as the results of the lesser talents, industry or acumen of the members of the deprived race or ethnic group; were it not for their innate faults, they would succeed like everyone else. To become like those whom they envy and wish to imitate would be within their reach if they wished and acted on their wishes.

This explanation is not possible, however, in the case of those members of the otherwise depressed category who succeed in market terms yet still find the gates to 'better styles of life' shut. Financially, they can afford the high fees of the club or the high charges of the hotel – and yet they are barred entry. The ascriptive character of their deprivation is thereby exposed; they learn that contrary to promise, money cannot buy everything and so there is more to human placement in society, to their well-being and dignity, than diligently earning money and spending it. This finding shatters their trust in the free market as a guarantee of human freedom. As far as we know, people may differ in their abilities to buy tickets, but no one can be refused a ticket if he or she can afford one. In a market society, ascriptive differentiation of opportunities is unjustifiable – and for this very reason unendurable. This is why a rebellion against discrimination on any but 'purchasing ability' grounds is led by the better-off, more successful members of the discriminated races, ethnic groups, religious denominations, linguistic communities (to a certain extent, the feminist struggle also draws its power from discriminations alien to the 'spirit', or at least the promise, of consumer society). The era of 'self-made persons', of the proliferation of life-style 'tribes', of differentiation through styles of consumption is also an era of resistance to racial, ethnic, religious and gender discrimination; an era of determined struggle for *human rights* — that is, for the removal of any restrictions except those which, in principle (according to the beliefs in our type of society), may be overcome by the effort of any human being as an individual.

Chapter Twelve

The Ways and Means of Sociology

Chapter by chapter, we have travelled together through the world of daily experience we share. Sociology was invited to accompany us as our guide: if our own daily concerns and problems marked the itinerary, sociology was offered the task of commenting on what we see and do. As on any guided tour, we hoped that our guide would make sure that we did not miss anything of importance and would bring to our attention things which if left to ourselves we would be liable to pass by unnoticed. We also expected the guide to explain to us things we knew only superficially — tell us stories about them we did not know. We hoped that at the end of our guided tour we would know more and understand things better than we did at the start; when we again go through our daily business of life after this trip, we should be better equipped to cope with the problems we face. Not that our attempts to solve them will necessarily be more successful; but at least we will know what the problems are and what their solution, if at all feasible, requires.

I think that sociology as we have come to know it during our tour acquitted itself reasonably well of the task we asked it to perform; but then, it would have disappointed us if we were expecting it to do more than provide us with a **commentary**, a series of explanatory footnotes to our daily experience. Commentary is exactly what sociology has to offer. Sociology is a refinement on that knowledge we possess and employ in our daily life — inasmuch as it brings into the open some finer distinctions and some not immediately evident connections which an unaided eye would fail to locate. Sociology charts more details on our 'world map'; it also extends the map beyond the horizon of our own daily experience, so that we can see how the territories we inhabit fit into the world we have had no chance to explore ourselves. The difference between what we know without sociology and what we know after we have heard its comments is not the difference between error and truth (though, let us admit, sociology may happen to correct our opinions here or there); it is, rather, the difference between believing that what we experience can be described and explained in one way and in one way only, and knowing that the possible — and plausible — interpretations are plentiful. Sociology, one may say, is not the end of our search for understanding, but an inducement to go on searching and an obstacle to that state of self-satisfaction in which curiosity wilts and the search grinds to a halt. It has been said that the best service sociology may offer is to 'prod sluggish imagination' — by showing apparently familiar things from unexpected angles and thus undermining all routine and self-confidence.

Generally however, two very different expectations are held regarding the services that sociology — as 'social science' (that is, as a body of knowledge which claims superiority over mere views and opinions and is believed to possess reliable, trustworthy, correct information about how things *truly* are) — can and should render.

One expectation puts sociology on a par with other kinds of expertise that promise to tell us what our problems are, what to do about them and how to get rid of them. Sociology is viewed as a sort of DIY briefing, or a textbook teaching the art of life: how to get what we want, how to jump over or by-pass anything that may stand in our way. What such an expectation boils down to is a hope that once we know how various elements of our situation depend on each other, we will be free to control that situation, to subordinate it to our purposes or at least force it to serve these purposes better. This is, after all, what **scientific knowledge** is all about. We hold it in such high esteem because we believe that the wisdom it supplies is of the kind that allows one to *predict* how things will turn out; and that the ability to predict the turn of events (and thus also the consequences of one's own action) will enable one to *act* freely and rationally — that is, to make such moves and only such moves as are guaranteed to bring the desired results.

Another expectation is closely related to the former one, but it throws open the assumptions underlying the instrumental usefulness idea — premises that the former expectation did not need to spell out. To be in control of the situation must mean, one way or another, luring, forcing or otherwise causing other people (who are always part of that situation) to behave in a way that helps us to get what we want. As a rule, control over the situation cannot but mean also control over other people (this is how the art of life is normally presented, after all — as the way 'to win friends and influence people'). In the second expectation this desire to control others comes to the fore. The services of sociology are enlisted in the hope that they will assist those efforts to create order and evict chaos which we found in a previous chapter to be a distinctive mark of our modern times. By exploring the inner springs of human actions, sociologists are expected to provide practically useful information about the way things ought to be arranged in order to elicit the kind of behaviour one would wish people to demonstrate; or, alternatively, to eliminate any conduct that the designed model of order makes unsuitable. So the factory owners may ask sociologists how to prevent strikes, commanders of armed forces occupying a foreign land may ask them how to fight the guerrillas, policemen may commission practical proposals on how to disperse crowds and keep potential rioters at bay, managers of trading companies may demand the best means to seduce prospective customers into buying their products, public relation officers may inquire how to make the politicians who hired them more popular and electable, the politicians themselves may seek advice on the methods of preserving law and order — that is, making their subjects obey the law, preferably willingly, but also when they do not like what they must obey.

What all such demands amount to is that sociologists should offer advice on how to reduce the freedom of some people so that their choice be confined and their conduct more predictable. A knowledge is wanted of how to transform the people in question from *subjects* of their own action into *objects* of other people's actions; how to implement in practice a sort of 'snooker ball' model of human action, in which what people do is wholly determined by pressures applied from outside. The more human action approximated such a 'snooker ball' movement, the more useful sociological services would be for the intended purpose. Even if people cannot stop being choosers and decision-makers, the external context of their actions should be so manipulated as to make it utterly improbable that the choices and decisions they make go against the wishes of the manipulators.

By and large, such expectations amount to the demand that sociology be *scientific*; that it shape its activity, and thus its products, after the pattern of established sciences which we all hold in high esteem because of their amply demonstrated practical usefulness – the tangible benefits it brings. Sociology ought to deliver recipes as exact, practically useful and effective as those offered by, say, physics or chemistry. From their inception those and similar sciences have been aimed at gaining a clearly defined kind of knowledge: such as may lead eventually to full mastery over the object of their study. That object, construed as 'nature', was denied its own will and purpose, so that it could without compunction be subordinated fully to the will and purpose of human beings wishing to exploit it for the better satisfaction of their own needs. The language of science used to describe its 'natural' objects was carefully purified of all terms referring to purpose or meaning; what remained after such a purge was an 'objective' language, a language construing its objects as far as they receive, not generate, action; as objects buffeted by external forces, invariably described as 'blind', that is, not aimed at any specific end and devoid of any intention. So described, the natural world was conceived as a 'free for all': a virgin territory waiting to be tilled and transformed into a purposefully designed plot better suited to human habitation. The objectivity of science expressed itself in reporting its findings in an unemotional, technical language that emphasized the unbridgeable gap between human bearers of ends and nature, destined to be shaped and moulded in accordance with such ends. The declared purpose of science was to aid the 'mastery of human kind over nature'.

The world was explored with this purpose in mind. Nature was to be studied so that human craftsmen would know how to give it the shape they desired (think, for instance, of sculptors and the slabs of marble they wish to transform into the likeness of a human figure. To implement their purpose, they must first know the inner qualities of the stone. There are only certain directions in which one can apply force to cut and chip the marble without breaking it. In order to impose on the marble the form they carry in their heads — to subordinate the stone to their designs — the sculptors must learn how to recognize such directions. The knowledge they seek would subordinate the dead stone to their will and allow them to reshape it in accordance with their ideas of harmony and beauty). This is how scientific knowledge was constructed: to *explain* the object of science was to acquire the ability to *predict* what would happen if this or that took place; with such an ability to predict, one would be *able to act* — that is, to impress upon a fragment of now conquered and docile reality the design that will better serve the selected purpose. Reality was seen as, first and foremost, a resistance to human purposeful acitivity. The aim of science was to find out how that resistance could be broken. The resulting conquest of nature would mean the emancipation of humanity from natural constraints; the enhancement, so to speak, of our collective freedom.

All knowledge worth its salt was exhorted and expected to match this model of science. Any kind of knowledge aspiring to public recognition, a place in the academic world, a share in public resources had to prove that it was like the natural sciences, that it could deliver a similarly useful, practical instruction which would permit us to make the world better suited to human purposes. The pressure to conform to the standard established by the natural sciences was enormous and virtually impossible to resist. Even if the role of the architects or draughtsmen of the social order did not cross their minds, even if the only thing they wanted was to comprehend the human condition more fully, the founding fathers of sociology could not but tacitly or overtly accept the dominant model of science as the prototype of 'good knowledge' and of the pattern of all comprehension. They had therefore to demonstrate that one could devise for the study of human life and activity methods as precise and objective as those which had been deployed by the sciences of nature; and that an equally exact and objective knowledge may result. They had to prove that sociology could elevate itself to the status of science and hence be admitted to the academic family on an equal footing with its older and trend-setting members.

This need goes a long way towards explaining the shape sociological discourse acquired once it settled down in the company of other sciences in the world of academic teaching and research. The effort to make sociology 'scientific' dominated the discourse; the task occupied the pride of place among the concerns of the participants. There were three strategies with which the budding academic sociology could respond to the challenge. All three were tried, and all three subsequently converged in the shape the established sociology assumed.

The first strategy is best illustrated by the teachings of the founder of academic sociology in France, **Emile Durkheim**. Durkheim took for granted that there was a model of science, shared by all areas of knowledge aspiring to scientific status. That model was characterized first and foremost by its *objectivity*, that is, by its treating the object of study as strictly separate from the studying subject, as a thing 'out there', which can be subjected to the gaze of the researcher, observed and described in strictly neutral and detached language. As all science behaves in the same way, scientific disciplines differ from each other only by directing the same kind of objective scrutiny to separate areas of reality; the world, so to speak, is divided into plots, each researched by a scientific discipline of its own. Researchers are all the same, they all command the same kind of technical skills and engage in an activity subjected to the same rules and code of behaviour. And the reality they study is the same for them all, always composed of things 'out there' waiting to be observed, described and explained. What sets scientific disciplines apart from each other is solely the division of the territory of investigation. Various branches of science divide the world between themselves, each one taking care of its own fragment, its own 'collection of things'.

If this is what sciences do, then for sociology to find a place in science — to become a science — it must find a section of the world which the extant scientific disciplines have not yet appropriated. Like a seafaring explorer, sociology should discover a continent over which no one has yet claimed sovereignty, so that it can establish its own uncontested domain of scientific competence and authority. The put it simply, sociology as a science and as a separate, sovereign, scientific discipline can only be legitimized if a hitherto neglected 'collection of things' is found that is still waiting to be subjected to the scientific gaze.

Durkheim suggested that specifically *social* facts — collective phenomena that do not belong to any person in particular (like shared beliefs and patterns of behaviour) — may be treated as such *things* and studied in an objective, detached fashion as other things are. Indeed, such phenomena appear to individuals like you and me much the same as the rest of the reality 'out there': they are tough and stubborn and independent of our will to recognize them as we cannot wish them away. They are there whether we know of them or not, much like a table or chair that occupies a certain place in my room whether or not I look at it or think of it. Moreover, I may ignore their presence only at my own peril. If I behave as if they did not exist, I would be severely punished (if I ignore the *natural* law of gravity and leave the room through the window rather than through the door, I'll suffer punishment — break a leg or an arm. If I ignore a *social* norm — the law and moral injunction against thieving — I'll also suffer punishment; I'll be put in jail or ostracized by my fellows). In fact, I learn of the presence of a social norm the hard way: when I breach it and hence inadvertently 'trigger' the punitive sanctions against me.

We can say, therefore, that social phenomena, though they obviously would not exist without human beings, do not reside *inside* human beings as individuals, but *outside* them. Together with nature and its inviolable laws, they constitute a vital part of the objective environment of every human being, of the outer conditions of any human action and human life as a whole. There would be no point in learning about those social phenomena by asking people subjected to their force (one cannot really study the law of gravity by collecting the opinions of people who must walk instead of flying). The information one may obtain by asking people would anyway be hazy, partial and misleading: the people to whom we address our questions have little to tell us, as they did not invent or create the phenomena under study, they found them already in place and ready made, and more often than not confronted them (that is, were made aware of their presence) but briefly and fragmentarily. So one must study social facts directly, objectively, 'from outside', by systematic observation; precisely as one studies the rest of the things 'out there'.

In one important respect, Durkheim agreed, social facts differ from the facts of nature. The connection between violating the law of nature and the damage that follows it is automatic: it has not been introduced by human design (or, for that matter, by anyone's design). The connection between violating the norm of society and the sufferings of norm-breakers is, on the contrary, 'human-made'. Certain conduct is punished because society condemns it and not because the conduct itself causes harm to its perpetrator (thus, stealing does no harm to the thief and may even be beneficial to him; if the thief suffers in its consequence, it is only because social sentiments militate against thieving). This difference, however, does not detract from the 'thing-like' character of social norms or from the feasibility of their objective study. The opposite is the case: it further adds to the norms' 'thing-like' nature, as they appear to be the real material and efficient causes of the regularity and non-randomness of human conduct and therefore of the social order itself. Such 'thing-like' social facts, and not the states of mind or emotions of individuals (such as are avidly studied by psychologists) offer the genuine explanation of human conduct. Wishing to describe correctly and to explain human behaviour, the sociologist is thus entitled (and exhorted) to by-pass the individual psyche, intentions, and private meanings that only the individuals themselves can tell us about — and that for this reason are bound to remain non-observable, impenetrable 'mysteries of the human soul' — and concentrate instead on studying phenomena which can be observed from outside and would in all probability look the same to any observer watching them.

This is one of the possible strategies one can follow to make a case for the scientific status of sociology. A very different strategy is associated with the work of **Max Weber**. The idea that there is one and only one way of 'being scientific' and that therefore sociology should selflessly imitate the practices of natural science is emphatically rejected. Instead, Weber proposes that sociological practice, without losing the precision expected from scientific knowledge, should be as different from that of the natural sciences as the human reality investigated by sociology is from the non-human world studied by the science of nature.

Human reality is different − indeed, unique − in that human actors put **meaning** in their actions. They have motives; they act in order to reach the ends they set for themselves. It is such ends that explain their actions. For this reason, human actions, unlike the spatial movements of physical bodies or chemical reactions, need to be understood rather than explained. More precisely, to explain human action means to *understand* it: to grasp the meaning invested into it by the actor.

That human actions are meaningful, and hence call for a special kind of investigation, was not Weber's discovery. On the contrary, this idea served long before as the foundation of **hermeneutics** − the theory and practice of 'recovery of meaning' embedded in a literary text, or a painting, or any other product of a human creative spirit. Hermeneutical investigations struggled in vain to attain scientific status. The theorists of hermeneutics found it difficult to demonstrate that the method, and the findings, of hermeneutical study may be as objective as the methods and results of science purport to be: that is, that one can codify the method of hermeneutical investigation so precisely that any researcher following the rules would have to arrive to the same conclusions. Such a scientific ideal seemed to the hermeneuticians unattainable. It seemed that in order to understand its meaning the interpreters of the text must 'put themselves in the author's place', see the text through the author's eyes, think the author's thoughts; in brief, try to be, to think, to reason, to feel like the author (such an effort to 'transfer' oneself into the life and spirit of the author, to relive and copy the author's experience, was called **empathy**). This requires a genuine congeniality with the author and the powerful exercise of the imagination; and the results would not depend on a uniform method *anybody* can apply with equal success, but on the *unique* talents of a single interpreter. Thus the whole procedure of interpreting belongs more to the arts than to science. If interpreters come forward with sharply different interpretations, one may choose one of the competing proposals because it is richer, more perceptive, profound, aesthetically pleasing or otherwise more satisfying than the rest; but these are not reasons that alllow us to say that the interpretation we prefer is *true*, while the ones we do not like are *false*. And an assertion which cannot be definitely corroborated as true, or proved wrong, cannot belong to science.

And yet Weber insisted that, being an investigation of human acts aimed at their understanding (that is, striving like hermeneutics to grasp their meaning), sociology can still reach the level of **objectivity** that is the distinctive mark of scientific knowledge. In other words, he insisted that sociology can, and should, achieve the objective knowledge of subjective human reality.

Not all human actions may be so interpreted, to be sure, as much of our activity is either traditional or affective − guided by habits or emotions. In both cases the action is *unreflective*: when I act out of anger or follow a routine, I do not calculate my action nor pursue particular ends; I do not design nor monitor my action as a means leading to a specific end. Traditional and affective actions are determined by factors my mind does not control − much like natural phenomena; and like natural phenomena, they are best comprehended when their cause is pointed out. What requires an understanding of meaning rather than a causal explanation are *rational* actions, that is *reflective* actions, *calculated* actions, actions that are consciously conceived and controlled and aimed at a consciously considered end (the 'in order to' actions). If traditions are manifold and emotions are thoroughly personal and idiosyncratic, the *reason* we deploy to measure our ends against the means we select in order to achieve them is common to all human beings. So I can wrest meaning out of the action I observe not by guessing what has been going on in the actors' heads, not by 'thinking their thoughts' (in other words, not by empathy), but by matching to the action a motive that makes sense and thus renders the action meaningful to me and to any other observer. Your hitting your fellow student in rage may fail to make sense to me if I happen to be a placid person who never experiences strong emotions. But if I see you 'burning the candle', late into the night and writing an essay, I can easily make sense of what I see (and so can anyone else) because I know that writing essays is an excellent, tested means of acquiring knowledge.

What Weber seemed to assume, in short, was that one rational mind may recognize itself in another rational mind; that as long as the studied actions are rational (calculated, following a purpose) they can be rationally understood: explained by postulating a meaning, not a cause. Sociological knowledge need not therefore be inferior to science. On the contrary, it has a clear advantage over science in that it can not only describe but also *understand* its objects — the human objects. However thoroughly explored, the world described by science stays meaningless (one can know everything about the tree, but one cannot 'understand' the tree). Sociology goes further than science — it recovers the *meaning* of the reality it studies.

There was also a third strategy aimed at lifting social study to the status of science: to show that, like science, sociology has direct and effective **practical** applications. This strategy has been applied with particular zeal by the pioneers of sociology in the United States of America — a country prominent for its pragmatic frame of mind and viewing practical success as the supreme criterion of value and, in the end, also of truth. Unlike their European colleagues, the first American sociologists had little time for theorizing about the nature of their enterprise; they did not concern themselves with the philosophical justification of sociological practice. Instead, they earnestly set out to demonstrate that the kind of knowledge sociological research can provide can be used in exactly the same way as scientific knowledge has been used for years with spectacular results: it can be employed to make predictions and to 'manipulate' reality, to change it in a way that agrees with our needs and intentions whatever they may be and however they have been defined and selected.

The third strategy concentrated on developing the methods of *social diagnosis* (surveys showing in detail the exact state of affairs in certain areas of social life) and the general theory of human behaviour (that is, of the factors that determine such behaviour; it was hoped that an exhaustive knowledge of such factors might render human conduct predictable and manipulable). From the start, sociology was given a practical edge. The edge was pressed against recognized social problems like rising criminality, juvenile delinquency, alcoholism, prostitution, the weakening of family ties, etc. Sociology grounded its bid for social recognition in a promise to assist the administration of social processes in the way geology and physics assist the builders of skyscrapers. In other words, sociology put itself at the service of the construction and maintenance of social order. It shared the concerns of social administrators, of people set on the task of managing other people's conduct. The promise of practical usefulness was addressed and taken up by ever new areas of managerial activity. The services of sociologists were deployed to defuse antagoism and prevent conflicts in factories and mines, to facilitate the adaptation of young soldiers in war-weary army units, to help the promotion of new commercial products, to rehabilitate former criminals, to increase the effectiveness of social welfare provisions.

This strategy came closest to Francis Bacon's formula 'to subdue nature by submission'; it blended truth with usefulness, information with control, knowledge with power. It accepted the power-holders' challenge to prove the validity of sociological knowledge by the practical benefits it may bring to the management of social order, to the solution of 'problems' as seen and articulated by the managers of order. By the same token, sociology that pursued such a strategy had to adopt the managerial perspective: to view society 'from the top', as an object of manipulation, as resistant material whose inner qualities must be known better in order to be made more pliable and more receptive to the shape one may wish to give it.

The merger of sociological and managerial interests may have endeared sociology to state, industrial or military administrations, but it exposed it to the criticism of those who perceived power control from the top as a threat to the values they cherished, and particularly to individual freedom and communal self-management. The critics pointed out that the pursuit of discussed strategy amounts to taking sides and an active support for the extant asymmetry of social power. It is not true — they insisted — that the knowledge and practical precepts proferred by sociology may serve equally well anyone that might wish to use them, and therefore may be seen as neutral and non-partisan. Not everyone can use knowledge construed from the managerial perspective; its application, after all, demands resources that only the managers command and can deploy. Sociology thus enhances the control of those who are already in control; it further shifts the stakes in favour of those who already enjoy a better hand. The cause of inequality and social injustice is thereby served.

Sociology therefore attracted controversy. Its work is subjected to pressures that are hard to reconcile. What one side asks sociology to do the other sees as an abomination and is determined to resist. The blame for controversiality cannot be put solely at sociology's door. Sociology falls victim to a real social conflict, an inner contradiction tearing apart society at large; a contradiction it is in no position to resolve.

The contradiction resides in the very project of *rationalization* inherent in modern society. Rationality is a two-edged sword. On the one hand, it helps human individuals to gain more control over their own actions. Rational calculation, as we have seen, may gear action better to the actor's ends and thus increase its effectiveness. On the whole, it seems that rational individuals are more likely to achieve their ends than such individuals as do not plan, calculate and monitor their actions. Put in the service of the individual, rationality may increase the scope of individual freedom. On the other hand, once applied to the environment of individual action — to the organization of the society at large — rational analysis may well limit the range of the individuals' choices or diminish the pool of means from which the individuals may draw to pursue their ends. It may achieve an exactly opposite effect: constrain individual freedom. So the possible applications of rationality are intrinsically incompatible and doomed to remain controversial.

The controversy that surrounds sociology only reflects the Janus-faced nature of rationality. There is little sociology can do to repair it, and so the controversy is likely to continue. The power-holders will go on accusing sociology of undermining their hold over their subjects and inciting what they see as social unrest and subversion. People defending their way of life against the stifling constraints imposed by the resourceful powers that be will go on being nonplussed or aggrieved when they see sociologists as counsellors and acolytes of their erstwhile adversaries. In each case, the virulence of the accusation will reflect the current intensity of conflict.

Attacked on two fronts, sociology finds its scientific status widely questioned. Its adversaries are vitally interested in delegitimizing the validity of sociological knowledge, and the denial of scientific status serves the purpose well. It is perhaps this double assault, such as few other branches of scholarship face, that makes sociologists so sensitive about the issue of their own status as scientists, and prompts ever renewed attempts to convince both academic opinion and the wider public that the knowledge sociologists produce can claim the truth value of the standard ascribed to scientific findings. Attempts remain inconclusive. They also turn attention away from the genuine service sociological thinking may offer to daily life.

All knowledge, being an orderly vision, a vision of order, contains an interpretation of the world. It does not, as we often believe, reflect things as they are by themselves; things are, rather, called into being by the knowledge we have: it is as if our raw, inchoate sensations condensed into things by sifting into containers our knowledge has prepared for them in the form of categories, classes, types. The more knowledge we have, the more things we see — the greater number of different things we discern in the world. Or, rather, to say, 'I have more knowledge' and 'I distinguish more things in the world' means the same. If I study the art of painting, my heretofore indiscriminate impression of 'redness' splits into an ever growing number of specific and highly distinct members of the 'family of red colours': I now see differently Adrianople red, flame red, hellebore red, Indian red, Japanese red, carmine, crimson, ruby, scarlet, cardinal red, sanguine, vermilion, damask, Naples red, Pompeian red, Persian red and a constantly increasing number of other reds. The difference between a person untrained, ignorant in arts, and an expert, a schooled artist or art critic, will express itself in the first person's inability to see the colours which for the second person appear blatantly (and 'naturally') distinct and separate. It may also express itself in the second person losing the first person's ability to see 'redness' as such, to perceive all the objects painted with various shades of red as being of the same colour.

In all areas, acquisition of knowledge consists of learning how to make new discriminations, how to make the uniform discrete, how to render distinctions more specific, split large classes into smaller ones, so that the interpretation of experience gets richer and more detailed. Often we hear of the education people possess being measured by the richness of the vocabulary they deploy (by how many words their language contains). Things may be described as 'nice' — but their 'niceness' may be made more specific, and then it transpires that things so described may be experienced as 'nice' for various reasons — for being enjoyable, or savoury, or kind, or suitable, or tasteful, or 'doing the right thing'. It seems that richness of experience and vocabulary grow together.

Language does not come into life 'from outside', to report what has already happened. Language is in life from the start. Indeed, we may say that language is a *form of life*, and every language — English, Chinese, Portuguese, working-class language, 'posh' language, the 'official' language of civil servants, the argot of the underworld, the jargon of adolescent gangs, the language of art critics, of sailors, of nuclear physicists, or surgeons or miners — is a form of life in its own right. Each brings together a map of the world (or a specific section of the world) and a code of behaviour — with the two orders, the two planes of discrimination (one of perception and another of behavioural practice), parallel and coordinated. Inside each form of life, the map and the code intertwine. We can think of them separately, but in practice we cannot pull them apart. Distinctions made between the names of things reflect our perception of the difference in their qualities — and hence also in their uses and in our actions towards them; but our recognition of the difference in quality reflects the discrimination we make in our actions towards them and the expectations from which our actions follow. Let us recall what we have found out already: to understand is to know how to go on. And vice versa: if we know how to go on, we have understood. It is precisely this overlapping, this harmony between the two — the way we act and the way we see the world — that makes us suppose that the differences are in the things themselves, that the world around us is by itself divided into separate parts distinguished by our language, that the names 'belong' to the named things.

Forms of life are many. Each one, of course, differs from another; their distinctions, after all, are what makes them into separate forms of life. But they are not separated from each other by impermeable walls; they should not be thought of as self-enclosed, sealed worlds, with inventories of contents all of their own, with all objects they contain belonging to them and to them alone. Forms of life are orderly, shared patterns − but often superimposed on each other. They overlap and vie for selected areas of the total life experience. They are, so to speak, different selections and alternative arrangements of the same portions of the total world and the same items drawn from the shared pool. In the course of one day, I move through many forms of life; but wherever I move, I carry a piece of other forms of life with me (so that the way I act in the research team where I work is 'tainted' by the regional and local particularities of the form of life of which I partake in my private life; my participation in that neighbourhood-bound form of life, in its turn, bears traces of a particular religious congregation to which I belong and whose life I share − and so on). In every form of life through which I pass in the course of my life I share knowledge and behavioural codes with a different set of people; and each of them might have a unique combination of forms of life of which he or she partakes. For this reason, no form of life is 'pure'; neither is it static, given once and for all. My entry into a form of life is not a passive process of rote learning on my part; not a process of twisting and moulding and trimming my ideas and my skills so that they conform to the rigid rules to which I now intend to submit myself. My entry into a form of life changes the form of life I enter; we *both* change, I bring with me a sort of dowry (in the shape of other forms of life which I carry in me) which transforms the contents of the form of life to which I am a newcomer, so that after my entry this form of life is different from before. And so it changes all the time. Each act of entry (of learning, of mastering and practising the language which constitutes a form of life) is a creative act: an act of transformation. To put this another way: languages, like the communities that share them, are wide-open and dynamic entities. They can exist only in a state of constant change.

This is why problems of understanding constantly arise (as well as the threats of confusion, of breakdown in communication). Renewed attempts to make communication foolproof (by 'freezing' the interpretations the language contains through enforcing a clear-cut, obligatory definition of every word) do not and cannot help, as the practitioners of language with their own and distinct interpretations constantly bring different sets of forms of life into interaction. In the course of such interaction, meanings undergo a subtle, yet steady and unavoidable change. They acquire new colouring, come to be associated with referents from which they used to be distant, displace older meanings and pass through many other changes that cannot but change the language itself. We can say that the process of communication — that action aimed at achieving joint understanding, at thrashing out the differences, at agreeing on interpretation — prevents any form of life from staying put. To grasp this amazing quality of the forms of life, think of whirls in a stream; each looks as if it had a steady shape and therefore 'remained the same', held its 'identity', over a protracted period of time — and yet, as we well know, it cannot keep a single molecule of water for more than a few seconds, its substance being in a state of permanent flux. In case you think this is a weakness of the whirl, and that it would be better for its security — for its 'survival' — if the flow of water in the river were stopped, remember that such an event would mean the 'death' of the whirl. It cannot 'live' (it cannot keep its shape, its form of separate and persistent identity) without a constant influx and outflow of ever new quantities of water (which, by the way, always carry somewhat different inorganic and organic ingredients).

We can say that languages, or forms of life, like whirls, or like rivers themselves, stay alive and preserve their identity, their **relative autonomy**, precisely because they are flexible, permanently in flux, able to absorb new material and let out the 'used up' one. This means, however, that forms of life (all languages, all bodies of knowledge) would die were they ever to become closed, stiff and repellent to change. They would not survive their final codification and that precision which prompts the attempts at codification. To put it differently, languages and knowledge in general need ambivalence to remain alive, to retain cohesion, to be of use.

And yet powers concerned with ordering the 'messy' reality cannot but view that ambivalence as an obstacle to their aims. They naturally tend to freeze the whirl, to bar all unwelcome input into the knowledge they control, to seal the 'form of life' for which they wish to secure monopoly. The search for unambiguous knowledge ('certain' thanks to the lack of competition) and the effort to make reality orderly, hospitable to self-assured, effective action, blend into one. To want full control over the situation is to strive for a clear-cut 'linguistic map' in which the meanings of words are not in doubt and never contested, in which each word unmistakably points to its referent and this one and only link is binding on all who use it. For these reasons, ambivalence of knowledge constantly prompts efforts to 'fix' certain knowledge as obligatory and unquestionable — as **orthodoxy**; to force through a belief that this knowledge and this knowledge alone is faultless, beyond reproach, or at any rate better (more trustworthy, reliable and useful) than its competitors; and to degrade by the same token the alternative forms of knowledge to the inferior, derisible status of superstition, prejudice, bias or manifestation of ignorance — but in any case a **heresy**, a condemnable deviation from the truth.

Such a double-pronged effort (to secure the position of the orthodoxy and to prevent or eliminate heresy) has control over interpretation as its objective. The power in question aims at gaining an exclusive right to decide which of the possible interpretations ought to be chosen and made binding as the *true* one (in the definition of truth, many of the competing versions may be false, but only one can be correct; errors are plentiful, while there is but one truth; the presumption of monopoly, of exclusivity, of non-competition is contained in the very idea of truth). The quest for monopoly of power expresses itself in casting the proponents of an alternative in the role of dissidents, in general *intolerance* of the pluralism of opinion, censorship and in extreme cases persecution (as in the burning of heretics by the Inquisition, the shooting of dissenters during Stalinist purges and of prisoners of conscience under contemporary dictatorial regimes).

By its nature sociology is singularly ill suited to the 'closing down' and 'sealing' job. Sociology is an extended commentary on the experience of daily life; an interpretation which feeds on other interpretations and is in turn fed into them. It does not compete, but shares forces with other discourses engaged in the interpretation of human experience (like literature, art, philosophy). If anything, thinking sociologically undermines the trust in the exclusivity and completeness of any interpretation. It brings into focus the plurality of experiences and forms of life; it shows each as an entity in its own right, a world with a logic of its own, while at the same time exposing the sham of its ostensible self-containment and self-sufficiency. Sociological thinking does not stem, but facilitates the flow and exchange of experiences. To put it bluntly, it adds to the volume of ambivalence as it saps the effort to 'freeze the flux' and shut the entry points. From the point of view of powers obsessed with the order they have designed, sociology is part of the 'messiness' of the world; a problem, rather than a solution.

The great service sociology is well prepared to render to human life and human cohabitation is the promotion of mutual understanding and tolerance as a paramount condition of shared freedom. Sociological thinking cannot but promote the understanding that breeds tolerance and the tolerance that makes understanding possible. In the words of the American philosopher Richard Rorty, 'if we take care of freedom, truth and goodness will take care of themselves'. Sociological thinking helps the cause of freedom.

Where to Find More: Further Reading

The best this book could offer you was a taste of sociology; an inkling of what one may learn from sociological findings and interpretations. You may by now have a fair idea of what sociology is about and how it can illuminate your own life and the world around you. Do not delude yourself, however, that your knowledge is complete. You have come as yet nowhere near to exhausting the richness of information sociology has accumulated and can deliver to those who wish to persevere in their study. Go to your college library and have a good look at the section filled with sociological books. You will find out how many books there are to be read and how attractive and appetite-whetting the topics these books talk about are. Indeed, sociology is a discipline of scholarship with a long tradition of thought that profoundly affected the whole of modern thinking as it dealt with issues central to our daily concerns. It is also a growing discipline, adding ever new research findings and new ideas to its already impressive achievement. It is quite possible that the visit to the library will leave you baffled; you may feel depressed by the sheer volume of knowledge awaiting you there, and thus lose some of your enthusiasm for further study, or give up the intention altogether.

Well, do not feel depressed, and do not surrender to the temptation to quit. Sociological knowledge may seem overwhelming, but most of it is geared to things you know and feel strongly about and chimes well with the experience you have. You will find the effort richly rewarding, and certainly not beyond your power. Besides, fortunately there are sociological publications written mostly to help you and other people facing a similar task: to lead into the main body of sociological knowledge in a relatively painless way. Some — by no means all — of these publications will now be listed and briefly discussed. What follows is a selection, not an exhaustive inventory. But as you go, you will grow ever more sure of where to make your next step; you will be ever more able to rely on your own judgement, you will know what you want to read about and where to find it.

Perhaps the book to start with is Anthony Giddens's *Sociology*. It offers the most comprehensive among the available maps of sociological territory; an up-to-date survey of all sociology's works — as complete as it can be. You will probably find it difficult to absorb the whole book in one go, but this is not the most important thing to do. Treat this book as a source of reference and a guide. It will tell you what you can find in the works of sociologists, and what sort of propositions you are likely to find there — and then you can pick and choose areas on which to concentrate and to study in depth. There will be less chance of getting lost on the way, as the itinerary will be well plotted before you embark on the journey.

While systematic summaries of the state of the art (of which Giddens's book is one of the best) are extremely useful and indispensable aids for any newcomer to the field, there is no substitute for a direct communication with the sources — the writings of such people as shaped sociological discourse and supplied its themes and essential concepts. One needs this insight into the work of mind-struggling to comprehend common experience and make sense of it; one needs to get a 'feel' of how the narrative is slowly and painstakingly built up and how it arrives at its present shape; one needs to understand what all those wise people were after, what 'made them tick', what they were curious about and what problems they wished to solve. For all these reasons you cannot consider your initiation into sociological thinking complete without reading 'the classics' — or at least a sample of the classic texts. There are several collections of such texts which have made the selection for you and hence make the daunting task easier to perform. A most comprehensive one is *Sociological Theory: A Book of Readings*, edited by Lewis A. Coser and Bernard Rosenberg (there were five editions altogether, each offering a partly revised selection). It conveniently divides the texts according to the major themes of sociological inquiry, so that you can see how various theoretical perspectives contributed to our understanding of the same topic and how these contributions criticize and at the same time complement each other. Other useful 'sample books' are organized differently, around one selected theory, one prominent author, so that you can see the cohesiveness of the total approach as it is consistently applied over a wide range of debated issues. Among the books in this category, the collections of readings from *Max Weber* (edited by J. E. T. Eldridge), from *Emile Durkheim* (edited by A. Giddens) and *Karl Marx* (edited by T. Bottomore and Rubel) deserve special mention. There is no comparable collection of Georg Simmel's writings, but you will get a good insight into his thought from his essays collected in *The Conflict in Modern Culture* (edited by K. P. Etzkorn) and *On Individuality and Social Forms* (edited by D. N. Levine).

If you require a general survey of sociological approaches presented in a relatively simple fashion, Stephen Mennell's *Sociological Theory: Uses and Unities* will go a long way towards meeting your need. An exceptionally illuminating introduction to the variety of sociological perspectives is offered by *Society*, a short book written by David Frisby and Derek Sayer; it clearly shows the difference a theoretical perspective can make to the way we perceive social reality. Finally, there are two important books that spell out in a powerful way the conflicts between the different understandings of the task sociology should perform and the role it is called upon to play in human life. One is C. Wright Mills's *The Sociological Imagination* − thirty years old, yet still fresh and topical. The other is Peter Berger's *Invitation to Sociology: A Humanistic Perspective*, which clearly conveys the concerns, doubts and choices faced by sociologists during the last decade.

However crucial it is to acquire reliable sociological skills, no amount of theoretical refinement will offer you what only the watching of 'sociology in action' can offer: the ability to use the cognitive perspective, and the stock of models concepts, for a better comprehension of phenomena apparently well familiar from private experience or popular discussion. There is no end to the vivid examples of the good works from which one can learn more sociological skills than from the most systematic of textbooks. Any selection must be arbitrary and very partial — and the one that follows is no exception.

Krishan Kumar's *Prophecy and Progress* will show you how one can think of the world we live in — the industrial world, the modern world — and the direction in which it is changing. You will find out that there is more than one way in which the story of this world can be told and that each story contains a grain or more of truth yet none is complete. You will see as well that with the passage of time stories once preferred fall out of favour and are replaced with others that now seem more credible; that other stories, on the contrary, outlive their time and thus tend to shape for us the meaning of new experiences they were not meant to report. Read Kumar's book carefully, and you will learn a lot about the intricate, two-directional relationship between knowledge and reality, between what we collectively think the world is like and the way we collectively act in making the world what it is.

Benedict Anderson's *Imagined Communities: Reflections on the Origin and Spread of Nationalism* complements Kumar's book. It shows how some of the most important stories, those of nations, national communities, national destinies, are produced and how they subsequently inform our actions, our loyalties and enmities, so that at the end of the day the reality those images pretended merely to reflect and report is conjured up; the images solidify, as it were, and become 'hard facts of life'. Since, however, the stories told and followed are manifold and often at odds with each other, the reality that emerges is far from lucid; the ambivalence of reality merely reflects the incompatibility of the images — the discrepancy between the clarity and precision they imply and the ambiguity that arises out of the subjection of human conditions to many mutually independent pressures.

Mary Douglas's *Purity and Danger* will tell you about the efforts we all make to find the way out of the incomplete and provisional nature of each and every story; about our urge to make the image of the world clear, straightforward and unambiguous, and to force the world to fit such an image (that is, to 'cut the corners', to draw exact boundaries and guard them against trespassing, to suppress all that spills over the boundary — all that carries more than one meaning).

You will learn from Mary Douglas that all such efforts are in vain, that ambivalence will stay with us for ever, as the life-world is much more 'fluid' than our knowledge construed of oppositions and clear-cut differences would admit and is able to absorb; but you will also learn that the efforts cannot stop and will never be given up, as we need clarity to go about our business life.

Erving Goffman's *Stigma* and *Presentation of Self in Everyday Life* will show you how each one of us tries to cope with such unavoidable ambivalence, with the possibility that things may not be what they seem or the need to make them seem different from what they are. The two books focus on our most poignant concerns: the laborious and never finished construction of self-identity and the keen yet often frustrated attempts to negotiate the acceptance of the results by the people around us. You will find out that to know how to perform a role well is one thing, but to convince others that you perform it well is quite another; and thus you will find out why we so often feel uneasy in the face of mere appearances and wish to go to the heart of the matter: find out what people around us truly are. On both sides, the efforts are bound to remain inconclusive, and it is ultimately on trust (which may or may not be well founded) that our interaction is based.

Hidden Injuries of Class by Richard Sennett and Jonathan Cobb will show you that in that labour to construct one's own identity and to make it accepted the situations of the negotiating sides are not equal. Some people tell or repeat stories that enjoy high influence — that carry authority; some others must look at themselves and weigh their own qualities in the light of such authoritative stories; their own story, even if they compose it, will stand little chance of being appreciated. As long as they stay in subordinate positions, these other people will go on resenting the authoritative stories that report their inferiority and blame them for it; but they will have little choice but to act as if those stories were true. The 'hidden injury' of the title is wounded dignity. The need to strive for values one does not respect is a most painful, though not immediately evident, offence that makes people feel hurt by class-related or any other inequality.

Dick Hebdidge's *Hiding in the Light* will teach you much about the problems of living under conditions marked simultaneously by ambivalence and inequality. You will learn about the difficulty of such living, but also of the ways of fighting back that successive generations of young people found and pursued. In the end you will better understand the apparently bizarre and baffling phenomena like 'youth culture': you will see beyond the exotic and shocking appearances into the need to transform humiliation into pride, to resist oppression, to cut out an island of freedom in the sea of dependence, to speak in a full voice and make oneself audible. Hebdidge's studies will help you to see better the complex, dialectical relationship between dependence and freedom, constraint and autonomy.

When you read these books (and the many others which, I hope, will follow), pay attention not only to what each one has to tell you, but also to the many different styles in which good sociological work can be done. Each of the named books is different in virtually everything: in the ways they select and pinpoint their topics, in the vantage points from which they look at them, in the ways they argue their respective cases. The differences are not between 'good' and 'bad' sociology (though, of course, you will find out in the end that there is as much 'bad' sociology as there is 'good'). The presence of differences testifies to the fact that our experience is manifold, multi-faceted, ambivalent and amenable to many, sometimes contradictory, interpretations. What unites the named books in spite of all their differences is the fact that they all concentrate on that experience, do not try to play down its complexity and imply clarity where there is no clarity, do not seek facile and simple explanations; on the contrary, it is the very complexity of our daily business of life that they wish to uncover and make sense of. This is precisely what makes them all examples of 'good sociology' — and such useful, such exciting reading.

Index

Note: uncommon concepts are in italics and names are in bold.

3